THE COSTS OF CONFLICT

THE COSTS OF CONFLICT

Prevention and Cure in the Global Arena

Edited by
Michael E. Brown
and
Richard N. Rosecrance

CARNEGIE COMMISSION ON PREVENTING DEADLY CONFLICT

CARNEGIE CORPORATION OF NEW YORK

ROWMAN & LITTLEFIELD PUBLISHERS, INC.
Lanham • Boulder • New York • Oxford

ROWMAN & LITTLEFIELD PUBLISHERS, INC.

Published in the United States of America
by Rowman & Littlefield Publishers, Inc.
4720 Boston Way, Lanham, Maryland 20706

12 Hid's Copse Road
Cumnor Hill, Oxford OX2 9JJ, England

British Library Cataloguing in Publication Information Available

Library of Congress Cataloging-in-Publication Data

The costs of conflict : prevention and cure in the global arena /
edited by Michael E. Brown and Richard N. Rosecrance.
p. cm.
Includes bibliographical references and index.
ISBN 0-8476-8893-3.—ISBN 0-8476-8894-1 (pbk.)
II. Rosecrance, Richard N.
JZ6368.C67 1999
327.1′7—dc21 98-41030
CIP

Printed in the United States of America

∞ ™ The paper used in this publication meets the minimum requirements of American National Standard for Information Sciences—Permanence of Paper for Printed Library Materials, ANSIZ39.48—1984.

ABOUT THE
Carnegie Commission on Preventing Deadly Conflict Series

Carnegie Corporation of New York established the Carnegie Commission on Preventing Deadly Conflict in May 1994 to address the threats to world peace of intergroup violence and to advance new ideas for the prevention and resolution of deadly conflict. The Commission is examining the principal causes of deadly ethnic, nationalist, and religious conflicts within and between states and the circumstances that foster or deter their outbreak. Taking a long-term, worldwide view of violent conflicts that are likely to emerge, it seeks to determine the functional requirements of an effective system for preventing mass violence and to identify the ways in which such a system could be implemented. The Commission is also looking at the strengths and weaknesses of various international entities in conflict prevention and considering ways in which international organizations might contribute toward developing an effective international system of nonviolent problem solving. The series grew out of the research that the Commission has sponsored to answer the three fundamental questions that have guided its work: What are the problems posed by deadly conflict and why is outside help often necessary to deal with these problems? What approaches, tasks, and strategies appear most promising for preventing deadly conflict? What are the responsibilities and capacities of states, international organizations, and private and nongovernmental organizations for undertaking preventive action? The Commission issued its final report in December 1997.

The books are published as a service to scholars, students, practitioners, and the interested public. While they have undergone peer review and have been approved for publication, the views that they express are those of the author or authors, and Commission publication does not imply that those views are shared by the Commission as a whole or by individual Commissioners.

Members of the Carnegie Commission on Preventing Deadly Conflict

David A. Hamburg, *Cochair*
President Emeritus
Carnegie Corporation of New York

Cyrus R. Vance, *Cochair*
Partner
Simpson Thacher & Bartlett

Gro Harlem Brundtland
Director-General
World Health Organization
Former Prime Minister of Norway

Virendra Dayal
Former Under-Secretary-General and Chef de Cabinet to the Secretary-General
United Nations

Gareth Evans
Deputy Leader of the Opposition and Shadow Treasurer
Australia

Alexander L. George
Graham H. Stuart Professor Emeritus of International Relations
Stanford University

Flora MacDonald
Former Foreign Minister of Canada

Donald F. McHenry
Distinguished Professor in the Practice of Diplomacy
School of Foreign Service
Georgetown University

Olara A. Otunnu
President
International Peace Academy

David Owen
House of Lords

Shridath Ramphal
Cochairman
Commission on Global Governance

Roald Sagdeev
Distinguished Professor
Department of Physics
University of Maryland

John D. Steinbruner
Senior Fellow
Foreign Policy Studies Program
The Brookings Institution

Brian Urquhart
Former Under-Secretary-General for Special Political Affairs
United Nations

John C. Whitehead
Chairman
AEA Investors Inc.

Sahabzada Yaqub-Khan
Former Foreign Minister of Pakistan
Chairman, Board of Trustees
Aga Khan International University–Karachi

Special Advisors to the Commission

Arne Olav Brundtland
Director, Studies of Foreign and Security Policy
Norwegian Institute of International Affairs

Herbert S. Okun
Visiting Lecturer on International Law
Yale Law School
Former U.S. Representative to the German Democratic Republic and to the United Nations

Jane E. Holl, *Executive Director*

The Carnegie Commission Series

Published in the series:

Bridging the Gap: A Future Security Architecture for the Middle East, by Shai Feldman and Abdullah Toukan

The Price of Peace: Incentives and International Conflict Prevention, edited by David Cortright

Sustainable Peace: The Role of the UN and Regional Organizations in Preventing Conflict, by Connie Peck

Turkey's Kurdish Question, by Henri J. Barkey and Graham E. Fuller

The Costs of Conflict: Prevention and Cure in the Global Arena, edited by Michael E. Brown and Richard N. Rosecrance

Forthcoming:

The Ambivalence of the Sacred: Religion, Violence, and Reconciliation, by Scott Appleby

Opportunities Missed, Opportunities Seized: Preventive Diplomacy in the Post–Cold War World, edited by Bruce Jentleson

Negotiating to Prevent Escalation and Violence, edited by I. William Zartman

Light Weapons and Civil Conflict: Controlling the Tools of Violence, edited by Jeffrey Boutwell and Michael Klare

Mediation and Arbitration to Prevent Deadly Conflict, edited by John Barton, Melanie Greenberg, and Margaret McGuinness

For orders and information please address the publisher:

Rowman & Littlefield Publishers, Inc.
4720 Boston Way
Lanham, Maryland 20706
1-800-462-6420

Reports Available from the Commission

David Hamburg, *Preventing Contemporary Intergroup Violence,* founding essay of the Commission, April 1994.

David Hamburg, *Education for Conflict Resolution,* April 1995.

Comprehensive Disclosure of Fissionable Materials: A Suggested Initiative, June 1995.

Larry Diamond, *Promoting Democracy in the 1990s: Actors and Instruments, Issues and Imperatives,* December 1995.

Andrew J. Goodpaster, *When Diplomacy Is Not Enough: Managing Multinational Military Interventions,* July 1996.

John Stremlau, *Sharpening International Sanctions: Toward a Stronger Role for the United Nations,* November 1996.

Alexander L. George and Jane E. Holl, *The Warning-Response Problem and Missed Opportunities in Preventive Diplomacy,* May 1997.

John Stremlau with Helen Zille, *A House No Longer Divided: Progress and Prospects for Democratic Peace in South Africa,* July 1997.

Nik Gowing, *Media Coverage: Help or Hindrance in Conflict Prevention,* September 1997.

Cyrus R. Vance and David A. Hamburg, *Pathfinders for Peace: A Report to the UN Secretary-General on the Role of Special Representatives and Personal Envoys,* September 1997.

Preventing Deadly Conflict: Executive Summary of the Final Report, December 1997.

Gail W. Lapidus with Svetlana Tsalik, eds., *Preventing Deadly Conflict: Strategies and Institutions,* Proceedings of a Conference in Moscow, Russian Federation, April 1998.

Scott Feil, *Preventing Genocide: How the Early Use of Force Might Have Succeeded in Rwanda,* April 1998.

Douglas Lute, *Improving National Capacity to Respond to Complex Emergencies: The U.S. Experience,* April 1998.

John Stremlau, *People in Peril: Human Rights, Humanitarian Action, and Preventing Deadly Conflict,* June 1998.

Tom Gjelten, *Professionalism in War Reporting: A Correspondent's View,* June 1998.

John Stremlau and Francisco R. Sagasti, *Preventing Deadly Conflict: Does the World Bank Have a Role?* June 1998.

Edward J. Laurance, *Light Weapons and Intrastate Conflict: Early Warning Factors and Preventive Action,* July 1998.

Donald Kennedy, *Environmental Quality and Regional Conflict,* November 1998.

To order *Power Sharing and International Mediation in Ethnic Conflicts* by Timothy Sisk, copublished by the Commission and the United States Institute of Peace, please contact USIP Press, P.O. Box 605, Herndon, VA 22070, USA; phone: (800) 868-8064 or (703) 661-1590.

Full text or summaries of these reports are available on the Commission's web site: http://www.ccpdc.org

To order a report or to be added to the Commission's mailing list, contact:
Carnegie Commission on Preventing Deadly Conflict
1779 Massachusetts Avenue, NW, Suite 715
Washington, DC 20036-2103
Phone: (202) 332-7900 Fax: (202) 332-1919

Contents

Tables

Acknowledgments

The authors are indebted to David Hamburg, Jane Holl, Esther Brimmer, Tom Leney, John Steinbruner, Barry Posen, John Stremlau, John Mueller, Greg Treverton, Carl Kaysen, Bill Stanley, Andrzej Korbonski, Catherine Sweet, and several anonymous reviewers for helpful comments and information.

Acronyms

ADB	Asian Development Bank
ARENA	Nationalist Republican Alliance Party (El Salvador)
ASEAN	Association of Southeast Asian Nations
BNL	Banca Nazionale del Lavoro
CARE	Cooperative for Assistance and Relief Everywhere
CDR	Coalition pour la défense de la république (Rwanda)
CENTCOM	Central Command (Somalia)
CGDK	Coalition Government of Democratic Kampuchea
CIREFCA	International Conference on Central American Refugees
CMAC	Cambodia Mine Action Center
COPAZ	National Committee for the Consolidation of Peace
CPK	Communist Party of Kampuchea
CPP	Cambodian People's Party
CSCE	Conference on Security and Cooperation in Europe
DK	Democratic Kampuchea
DMZ	Demilitarized Zone
EBRD	European Bank for Reconstruction and Development
EC	European Community
ECLA	Economic Commission for Latin America
ERP	People's Revolutionary Army (El Salvador)
EU	European Union
FAO	Food and Agriculture Organization
FDI	Foreign Direct Investment

FDR	Democratic Revolutionary Front (El Salvador)
FMK	Independent Hungarian Initiative
FMLN	Farabundo Martí National Liberation Front
FPL	Popular Forces of Liberation (El Salvador)
FUNCINPEC	National United Front for an Independent, Neutral, Peaceful, and Cooperative Cambodia
FYROM	Former Yugoslav Republic of Macedonia
GEF	Global Environment Facility
HCDM	Hungarian Christian Democratic Movement
HCNM	High Commissioner on National Minorities
HPP	Hungarian People's Party
ICFY	International Conference on Former Yugoslavia
ICJ	International Court of Justice
ICORC	International Conference on the Reconstruction of Cambodia
IDA	International Development Association
IDB	Inter-American Development Bank
IFC	International Finance Corporation
IFOR	NATO Implementation Force (Bosnia)
IMET	International Military Education and Training
IMF	International Monetary Fund
JNA	Yugoslav People's Army
KLA	Kosovo Liberation Army
KPNLF	Khmer People's National Liberation Front
MDS	Public Against Violence—for a Democratic Slovakia
MICIVIH	International Civilian Mission in Haiti
MNF	Multinational Force (Haiti)
MRND	Mouvement révolutionnaire national pour le développement (Rwanda)
NCP	National Campaign Plan (El Salvador)
NFL	National Liberation Front (Vietnam)
NGO	Nongovernmental Organization
OAS	Organization of American States
OAU	Organization of African Unity
ODA	Overseas Development Assistance

OECD	Organization for Economic Cooperation and Development
ONUMOZ	United Nations Operation in Mozambique
ONUSAL	United Nations Observer Mission in El Salvador
OPEC	Organization of Petroleum Exporting Countries
OSCE	Organization for Security and Cooperation in Europe
OXFAM	Oxford Committee for Famine Relief
P-5	The five permanent members of the United Nations Security Council: China, France, Russian Federation, United Kingdom, United States
PAV	Public Against Violence (Slovakia)
PDC	Christian Democratic Party (El Salvador)
PFP	Partnership for Peace
PNC	National Civil Police (El Salvador)
PPD	Party for Democratic Prosperity (Macedonia)
PRK	People's Republic of Kampuchea
RCAF	Royal Cambodian Armed Forces
RGA	Rwandan Government Forces
RPF	Rwandan Patriotic Front
RRF	Rapid Reaction Force
SDA	Muslim Party of Democratic Action
SEED	Support for East European Development
SFOR	NATO Stabilization Force (Bosnia)
SNC	Supreme National Council (Vietnam)
SNM	Somalia National Movement
SOC	State of Cambodia
SPM	Somali Patriotic Movement
UNAMIC	United Nations Advance Mission in Cambodia
UNAMIR	United Nations Assistance Mission for Rwanda
UNDPI	United Nations Department of Public Information
UNHCR	United Nations High Commissioner for Refugees
UNICEF	United Nations Children's Fund
UNITAF	Unified Task Force
UNMIBH	United Nations Mission in Bosnia and Herzegovina
UNMIH	United Nations Mission in Haiti
UNO	National Opposition Union (El Salvador)
UNOMUR	United Nations Observer Mission Uganda-Rwanda
UNOSOM	United Nations Operation in Somalia, I and II

UNPREDEP	United Nations Preventive Deployment Force
UNPROFOR	United Nations Protection Force
UNSMIH	United Nations Support Mission in Haiti
UNTAC	United Nations Transitional Authority for Cambodia
UNTAES	United Nations Transitional Administration for Eastern Slavonia, Baranja and Western Sirmium
UNTMIH	United Nations Transition Mission in Haiti
USAID	United States Agency for International Development
USC	United Somali Congress
USFORSOM	U.S. Forces in Somalia
VMRO-DPMNE	Internal Macedonian Revolutionary Organization–Democratic Party for Macedonian National Unity
WEU	Western European Union
WFP	World Food Programme
WHO	World Health Organization
WPK	Worker's Party of Kampuchea

Maps

BOSNIA AND HERZEGOVINA
International boundary
Republic boundary
Provincial boundary
National capital
Town, village
Major airport
Railroad
Main road
Secondary road
CROATIA
FEDERAL REPUBLIC OF YUGOSLAVIA
MONTENEGRO (FRY)
SERBIA (FRY)
VOJVODINA (FRY)
ALBANIA
ADRIATIC SEA
Sarajevo
Banja Luka
Mostar
Tuzla
Zenica
Bihać
Prijedor
Doboj
Bijeljina
Trebinje
Dubrovnik
Split
Podgorica
Lake Scutari
The boundaries and names shown on this map do not imply official endorsement or acceptance by the United Nations.
0 10 20 30 40 50 60 70 80 km
0 10 20 30 40 50 mi

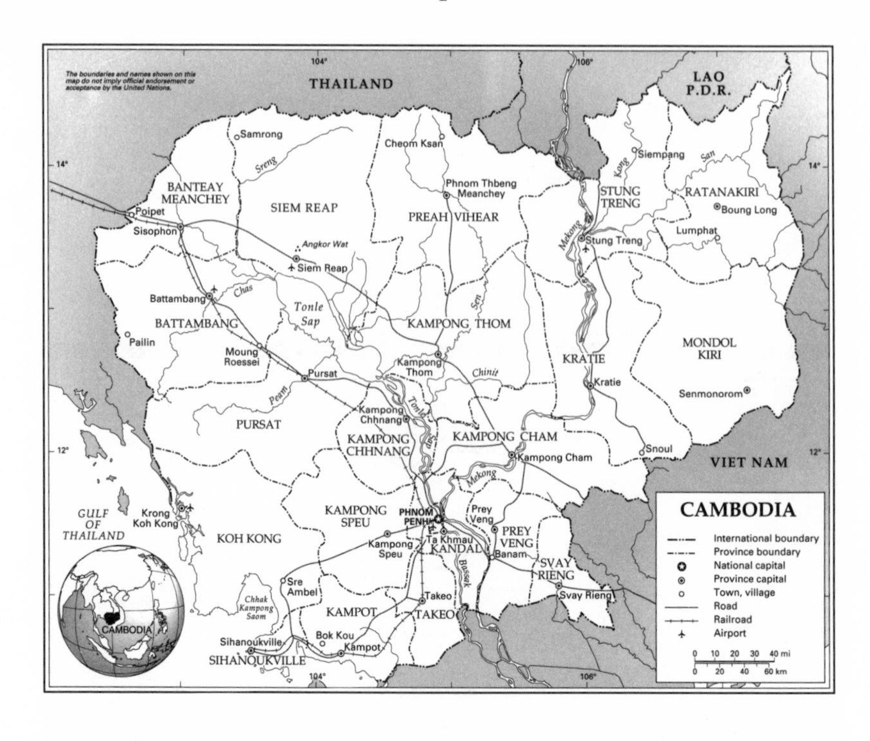
The boundaries and names shown on this map do not imply official endorsement or acceptance by the United Nations.
THAILAND
LAO P.D.R.
VIET NAM
GULF OF THAILAND
CAMBODIA
BANTEAY MEANCHEY
SIEM REAP
PREAH VIHEAR
STUNG TRENG
RATANAKIRI
BATTAMBANG
KAMPONG THOM
MONDOL KIRI
KRATIE
PURSAT
KAMPONG CHHNANG
KAMPONG CHAM
KAMPONG SPEU
KOH KONG
PREY VENG
KANDAL
SVAY RIENG
KAMPOT
TAKEO
SIHANOUKVILLE
Samrong
Cheom Ksan
Siempang
Phnom Thbeng Meanchey
Boung Long
Poipet
Sisophon
Lumphat
Stung Treng
Angkor Wat
Siem Reap
Battambang
Pailin
Tonle Sap
Moung Roessei
Kampong Thom
Pursat
Kratie
Senmonorom
Kampong Chhnang
Snoul
Kampong Cham
Krong Koh Kong
PHNOM PENH
Prey Veng
Kampong Speu
Ta Khmau
Banam
Sre Ambel
Svay Rieng
Takeo
Chhak Kampong Saom
Sihanoukville
Bok Kou
Kampot
Sreng
Chas
Sen
Chinit
Peam
Kong
San
Mekong
Tonle Sap
Bassak
104°
106°
14°
12°
International boundary
Province boundary
National capital
Province capital
Town, village
Road
Railroad
Airport
0 10 20 30 40 mi
0 20 40 60 km

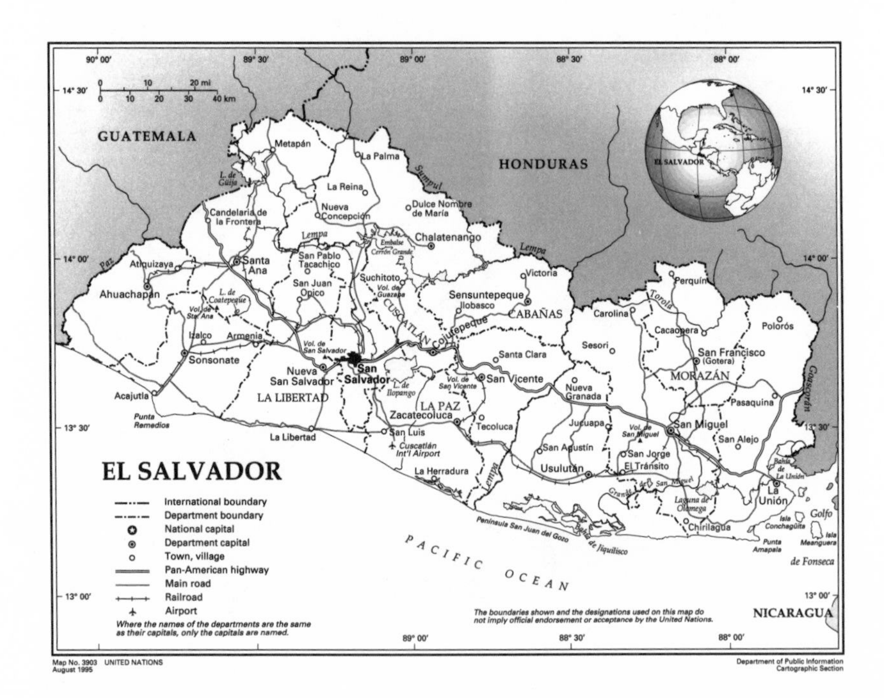
EL SALVADOR
GUATEMALA
HONDURAS
NICARAGUA
PACIFIC OCEAN
Golfo de Fonseca
Metapán
La Palma
L. de Güija
La Reina
Nueva Concepción
Dulce Nombre de María
Candelaria de la Frontera
Chalatenango
Embalse Cerrón Grande
Atiquizaya
Santa Ana
San Pablo Tacachico
Victoria
Perquín
Ahuachapán
San Juan Opico
Suchitoto
Sensuntepeque
Ilobasco
CABAÑAS
CUSCATLÁN
L. de Coatepeque
Vol. de Sta. Ana
Carolina
Torola
Polorós
Izalco
Armenia
Vol. de San Salvador
Cojutepeque
Cacaopera
Sesori
Sonsonate
Nueva San Salvador
San Salvador
L. de Ilopango
Santa Clara
San Francisco (Gotera)
Vol. de San Vicente
San Vicente
Nueva Granada
MORAZÁN
Acajutla
LA LIBERTAD
LA PAZ
Zacatecoluca
Tecoluca
Jucuapa
Vol. de San Miguel
San Miguel
Pasaquina
Punta Remedios
La Libertad
San Luis
Cuscatlán Int'l Airport
San Agustín
San Jorge
San Alejo
Usulután
El Tránsito
La Herradura
Bahía de La Unión
La Unión
Laguna de Olomega
Chirilagua
Península San Juan del Gozo
Bahía de Jiquilisco
Isla Conchagüita
Isla Meanguera
Punta Amapala
Lempa
Paz
Sumpul
Goascorán
Grande de San Miguel
90° 00'
89° 30'
89° 00'
88° 30'
88° 00'
14° 30'
14° 00'
13° 30'
13° 00'
0 10 20 mi
0 10 20 30 40 km
International boundary
Department boundary
National capital
Department capital
Town, village
Pan-American highway
Main road
Railroad
Airport
Where the names of the departments are the same as their capitals, only the capitals are named.
The boundaries shown and the designations used on this map do not imply official endorsement or acceptance by the United Nations.
Map No. 3903 UNITED NATIONS
August 1995
Department of Public Information
Cartographic Section

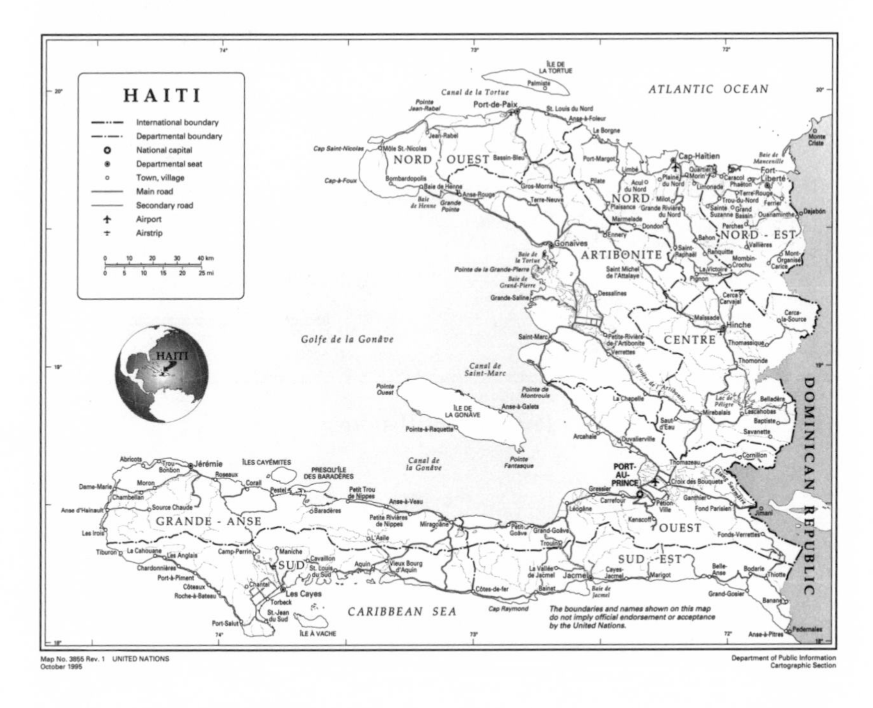

Map No. 3855 Rev. 1 UNITED NATIONS
October 1995

Department of Public Information
Cartographic Section

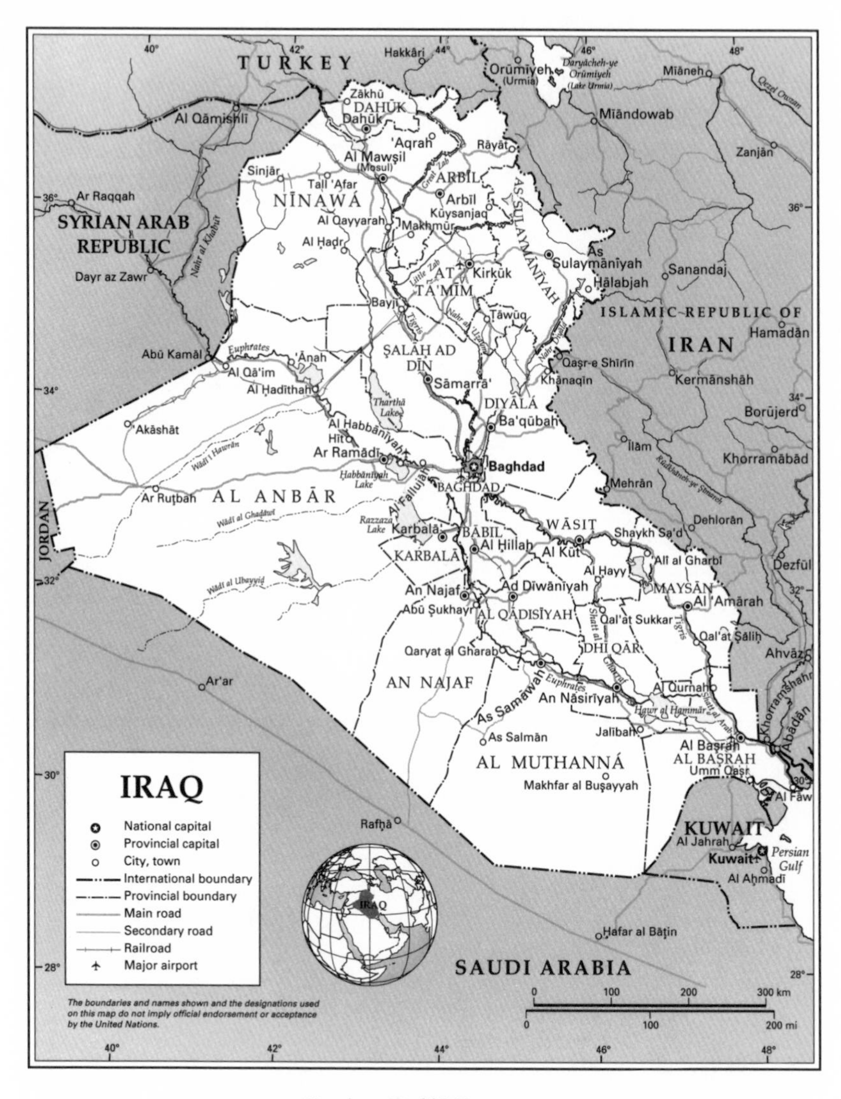

Persian Gulf War area

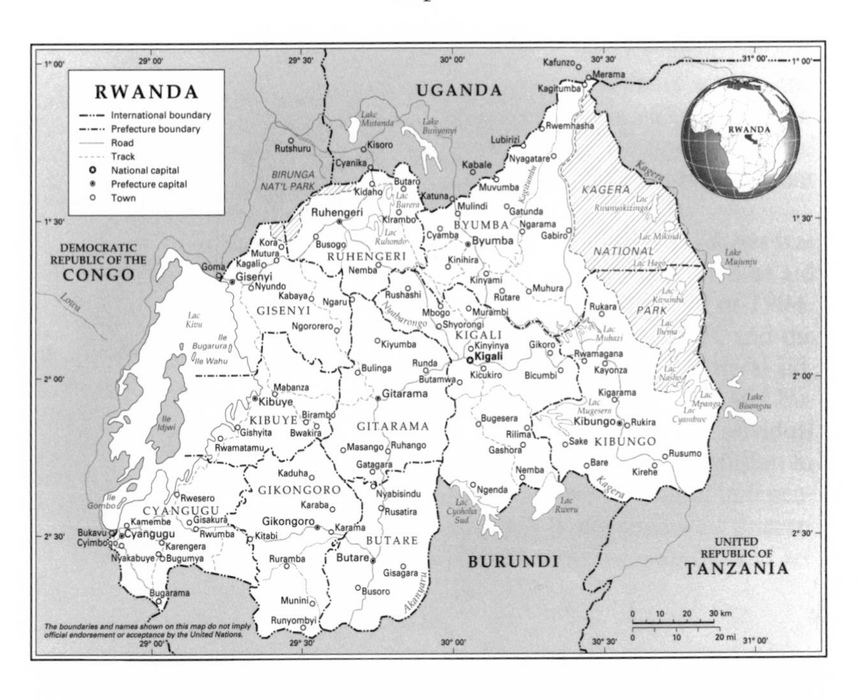
RWANDA
International boundary
Prefecture boundary
Road
Track
National capital
Prefecture capital
Town
UGANDA
DEMOCRATIC REPUBLIC OF THE CONGO
BURUNDI
UNITED REPUBLIC OF TANZANIA
Kigali
Ruhengeri
Gisenyi
Kibuye
Gitarama
Byumba
Kibungo
Gikongoro
Cyangugu
Butare
RUHENGERI
GISENYI
KIBUYE
GITARAMA
BYUMBA
KIGALI
KIBUNGO
GIKONGORO
CYANGUGU
BUTARE
BIRUNGA NAT'L PARK
KAGERA NATIONAL PARK
Lac Kivu
Ile Idjwi
Goma
Bukavu
Lake Mutanda
Lake Bunyonyi
Lac Burera
Lac Ruhondo
Lac Muhazi
Lac Rweru
Lac Cyohoha Sud
Lake Mujunju
Lake Bisongou
Kagera
Akanyaru
Nyabarongo
Kafunzo
Merama
Kagitumba
Rwemhasha
Nyagatare
Kabale
Rutshuru
Kisoro
Cyanika
Butaro
Kidaho
Katuna
Mulindi
Gatunda
Ngarama
Gabiro
Kirambo
Busogo
Cyamba
Kora
Mutura
Kagali
Nyundo
Kabaya
Ngaru
Nemba
Kinihira
Kinyami
Rutare
Muhura
Rushashi
Mbogo
Shyorongi
Murambi
Rukara
Ngororero
Kiyumba
Kinyinya
Gikoro
Rwamagana
Kayonza
Bulinga
Runda
Butamwa
Kicukiro
Bicumbi
Mabanza
Kigarama
Birambo
Gishyita
Bwakira
Bugesera
Rilima
Rukira
Sake
Gashora
Masango
Ruhango
Rwamatamu
Gatagara
Rusumo
Bare
Kirehe
Nemba
Kaduha
Nyabisindu
Ngenda
Rwesero
Karaba
Rusatira
Gisakura
Kamembe
Gikongoro
Karama
Rwumba
Kitabi
Cyimbogo
Karengera
Ruramba
Gisagara
Nyakabuye
Bugumya
Busoro
Bugarama
Munini
Runyombyi
Ile Bugarura
Ile Wahu
Ile Gombo
30 km
20 mi
The boundaries and names shown on this map do not imply official endorsement or acceptance by the United Nations.

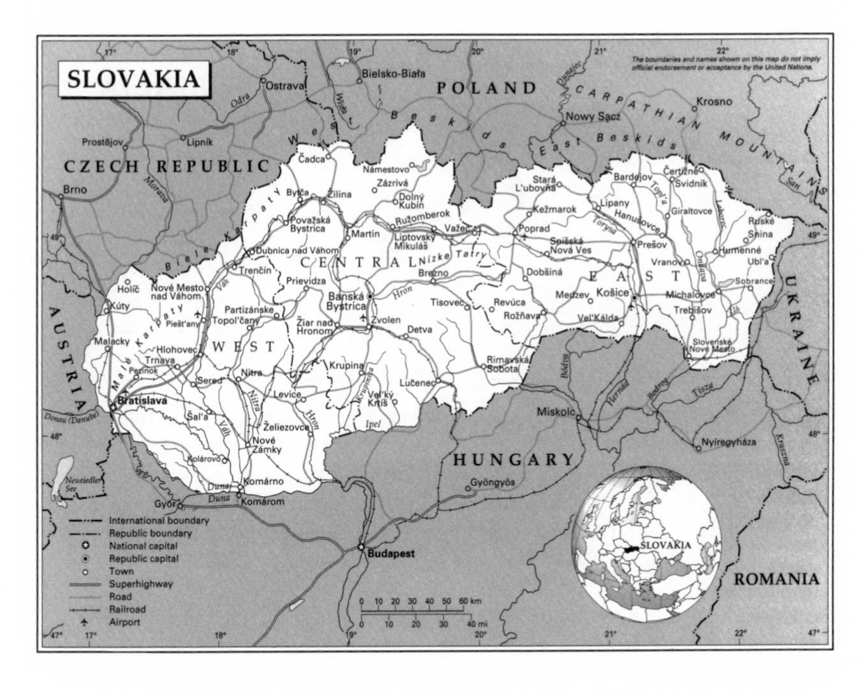
SLOVAKIA
POLAND
CZECH REPUBLIC
AUSTRIA
HUNGARY
UKRAINE
ROMANIA
CARPATHIAN MOUNTAINS
West Beskids
East Beskids
Biele Karpaty
Malé Karpaty
Nízke Tatry
WEST
CENTRAL
EAST
Bratislava
Budapest
Ostrava
Bielsko-Biała
Krosno
Nowy Sącz
Prostějov
Lipník
Brno
Čadca
Namestovo
Zázrivá
Dolný Kubín
Stará L'ubovňa
Bardejov
Čertižné
Svidník
Bytča
Žilina
Považská Bystrica
Martin
Ružomberok
Liptovský Mikuláš
Važec
Poprad
Kežmarok
Lipany
Hanušovce
Giraltovce
Ruské
Snina
Humenné
Ubl'a
Dubnica nad Váhom
Trenčín
Spišská Nová Ves
Prešov
Vranov
Sobrance
Prievidza
Brezno
Dobšiná
Michalovce
Trebišov
Košice
Medzev
Holíč
Nové Mesto nad Váhom
Banská Bystrica
Tisovec
Revúca
Rožňava
Vel'Kálda
Kúty
Partizánske
Topol'čany
Piešťany
Žiar nad Hronom
Zvolen
Detva
Malacky
Hlohovec
Trnava
Pezinok
Sered'
Nitra
Krupina
Rimavská Sobota
Slovenské Nové Mesto
Levice
Vel'ký Krtíš
Lučenec
Miskolc
Šal'a
Želiezovce
Nové Zámky
Kolárovo
Komárno
Komárom
Győr
Gyöngyös
Nyíregyháza
Neusiedler See
Donau (Danube)
Duna
Odra
Morava
Váh
Hron
Ipel
Dunajec
Wisła
Torysa
Ondava
Laborec
Bodrog
Hornád
Tisza
Sajó
San
Krasna
Topl'a
Bodva
International boundary
Republic boundary
National capital
Republic capital
Town
Superhighway
Road
Railroad
Airport
60 km
40 mi
The boundaries and names shown on this map do not imply official endorsement or acceptance by the United Nations.

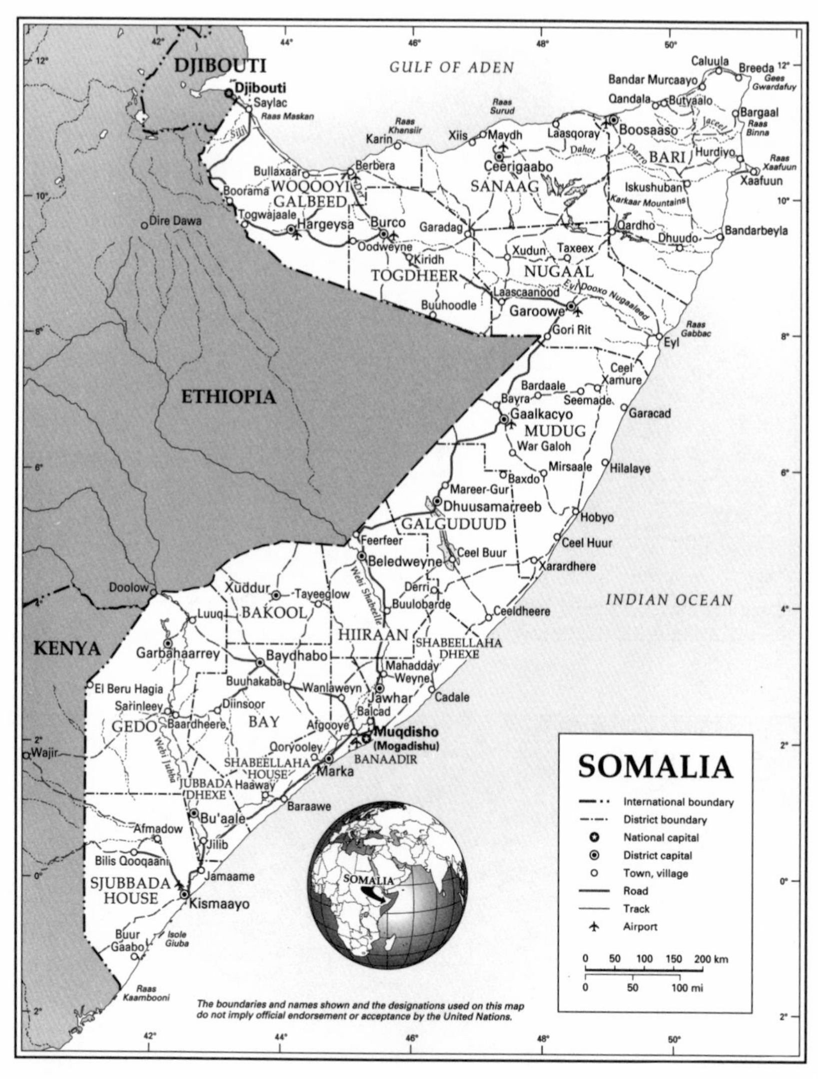

Source: Maps courtesy of the United Nations Department of Public Information, *Bosnia and Herzegovina:* 3729 rev. 1, August 1995; *Cambodia:* 3860 rev. 1, August 1995; *El Salvador:* 3903, August 1995; *Former Yugoslav Republic of Macedonia:* 3789 rev. 1, October 1995; *Haiti:* 3855 rev. 1, October 1995; *Iraq and Persian Gulf War area:* 3835 rev. 2, August 1996; *Rwanda:* 3717 rev. 1, December 1997; *Slovakia:* 3803, March 1994; *Somalia:* 3690 rev. 4, August 1997.

1

Comparing Costs of Prevention and Costs of Conflict: Toward a New Methodology

Michael E. Brown and Richard N. Rosecrance

It is often said that an ounce of prevention is worth a pound of cure. In this study, we investigate whether this is true with respect to deadly conflicts. More specifically, we try to determine whether conflict prevention makes sense in selfish cost-benefit terms to neighboring states, regional powers, and the international community in general. Is conflict prevention cost-effective from the standpoint of outside parties?

We focus on these cost considerations because one of the main barriers to conflict prevention is motivating outside powers to take action. Contrary to what one might think, we know that international powers have often received early warning of impending trouble. As Boutros Boutros-Ghali, the former secretary general of the United Nations observed, "Experience has shown that the greatest obstacle to success in these [preventive] endeavors is not, as is widely supposed, lack of information, analytical capacity, or ideas for United Nations initiatives."[1] It was widely recognized in the first few months of 1992, for example, that Bosnia was about to plunge into chaos. Similarly, it was well understood in late March and early April 1994 that the situation in Rwanda was moving toward violence. Even so, the international community failed to take firm, effective action to prevent these countries from exploding.

One might like to think that well-meaning people around the world will be motivated to act when human suffering is intense, when important moral principles are being trampled, and when crimes against humanity are being committed. Sadly, humanitarian impulses and moral motivations are often insufficient, as we have seen in Bosnia, Iraq, Liberia, Rwanda, Sudan, and many other places. The international community stood back and watched while genocide was committed and more than 800,000 people were murdered in Rwanda in the spring and early summer of 1994. And since scenes of slaughter were broadcast throughout the world, policymakers in distant capitals cannot hide behind the excuse that they were unaware of what was taking place in Rwanda. They knew that genocide was being carried out, but their moral outrage was insufficient to spur them into action.[2]

The premise behind this study is that policymakers in foreign lands might be more inclined to take steps to prevent disputes from becoming violent in the future if they understood that conflict prevention makes sense on cost-effective grounds. If the costs of preventive actions are less than the military, economic, and political costs that have to be borne by outside powers when conflicts unfold, then the case for conflict prevention on national interest grounds becomes very strong.

That said, our obligation is to treat this as a question to be answered, not as a case to be made: How do the costs of conflict prevention compare with the costs of conflicts themselves? To answer this question, we need to explain how we will compare the costs of preventive actions to the costs of conflicts to outside parties.

We stress here that we are not seeking to estimate the costs of conflict to the parties themselves—in terms of loss of life, damaged facilities, or production forgone. This is not only because these costs are difficult to measure. (What, for example, is the appropriate value to attribute to human life?) It is also because we assume that outside powers become involved essentially selfishly to prevent later costs impinging on themselves. If the internal costs of conflict were to be included, they would make an even stronger case for early conflict prevention efforts because the costs thereby forestalled would be much greater.

Research Design

In analyzing the cost-effectiveness of conflict prevention, we confront a difficult task. First, few international actions have been undertaken since the end of the Cold War with conflict prevention, and prevention alone, in mind. As a result, it is hard to make estimates of the costs of actual conflict prevention operations. One such operation is the ongoing deployment of military personnel from the United States, Western Europe, and other parts of the world in Macedonia. This operation, which was authorized by the UN Security Council in December 1992, was designed to prevent the conflict in the former Yugoslavia from spreading to Macedonia and perhaps to other parts of the Balkans.[3] The international deployment in Macedonia, however, is a modest undertaking and not necessarily representative of the kinds of activities that more ambitious conflict prevention operations would involve.

Second, even when conflict prevention operations are launched, it can be difficult to determine the extent to which international actions have influenced the course of events. It is certainly true, for example, that the war in the former Yugoslavia has not spread to Macedonia, but one cannot be sure that the international community's deployment of troops in Macedonia is responsible for this. There is a good case to be made that the war has not spread to Macedonia because Slobodan Milosevic's ambitions to create a Greater Serbia foundered in Bosnia. The presence of U.S. and Western European troops in Macedonia undoubtedly had some impact on his and Serbian calculations and contributed in some way to stability in Macedonia; it is uncertain, however, how much of the credit should be given to this particular conflict prevention effort.

Third, if conflict prevention efforts are successful, it is impossible to compare the costs of prevention to the costs of armed conflict because the latter never materialize. By the same token, if conflict prevention efforts are not launched or if they fail and war subsequently breaks out, one cannot be sure what the costs of a successful preventive effort would have been. We can therefore make only indirect comparisons of the costs of prevention and the costs of armed conflict.

We nonetheless argue in this book that early preventive action makes sense in political, military, and economic terms. Subsequent conflict can thereby be circumscribed, or in some cases entirely prevented. The null hypothesis that must be rejected, therefore, is that actions taken to prevent the outbreak and development of conflict are just as onerous and costly as allowing the conflict to unroll without preventive intervention.[4] In the cases we consider, the null hypothesis would amount, inter alia, to the following assertions:

1. Conflict prevention in *Bosnia* would have been as difficult and costly as the conflict itself proved to be.
2. Conflict prevention in *Rwanda* would have been as expensive to the outside world as the extremely costly civil/international conflict that actually occurred.
3. Conflict prevention in *Haiti* would have been as costly and difficult

for outside powers as coping with the later costs of permitting the civil violence there to spread unchecked.

4. Conflict prevention in *Somalia* (to prevent the warlords from instituting anarchy) would have been very expensive—as costly as the conflict that ultimately ensued—and perhaps would have created a quagmire like that in Vietnam.
5. Conflict prevention via early intervention in regard to *Iraq* could not have prevented the invasion of Kuwait or forestalled the Gulf War.

As we contend in the chapters that follow, we reject each of these formulations of the null hypothesis.

1. In regard to Bosnia, the breakup of Yugoslavia could at least have been delayed by the continuance of military and economic assistance to the collective regime in power in Belgrade.[5] The violence that ensued might later have been damped by strong warnings to Milosevic, who was clearly set on carving out a Greater Serbia. Still later intervention in February 1992 would undoubtedly (as we show) have been expensive. It would not, however, have been as costly or long-lived as the NATO Implementation Force (IFOR) and NATO Stabilization Force (SFOR) operations actually undertaken.

2. The situation in Rwanda was undoubtedly worsened by the fall in the international coffee price in 1987–89, leading to increased unemployment and a domestic recession. Even before the plane crash on April 6, 1994, that killed moderate Rwandan President Juvenal Habyarimana and Burundian President Cyprien Ntaryamira, clashes between the Hutu-led Rwandan Patriotic Front and the Rwandan government forces had occurred. If, in response to repeated requests, the UN humanitarian relief forces had been reinforced militarily and provided with new rules of engagement to prevent civil conflict, the carnage could have been prevented or contained at a fraction of the cost that the international community ultimately bore.

3. In regard to Haiti, we contend that early intervention to support President Jean-Bertrand Aristide after his election in December 1990, or after the conclusion of the Washington Accord in February 1992, would have achieved the same result as the later (September 1994) United States–United Nations intervention at less cost.

4. Somalia presents a difficult case for conflict prevention. By the advent of United Nations Operation in Somalia (UNOSOM II) (with the United States providing the bulk of the troops), mission tasks had been increased but fewer troops were actually provided. The warlords had not been disarmed, though French troops partly succeeded in this objective in their sector. In Mogadishu, however, U.S. Rangers needed backup and

different rules of engagement. They were not able to disarm the contending factions or to capture General Mohammed Farah Aideed. After a decisive engagement in which the Rangers suffered eighteen killed and seventy-five wounded, President Bill Clinton authorized American withdrawal in March 1994. Alternatively, if U.S. economic and military aid had been continued for a time after 1989, the economic crisis and ensuing disorganization of production might not have occurred. Or an intervention force in early 1991 after the fall of the Siad Barre regime would have been able to prevent anarchy. At that time, no military force capable of opposing an American-led intervention existed in Somalia. But neither of these options occurred. Both would have been considerably less costly than the result that transpired.

5. Finally, even more difficult was dealing with Saddam Hussein, dictator of Iraq. Saddam needed money and a higher oil price. Both, he believed, could be provided by a compliant Kuwait. After Kuwait had been invaded and occupied on August 2, 1990, there were few options open to the international community to reverse the Iraqi absorption of Kuwait. Military force had to be used, and the prospect of it was not compelling to a leader who was willing to suffer defeat at the hands of the United States and the coalition forces rather than concede in front of Arab opinion. On the other hand, resolute action before August 2 (for example, in May 1990) might have deterred Iraqi action. The sending of a few brigades to Kuwait or the dispatch of a carrier task force to the Persian Gulf would have signaled much stronger American and international intentions than were actually conveyed at the time. The resulting outcome would have been much cheaper than the waging of the Gulf War.

It is not our purpose to convince the reader now that the null hypothesis should be rejected. But the previous five paragraphs give evidence of our intention to engage and contest the null hypothesis in the case studies to follow.

The Problem of Counterfactuals

In this study we are constantly estimating the costs and outcomes of actions that did not happen, or counterfactual events. For large N studies, comparable cases can be assessed on the basis of a few key variables in regression equations. But there is still a problem of counterfactuals.[6] The analyst must convince himself or herself that small differences in the case studies do not matter to the result obtained. This may or may not be true, but the investigator posits it nonetheless.

In small N studies, one assumes that a change in one variable or initial condition might have greatly influenced the result (without changing the whole complex of the case). This is our problem here: to say what might have happened if earlier conflict prevention efforts had occurred. To do this, one must make a case that such interventions were among the options known or considered at the time and were politically feasible ones. This assertion may raise historical hackles. It is always open to the historian to contend that only what actually occurred was possible. History then becomes a deterministic and irreversible process. For those who are convinced this is true, the rest of the analysis will appear an exercise in academic futility.

As opposed to historians, however, policymakers can hardly adopt this stance. They know they might have done better. Most policymakers after World War II contended that the world did not have to countenance the results of the Munich Conference in September 1938 in which British Prime Minister Neville Chamberlain gave way to German Chancellor Adolf Hitler. This and other outcomes could and should have been changed. Some informed observers believe that Hitler was the only figure among the German elite who favored going to war in 1939.[7] If he had been removed, the other leaders, both military and political, would have hesitated to attack Poland, France, the United Kingdom, and their allies. In another case, many are convinced that Winston Churchill was the only British leader who would not have compromised with Hitler in June 1940.[8] Other members of the cabinet appear to have been ready for a deal.[9] If these contentions are true, World War II might have been averted or altered by hypothesized counterfactual interventions to change the leadership on one or both sides. One does not have to agree, however, with these particular assertions to accept the notion that policymakers can do better. They can learn from mistakes. From a study of many cases, we have come to the conclusion that conflict prevention actions in conflict situations can be both more effective and better timed than they have been.

Early intervention is difficult perhaps because many leaders think that domestic public opinion is willing to accept action only when the conflict has reached a peak. By that time, however, it may be too late or require too great a commitment to engage in conflict prevention actions. Actual ease of involvement may be inverse to that commended by domestic politics. Intervention is easier at the very beginning or at the end of a conflict period when the parties are tired and seek a respite from civil or external strife (see figure 1.1).

But this does not mean that early actions are impossible. It just means that executive leadership is required to create the climate of opinion in which conflict prevention can take place. Public opinion did not favor American participation in actions in either Bosnia or Haiti when they occurred. But it did legitimize them afterward. The key lesson for leadership

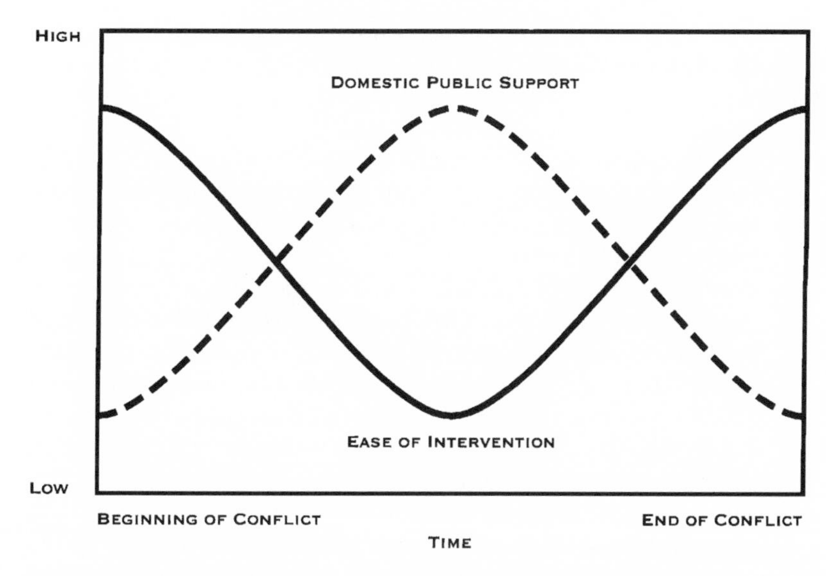

Figure 1.1 Ease of Intervention versus Domestic Public Support for Intervention

is to intervene in such a way as to resolve the issue, limiting long-term involvement.

Thus, we contend that a survey of what might have been done (using intelligently framed counterfactual analysis) is crucial to the development of better international policy. In our case we recognize that no single approach to counterfactual action is adequate. We must, rather, consider different strategies for different cases, imagine early conflict prevention where it did not occur, and hypothesize conflict occurrence where it did not take place. We posit three different ways of dealing with the problem.

Option 1

First, one can engage in counterfactual analysis by comparing the costs of *actual* conflicts to *estimates* of what it would have cost to prevent these conflicts from taking place. To engage in this kind of counterfactual analysis one must do two things. First, one must identify a moment when international action could have been taken to prevent the dispute in question from becoming violent. Second, one must ascertain what kinds of international actions would have been needed to prevent violence from breaking out. To guard against the charge that one is skewing the analysis in favor of conflict prevention, one should assume that conflict prevention operations would have been robust and that they would have been of long duration.

Cost estimates could be based in part on the costs of comparable operations launched elsewhere in the world. Three baselines can be utilized in this context.

1. For multifunctional operations with *small* military forces (a few thousand troops), undertaken with the consent of the local parties, such as the UN operations in El Salvador, Nicaragua, Namibia, Mozambique, and Cambodia.[10]
2. For multifunctional operations with *medium-size* military contingents (tens of thousands of troops), undertaken with the consent of local parties but where consent might break down and military operations might be needed, such as the U.S./UN operation in Haiti (20,000 troops); IFOR in Bosnia (60,000 troops) along with the European Union (EU) contingent involved in implementing the civilian aspects of the Dayton Accord.[11]
3. For *large-scale* military operations (hundreds of thousands of troops), undertaken in places where the consent of the local parties has not been obtained and where international forces are expected to engage in open warfare, such as Operation Desert Shield and Operation Desert Storm (500,000 troops).[12]

Option 2

Second, one can engage in counterfactual analysis by comparing the costs of *actual* conflict prevention efforts to the *estimated* costs to regional and international powers of conflicts that might have taken place.[13] For example, one could determine the costs of the international efforts to prevent conflict in Macedonia and the southern Balkans to the estimated costs of a wider Balkan war. One could also determine the costs of international efforts to dampen tensions between Hungary and Slovakia over the latter's mistreatment of its Hungarian minority, and compare these costs to estimates of what an armed conflict between these two states might have entailed. To engage in this kind of counterfactual analysis, one must make assumptions about how conflicts might have been escalated and spread. In this case one analyzes initial prevention efforts.

Option 3

Third, one can analyze the costs of multifunctional (diplomatic, political, economic, miliary) peace operations in places such as El Salvador, Nicaragua, Namibia, Mozambique, and Cambodia.[14] Although these are usually characterized as conflict resolution efforts because they aim to resolve conflicts that have already taken place, they are also conflict prevention efforts in that they seek to keep war from breaking out again. In cases such as these, one can determine the *actual* costs that these wars have imposed on regional and international powers, and compare them to the *actual* costs of international efforts to keep them from breaking out again. This is a hard case for conflict prevention because the international community is helping to rebuild political and economic systems that have been torn apart by years of war. These costs are higher than the costs the international community would have paid to prevent these conflicts from breaking out in the first place.[15] In this instance one analyzes mid-course intervention in a conflict process.

Obviously, these baselines would provide only a starting point for estimating the costs of hypothetical conflict prevention operations. Assumptions would have to be made in each case about the kinds of operations and forces that would have been needed, and cost estimates would have to be adjusted accordingly.

Our Approach

There is no direct way of comparing the costs of a successful preventive operation with an actual conflict: if prevention succeeds, no war ensues. We therefore employ all three of these "indirect" methodological options in our analysis of the problem. This methodological checks and balances system minimizes the chance of bias skewing our final results. This, in turn, gives our study a strong analytical foundation.

Calculating the Costs of Prevention

Conflict prevention efforts are not just military undertakings. To the contrary, they usually involve a wide range of diplomatic, political, economic, and military activities undertaken by states (acting unilaterally or multilaterally), international organizations, and nongovernmental organizations (NGOs). In addition, both long-term efforts to address the underlying causes of conflicts and focused efforts to address the proximate causes of conflicts need to be taken into account.[16] (See table 1.1.) In our analysis of the costs of actual and hypothetical conflict prevention efforts, we will endeavor to take the full range of actions and options into account.

Long-Term Efforts

Long-term efforts to address the underlying causes of conflicts include measures aimed at reducing security concerns, promoting political justice

TABLE 1.1
Elements of Conflict Prevention

Long-Term Efforts:
- To reduce security concerns
- To promote political justice and human rights
- To promote economic development and justice
- To overturn patterns of cultural and social discrimination

Focused Efforts to Address Impending Crises:
- Fact-finding missions
- Mediation missions
- Confidence-building measures
- Traditional peacekeeping operations
- Multifunctional peacekeeping operations
- Military and economic technical assistance
- Arms embargoes and economic sanctions
- Judicial enforcement measures
- The threat or use of military force

and human rights, promoting economic development and justice, and overturning patterns of cultural and social discrimination.[17]

Reducing Security Concerns

Security concerns and arms races contribute to instability and the potential for violence. One way to reduce the uncertainties that often drive arms races is to promote transparency and adopt confidence-building measures. In many cases, the challenge will be convincing governments that they face these kinds of instability problems and that they should agree to outside involvement in delicate security matters. Securing and protecting arms caches (against seizures, as could have been done in Rwanda and Somalia, or preemption of the kind that took place in the Serbian and Albanian cases) would be extremely useful.

Promoting Political Justice and Human Rights

When people feel that existing political arrangements are unjust and incapable of being changed peacefully, the potential for intrastate violence increases dramatically. International actors can help promote peaceful political change by extending technical advice about constitutional and electoral reforms, for example. They can also exert considerable influence by linking financial assistance and the development of closer economic ties to political reforms—that is, by making financial aid and economic relationships conditional. They can also link membership in international economic, military, and political institutions to domestic political reforms. This has worked fairly well in East-Central Europe, where states are eager to join the EU and the North Atlantic Treaty Organization (NATO) and willing to do whatever is necessary to improve their chances of being offered early admission to Western institutions.

Promoting Economic Development and Justice

A country's economic situation and economic prospects have tremendous implications for its potential for violence. If international actors are serious about preventing internal conflict and civil war, they have to do more than treat the military dimensions and military manifestations of the problem; they have to address the economic sources of conflict in troubled societies. International actors can help promote economic reforms the same way they can help promote political reforms: by extending technical assistance; by linking financial assistance and economic relationships to the implementation of reforms; and by linking membership in international organizations and institutions to reforms. States, international financial institutions, other international organizations, and NGOs can work together to develop "mini–Marshall Plans" for countries in need of special economic attention.

Overturning Patterns of Discrimination

Finally, international actors can help to address the cultural and perceptual factors that lead some countries toward violence. This means working to overturn patterns of cultural discrimination by safeguarding rights with respect to language, religion, and education. This also means working to revamp the distorted histories groups often have of each other. Governments could be asked to enter into international dialogues about group histories and to publish foreign criticisms of school curricula and textbooks.[18]

Focused Efforts

When political problems intensify and violence is looming, international actors interested in preventing violent conflicts have nine main policy instruments at their disposal.[19] Six are cooperative measures that depend in important ways on the consent of local parties: fact-finding missions; mediation missions; confidence-building measures; traditional peacekeeping operations; multifunctional peacekeeping operations; and military and economic technical assistance. Three instruments are fundamentally coercive: arms embargoes and economic sanctions; judicial enforcement measures; and military force.

Fact-Finding Missions

Launching a fact-finding mission is a first step that the United Nations and regional organizations can take—and often do take—to help prevent disputes from becoming violent. The idea is to provide a detailed, impartial report on the issues in dispute. Fact-finding missions come in many forms. Some come at the initiative of the state or states in question. Others come at the initiative of the UN Security Council, the General Assembly, the secretary general, or regional bodies. Any of these actors can conduct a fact-finding mission, but all fact-finding missions to the territory of a state require an invitation from or the consent of the state or states being examined. Some missions consist of a single person; others are larger undertakings. The mandates of fact-finding missions also vary. Some try to determine the causes of a conflict, while others examine the role of neighboring powers in a conflict. Many investigate human rights abuses. Some fact-finding missions are launched before violence breaks out, and are therefore conflict prevention efforts. Others are launched during conflicts, and can be seen as conflict management or conflict resolution measures. Fact-finding missions frequently lead to other initiatives, such as good offices and mediation efforts, peacekeeping operations of various kinds, and the employment of coercive instruments, including arms embargoes, economic sanctions, judicial actions, and the use of military force.

Mediation Missions

When trouble is brewing and especially when violence breaks out, third parties, regional organizations, and the United Nations often offer to mediate disputes.[20] Since mediation efforts are not expensive undertakings, the international community naturally gravitates toward them. Policymakers can claim that they are "doing something" about trouble spots, but they do not have to bear the costs of imposing economic sanctions or run the risks of taking military action.

Confidence-Building Measures

Security concerns often lead to arms races and to the onset of violence. One way to reduce the uncertainties that drive arms races and undermine peace processes is to promote transparency. International actors can encourage local parties to make declarations about the size and deployment of their military forces and about arms acquisitions and transfers. They can help to create buffer zones from which heavy weapons are excluded. They can help to form joint consultative committees, with representatives from all of the relevant local parties, to discuss and resolve these and other security problems.[21] International actors can play two main roles in this effort. First, they can help to devise transparency and confidence-building measures and, through mediation efforts, get local parties to agree to them. Second, international actors can help to implement agreements through the deployment of international monitors. The latter are frequently incorporated into the frameworks for traditional peacekeeping and multifunctional peacekeeping operations.

Traditional Peacekeeping Operations

A traditional peacekeeping force is an outside military force positioned between two or more disputants. It is deployed with the consent of the relevant local parties, and its main mission is to monitor an agreed-upon cease-fire. In such an operation peacekeepers are authorized to use force in self-defense and to deter small-scale attacks, but they do not have any significant coercive capabilities or enforcement authority. Traditional peacekeeping operations are usually accompanied by diplomatic efforts to resolve the underlying political conflict, and they are usually authorized by the Security Council.

Traditional peacekeeping operations can help to reinforce peace and bolster peace processes in a number of ways.[22] First, they can monitor the cantonment and separation of warring factions. The UN peacekeeping missions in Cyprus and Georgia, as well as the initial deployment of the United Nations Protection Force (UNPROFOR) in the former Yugoslavia are examples. Second, peacekeeping forces can monitor and verify the withdrawal of foreign troops from a conflict zone. Examples include the UN operations in the Congo, which oversaw the withdrawal of Belgian troops from the region; Angola, which oversaw the withdrawal of Cuban troops; and Afghanistan, which oversaw the withdrawal of Russian troops. Third, peacekeeping forces can monitor the cessation of aid to irregular forces and insurrectionist movements. Examples include the UN missions in Lebanon and Yemen. Fourth, peacekeeping forces can help ensure that the territory of one state is not used for attacks on others. Cases where UN forces sought to do this include Yemen, Lebanon, Central America, and Tajikistan. Fifth, peacekeeping forces can help discourage one state or party from attacking another. The preventive deployment of UN troops in Macedonia was designed with this in mind.

Multifunctional Peacekeeping Operations

Multifunctional peacekeeping operations were developed by the United Nations to address the complex problems posed by intrastate and regional conflicts and to take advantage of the political opportunities that emerged after the end of the Cold War.[23] Traditional peacekeeping operations and multifunctional peacekeeping operations are similar in that they both depend on the full consent of the local parties, the use of force is basically limited to self-defense, and they have limited coercive or enforcement capabilities. However, they differ in three important respects.

First, traditional peacekeeping forces can be deployed once a cease-fire is reached, but multifunctional peacekeeping operations can only be launched after a comprehensive peace agreement has been reached. Multifunctional operations are strictly postconflict undertakings. However, as noted above, they can also be thought of as conflict prevention efforts in that they aim to keep conflicts from breaking out again in the future. Second, traditional peacekeeping operations concentrate mainly on military problems—monitoring cease-fires and keeping combatants separated, for example—whereas multifunctional peacekeeping operations seek to address a wide range of military, political, and economic problems. Multifunctional operations often include a traditional peacekeeping element, but they also help to demobilize armed forces and collect weapons; monitor the provisions of political settlements; design and supervise constitutional, judicial, and political reforms; organize and monitor elections; train local police; monitor potential human rights problems; and help promote economic recovery and economic development. Third, traditional peacekeeping operations are military undertakings that involve few civilians, whereas multifunctional peacekeeping operations involve a wide range of military and civilian personnel. In some multifunctional operations separate organizational elements are set up for electoral, human rights, and humanitarian issues, for example. Most multifunctional operations have large numbers of people involved in the maintenance of law and order, and the training of local police forces.

Military and Economic Technical Assistance

The military and economic levels of power can be used either to persuade—through military and economic technical assistance—or to coerce—through the imposition of arms embargoes and economic sanctions. The extension of military assistance is usually the province of states, because regional and international organizations lack independent military resources of their own. Economic assistance, however, can be channeled through a wider range of international actors, including the United Nations and international financial institutions, such as the International Monetary Fund (IMF) and the World Bank.

When extending military assistance as part of an effort to prevent, manage, or resolve a conflict, international actors face difficult choices. Building up one party to a conflict can aggravate the security concerns of others who can in turn seek to acquire more arms for themselves. Arms races and escalatory spirals can ensue. Now that the Cold War is over, most arms producers are desperate for markets because they have excess production capacities and large stockpiles of weapons; they will therefore sell just about anything to just about anybody. In addition, the black market in arms has grown considerably. As a result, international actors have little control over the international arms market, and they therefore have a limited ability to fine-tune military balances in troubled regions.[24]

One of the developments on the economic front since the 1970s has been the emergence of what is known as "conditionality." That means attaching conditions or strings to economic grants or loans. The IMF and the World Bank, for example, often link economic packages to local commitments to pursue certain kinds of fiscal and political initiatives. In war-torn regions, economic assistance can be and often is linked explicitly to conflict prevention and conflict resolution measures, which can have salutary effects on the prospects for peace processes.

Arms Embargoes and Economic Sanctions

The international community also has a range of coercive instruments at its disposal, starting with the imposition of arms embargoes and economic sanctions on troublemakers. Although embargoes and sanctions can be imposed by individual states or small groups of states, international actions are often coordinated through and authorized by regional organizations or the United Nations.

The adoption of mandatory arms embargoes and economic sanctions under Chapter VII of the UN Charter has increased dramatically since the end of the Cold War.[25] During the Cold War, the United Nations imposed mandatory sanctions only twice, against Rhodesia in 1966 and South Africa in 1977. Since 1990, mandatory Chapter VII embargoes and sanctions have been imposed eight times, six in the context of internal conflicts: in the former Yugoslavia in 1991 and 1992; in Somalia in 1992; in Liberia in 1992; in Angola in 1993; in Haiti in 1993 and 1994; and in Rwanda in 1994. The increased utilization of Chapter VII measures is a reflection of several broad developments: the end of Cold War antagonisms between Washington and Moscow; the resulting revitalization of the UN Security Council; and the Security Council's willingness to address threats to international peace and security in a more resolute and forceful manner. In addition, many policymakers hope that the utilization of arms embargoes and economic sanctions will enable them to avoid sending their own troops into the fray.

Judicial Enforcement Measures

The UN Security Council's frustrations with respect to the former Yugoslavia and Rwanda led it to create an ad hoc international criminal tribunal for the former in 1993 and one for the latter in 1994. The tribunals have three main tasks: to prosecute persons responsible for serious violations of international humanitarian law; to deter further crimes; and to contribute to the restoration and maintenance of peace. The establishment of these tribunals has been met with a fair amount of skepticism. The capacities of the tribunals to bring to justice those who violated humanitarian law in the former Yugoslavia and Rwanda are limited. Although Chapter VII resolutions are legally binding on all member states of the United Nations, this does not necessarily mean that cooperation will be forthcoming. Indeed, much will depend on the extent to which authorities in the former Yugoslavia and Rwanda are willing to provide evidence to international investigators and hand over indicted persons. Another major problem is that the legal requirement to bring war criminals to justice is in conflict with the political requirement to bring conflict to an end: leaders in the former Yugoslavia and Rwanda will be unwilling to agree to peace settlements if legal indictments are sure to follow. Although these tribunals clearly face problems, they may nonetheless play important roles in promoting reconciliation in war-torn countries. By attributing war crimes to specific individuals rather than blaming entire groups, they may make it easier for people to end hostilities and rebuild civil societies—and thereby help to keep conflicts from breaking out again in the future.

The Use of Military Force

The ultimate enforcement instrument at the disposal of states—acting unilaterally or multilaterally through regional organizations or the United Nations—is the use of military force.[26] In the first half of the 1990s, the UN Security Council authorized the use of force with respect to several internal conflicts: Bosnia, Somalia, Rwanda, and Haiti.

Three conditions must be met if the Security Council is to use military force effectively under Chapter VII of the Charter. First, none of the five permanent members of the council (known in UN circles as the P-5) can oppose the use of force: any one of the five can veto a Security Council resolution authorizing military action. It is extremely important, moreover, for most of the P-5—the United States, in particular—to actively support the military action in question. Second, if military force is to be used effectively, the Security Council must identify and enunciate clear and consistent political objectives. This was done in Haiti; Operation Restore Democracy has consequently been a success. This was not done in Bosnia,

Somalia, and Rwanda, where UN missions have been markedly less successful. Third, sufficient military forces have to be made available to the Security Council. The fact that the council lacks military forces it can call upon, as provided for in Article 43 of the Charter, severely limits its ability to act. Although this does not preclude action, it makes UN operations totally dependent on the willingness of states, especially the P-5, to make troops available at specific points in time. The United States is particularly key: it alone has the firepower, transport, command and control, communications, intelligence, logistics, and power projection capabilities needed for large-scale operations.

What many people think of as "UN enforcement actions" and "UN military operations" have been and will continue to be actions authorized by the UN Security Council but carried out by individual states or groups of states. Whether these kinds of operations will be launched, therefore, will depend to a significant degree on the extent to which state interests are engaged by particular problems.

Calculating the Costs of Conflicts to Outside Powers

Estimating the costs of conflicts to regional and international powers is another uncertain task.[27] It involves looking at a range of quantifiable and nonquantifiable costs. Both are important, although the latter are hard to evaluate on a comparative basis. One should also try to distinguish between the costs to contiguous states and the costs to distant powers. The former usually bear more costs than the latter, but the latter are usually the key to nonpartisan, effective conflict prevention. In this study, we distinguish between and attempt to estimate five main sets of costs: refugee costs, military costs, economic costs, instability costs, and the costs associated with international humanitarian operations, conflict management operations, and conflict resolution operations. (See table 1.2.)

Refugee Costs

When violent conflicts break out, people often flee across international borders in large numbers. In many cases, refugees have to be counted in tens and hundreds of thousands—even millions. Refugees often create heavy economic burdens for neighboring states, and these states are often ill equipped to take on sudden burdens of this kind. In addition to these economic costs, which are quantifiable, refugees also create a range of other problems that are not quantifiable. Complaints about the economic burdens created by refugees can cause domestic political problems in host countries. Refugees can also upset ethnic balances within host countries,

TABLE 1.2
Costs to Outside Powers

Refugee Costs
- Economic burdens
- Political and social problems
- Military complications

Direct Economic Costs and Economic Opportunity Costs
- Lost investments
- Lost imports
- Lost export markets
- Disruptions to labor supplies
- Regional burdens

Military Costs
- Territorial infringements
- Military skirmishes
- Higher defense budgets

Instability Costs
- Ethnic radicalization
- Drug trafficking
- Nationalistic and diversionary campaigns
- Opportunistic interventions and invasions

Costs of International Peace Operations
- Humanitarian relief efforts
- Multifunctional conflict resolution operations

thereby leading to political turmoil. In addition, fighters often use refugee bases for rest, recuperation, reorganization, and rearming; when refugee camps become military bases, military skirmishes often follow.[28] In many cases, these skirmishes involve military forces from host countries; in others, they involve interdiction forces from home countries; in still others, they involve both, and lead to interstate confrontations. In short, refugees create a multitude of quantifiable and nonquantifiable costs for neighboring states, and often distant international powers as well.

Other Direct Economic Costs and Economic Opportunity Costs

When violent conflicts break out, the direct economic costs and economic opportunity costs to outside powers are many and varied. They include lost investments in local and joint projects; lost imports (in some cases involving strategic resources such as oil); lost export markets (which in some but not all cases can be replaced in the long run); and disruptions to labor supplies. Lost investments and opportunity costs can be quantified (although assumptions have to be made about future trends). Other economic costs are harder to estimate, especially indirect economic costs borne by other states in the region in question. If the region as a whole is perceived by international powers as unstable, capital might cost more, loans might become more difficult to obtain, and inflation rates might go up. The economic costs generated by violent conflicts are not confined to regional powers, however; distant powers often pay a heavy price as well.

Military Costs

Rebel groups frequently use outlying regions of neighboring states as sanctuaries. This often leads home states to carry out hot-pursuit operations, which in turn often lead to skirmishes between the military forces of the home and host states. Therefore, when a conflict breaks out in one state, the costs to neighboring states can include the costs of strengthened border controls; the costs of additional troop deployments in troubled regions; higher levels of defense spending; and combat casualties. In some cases, rebels attack targets in host countries to attract attention to their plight; this happened in Irian Jaya in 1995, for example. Harder to quantify (but still important) are the instability problems created when warring factions use the territory of neighboring states for their own purposes: sovereignty is undermined; political instability is created; and the possibility of interstate conflict increases.

Instability Costs

These costs are very difficult (perhaps impossible) to measure, but they nonetheless need to be taken into account. As already noted, refugees and rebel forces can create instability problems in neighboring states. In addition to these problems, conflicts can undermine stability in neighboring states in other ways. Ethnic groups can become radicalized if they see their brethren being persecuted; this can lead to calls for protective interventions. Ethnic groups can also become mobilized if their brethren are rising up (successfully or unsuccessfully) in revolt; successful uprisings can be inspirational because they raise hopes about the successful use of coercion and force; existing social contracts might begin to crumble. Ethnic groups can become more willing to use force if they see other ethnic groups in other states becoming more assertive, and especially if groups in other states are able to use coercion or force successfully; again, existing social contracts might begin to crumble. Another problem is drug trafficking.

Rebel groups often resort to drug trafficking to finance their campaigns. Their drug operations often take on a life of their own. This can lead to drug use problems, political instability, and a loss of control over territory in neighboring states.

At a state-to-state level, trouble in Country A might lead policymakers in that country to employ nationalistic appeals, which could lead to regional instability. Simultaneously or alternatively, policymakers in Country A might launch a diversionary war against Country B. Another potential problem is that trouble in Country A could lead policymakers in Country B to launch an opportunistic intervention (supporting a rebel faction) or an opportunistic invasion—this would create security concerns and instability problems for other countries in the region. In short, turmoil in one place can lead to regional instability in a number of ways.

Costs of International Peace Operations

In calculating the costs of a conflict to outside powers, we think it is reasonable to include the costs of all the things that neighboring states, distant powers, international organizations, and NGOs eventually do because they failed to prevent conflicts from breaking out in the first place. In Bosnia, for example, the costs of UNPROFOR, NGO humanitarian efforts, UN economic sanctions, and IFOR (and all sorts of other international actions) should be taken into account. Similarly, in Rwanda, the costs of the humanitarian relief efforts in all of the refugee camps and the costs of the international criminal tribunal should be counted. In addition, one should include the long-term costs of multifunctional peacekeeping and reconstruction efforts in places like El Salvador, Nicaragua, Mozambique, and Namibia: How much is it costing regional and international powers to demobilize armed factions and rebuild political and economic systems? How much does it cost to rebuild and revitalize war-torn states? These are costs outside powers would have avoided if they had taken effective conflict prevention efforts at the outset. Since conflict prevention efforts undertaken by a coalition of nations enjoy a special legitimacy that did not exist during the Cold War, these offer a new and viable instrument, politically and internationally.

Case Selection

In this study, we focus on the post–Cold War era because the dynamics of internal and regional conflicts and the dynamics of international intervention have changed in fundamental ways with the end of the global competition for power between Washington and Moscow. During the Cold War, the superpowers sparked and escalated many internal and regional conflicts, and the competition between Washington and Moscow made concerted conflict prevention efforts virtually impossible. With the end of the Cold War, the prospects for conflict prevention have changed because the prospects for international consensus and joint action have improved.

Since it is not feasible to analyze all of the dozens of trouble spots (and potential trouble spots) around the world or all of the dozens of international actions that have been taken (or could have been taken) since the end of the Cold War to prevent, manage, or resolve internal or regional conflicts, we look at a representative sample of cases in this investigation of the problem. (See table 1.3.)

The first category of cases we examine are cases where the costs of *actual* conflicts are compared to the *estimated* costs of conflict prevention efforts that could have been taken but were, in the event, not taken. (This is Option 1 in the framework outlined above.) In this study, we examine the conflicts in Bosnia, Rwanda, Somalia, and Haiti, as well as the Gulf War.

The second category are cases where the costs of *actual* prevention efforts are compared to the *estimated* costs of conflicts that did not follow. (This is Option 2 in the framework outlined above.) In this study, we analyze the conflict prevention efforts undertaken in Macedonia and Slovakia.

The third category are cases where the costs of *actual* conflicts are compared to the costs of the *actual* conflict resolution and conflict prevention efforts that followed. (This is Option 3 in the framework outlined above.) In this study, we analyze the costs associated with the conflicts in Cambodia and El Salvador. As opposed to the other conflicts we examine, both of these originated during the Cold War, though they continued beyond its end.

Most post–Cold War conflicts have been internal conflicts, and our sample follows suit. However, it includes one notable case of interstate aggression—the Iraqi invasion of Kuwait, and the international response to this act of aggression. Some conflicts have caused many casualties, produced

TABLE 1.3
Case Selection

Failed Prevention	Initial Prevention
• Bosnia	• Macedonia
• Rwanda	• Slovakia
• Somalia	
• Haiti	**Mid-Course Prevention**
• The Persian Gulf	• Cambodia
	• El Salvador

large numbers of refugees, and imposed high costs on regional and international powers. Others were more isolated, and imposed comparatively low costs on outside powers. We look at examples of both: Bosnia, Rwanda, El Salvador, and the Gulf War imposed high costs on neighboring and international powers; Haiti, Cambodia, and Somalia had comparatively modest effects on neighboring states and distant powers. Some problems eventually triggered aggressive international action, while others triggered more limited responses. Again, we look at both: the Gulf War and Bosnia are examples of the former; Haiti, El Salvador, Cambodia, Somalia, and Rwanda are examples of the latter.

Part One

Failed Prevention

2

Bosnia

Andrea Kathryn Talentino

Case Preview

EUROPE WAS UNPREPARED for the violence that exploded in the former Yugoslavia just as the end of the Cold War seemed to promise greater possibilities for international cooperation. Instead of peace, the new decade brought more than four years of war to the Balkans and the largest refugee crisis in Europe since World War II. Though the media popularized the problem as one of deep and ancient hatreds between ethnicities and religions, in reality the country's collapse was the work of elites who sought to maximize their individual power by using economic crisis to catalyze nationalism, defined in the 1990s by ethnic and republican, rather than national, borders. The Serbo-Croatian war of 1991 was only a prelude, its six short months foretelling the ferocity of events to come. The Bosnian war began when Bosnian Serb forces repudiated Bosnian independence and attacked Sarajevo and predominately Muslim towns in April 1992. Bosnian Croats subsequently joined the conflict, making a trio of warring parties—Bosnian Serbs, Bosnian Croats, and Bosnian Muslims (government forces)—who were variously joined, covertly and overtly, by regular Serb and Croat forces. Alliances among the three main belligerents proved flexible, as political possibilities demanded, but the conflict was primarily defined by the Bosnian Serbs and their hopes of creating a Greater Serbia or an autonomous republic in confederation with Serbia proper.

Initially supported by the Serbian remnant of the former Yugoslav army, the Serbs managed to claim large chunks of Bosnian territory. Their methods, however, which from the start included slaughter and intimidation—portrayed by the perpetrators as "ethnic cleansing"—also came to include the use of UN soldiers as human shields and indiscriminate bombing of civilian areas. The last ultimately produced the international intervention that brought the fighting to a halt in December 1995.

The European Union (then the European Community) recognized Bosnia as a sovereign state in April 1992. This recognition triggered the Serb offensive. International attention until then had been occupied with the Serb-Croat conflict in Croatia, where recognition of Croatia had caused violence in that republic, initiated by Croatian Serbs who, like their counterparts in Bosnia, wanted to join the Greater Serbia promoted by Serbian President Slobodan Milosevic. The ramifications of this for Bosnia, which had an even larger Serbian minority than Croatia, were largely ignored, even though Bosnian Serbs had already declared their intention to thwart independence by force if necessary. Recognition was extended to Bosnia nonetheless, and remained the single most influential international action on the conflict until the Dayton peace talks.

The United Nations Protection Force (UNPROFOR) arrived in June 1992 with a mainly humanitarian mandate, and succeeded in opening Sarajevo's airport to humanitarian aid, but its attempts to deliver relief throughout the country were hindered over the next several years by the continuing violence and Serb animosity. Diplomatic efforts to resolve the crisis began in August 1992, with the opening meeting of the International Conference on the Former Yugoslavia (ICFY), which regularly produced plans for peace that were just as regularly rejected by the Bosnian Serbs. Increasing levels of economic sanctions were added to the arms embargo imposed by the Security Council in September 1991. The embargo and sanctions were monitored and enforced by NATO forces, as was the no-fly zone, which was imposed in November 1992 and strengthened by direct NATO overflights in April 1993, but none of this had much effect on the war. Both sides were able to obtain arms from various sources. The Serbs continued to attack since the West seemed disinclined to stop them, while the Muslims hung on expecting the West to intervene at any time. The creation of a Croat-Muslim alliance helped push back the Serbs in 1994, but intensified the violence. The continuing conflict, the vulnerable position of UN troops, and the continued destruction wreaked on the civilian population led the United States to commit both its troops and its diplomatic muscle in 1995. The Dayton Accord was signed in November of that year, providing for a cease-fire, separation and demobilization of forces, and deployment of a combat-ready NATO force in December 1995.

The inability of outside powers to agree on the need for intervention to dampen the violence that characterized Bosnia's first four years of conflict represents for many all that is wrong with the international system today. Some believe that the West's failure to act was a moral and ethical failure of the highest degree. It is even difficult to understand in terms of self-interest. Western states lay next to Bosnia and Croatia. They had to deal with the war's effects in terms of refugees. Indeed, initially the European states claimed that it was a European issue and was best dealt with on that level. As later action showed, deployment of an international force was not that difficult, logistically speaking, although the European Community by itself had neither the diplomatic nor military wherewithal to resolve the crisis. Thus, Bosnia is an important case for the study of the costs of conflict prevention. The episode also provides a lesson in the value of early action. The international community did not take decisive action until late in the conflict, first spending years dithering about partitions of territory and how and when to use force. It wasted precious dollars as well as the lives of UN peacekeepers.

The dollar cost of the Bosnian conflict to the international community has been enormous, reaching a total of at least $53.68 billion between 1992 and 1998. The military costs alone, which include the UN mission beginning in 1992 and the costs of NATO's operation, which has run into 1999, are over $19 billion. The total figure includes the cost of UNPROFOR and its associated operations, NATO military actions, humanitarian aid efforts—both public and private—and rehabilitation programs. Of this total, the $6 billion World Bank estimate for rehabilitation of the country's economy and infrastructure is just 13 percent of what the Bosnian government estimates is needed.[1] The total figure will also rise since humanitarian aid and rehabilitation efforts can be expected to continue as long as the NATO forces keep the conflict stabilized. The exit date has now been left open-ended.

Bosnia's story holds particular relevance because no one should have been surprised when the country fell apart.[2] The Serbo-Croatian war of late 1991 amply displayed the tensions involved in the breakup of Yugoslavia and clearly evinced Serb willingness to resort to violent means to achieve their goals. The situation in Bosnia promised to be far worse, however, since it was the most ethnically mixed of all the Yugoslav republics. The theme of this study is the financial benefit of preventive action, and Bosnia is clearly a case where action should have been taken early, when tensions but not violence were the norm. Part of the task lies in identifying when international action should have been taken, and early 1992 proved a critical window of lost opportunity.

From January to March 1992 the international community had a clear opportunity to take preventive action against the collapse of Bosnia. Early in the conflict the main perpetrators of the violence were bands of Serbian criminals, released explicitly in order to create mayhem, who joined the various ethnically based paramilitary groups of extremists and "mercenary thugs."[3] The first Bosnian and Croat fighting forces were similarly composed of criminals and extremists, often recruited from street gangs, operating in small and undisciplined bands. The first months of 1992 can be clearly identified as a time when international action could have averted tragic and continuing violence. The warring bands on all sides were small, disorganized, and composed of fanatics and criminals. Nationalism had not yet taken on the quality of mass hysteria that the war of ethnic cleansing would give it, and the possibility existed to demobilize and neutralize the paramilitary thugs. Despite the inflammatory rhetoric of nationalists like Serbia's Slobodan Milosevic and Croatia's Franjo Tudjman, the violence was primarily the province of the radical fringe rather than a mass movement. An international force with an offensive capability could have largely controlled these groups and significantly altered the first years of Bosnia's nationhood.

Even at that time, however, a large force might have been necessary, given the potential for internal violence. Pentagon officials later estimated that up to 300,000 troops would have been required to monitor and enforce a peace agreement and protect Muslim towns.[4] A force of this size, composed mainly of infantry, would have cost approximately $25 billion per year. Using the Pentagon's estimate of need, therefore, preventive action would have cost $34–$40 billion at most. This estimate is based on a force of 300,000 operating for four years, with gradual reductions in size. This would be massive for a preventive force, however, and represents an extreme upper limit of what was needed to deal with the conflict.

In all likelihood somewhat fewer troops would have been sufficient if the force had been inserted before the violence began. Such an operation would have been much cheaper than the course actually taken if the troops had promptly imposed order. Warren Zimmermann, the American ambassador during Yugoslavia's collapse, has suggested that even a limited show of Western force in late 1991 or early 1992 would have deterred the Bosnian Serbs.[5] A force of 30,000–50,000 troops would have been sufficient if they had been put in place early, and would have cost approximately $2.7 billion per year. Assuming a four-year operation, preventive action would have cost $10.8 billion, and probably less when accounting for force reductions over time. Such an operation would have been effective at preventing the violence, and would have been far more cost-effective than the Pentagon's proposal.

Origins of the Conflict

Although Serb aspirations and the ethnic composition of the Balkans had created international tensions since the nineteenth century, the Bosnian conflict developed out of the economic crises of the 1980s and the willingness of local republican leaders to maximize their own power by any means possible. Virulent nationalists like Milosevic in Serbia and Tudjman in Croatia cleverly revived historic grievances and fanned nationalist flames in order to consolidate and expand their own power. Their popularity grew as the economic situation worsened. The West's inclination to shirk responsibility for the problem by ascribing it to deep animosities dating back centuries obscures the economic issues and manipulation by elites that lay at its heart. Historical experiences certainly contributed to the breakup of the former Yugoslavia but were not the original or even the most intransigent forces that caused political cleavage. Instead, a heady mixture of political change and economic conditions led to dissatisfactions that were manipulated by nationalist leaders to attain their ends.[6]

Several developments in the late 1980s paved the way for leaders willing to use the language of ethnic nationalism. First, economic conditions worsened dramatically as a result of unsuccessful austerity measures imposed by the government in 1979, and the subsequent need for International Monetary Fund (IMF) loans that were granted on the condition of radical, institutional reforms and shock therapy programs. Second, the reforms had to be undertaken by a weak central state that had, in the late 1970s and early 1980s, ceded economic control to its constituent republics. The wealthier republics refused to pay for the problems of their poorer siblings, and they sought to resist central reforms while dealing with international bodies on their own terms. Simultaneously, the poorer republics sought to preserve the federal state in order to maintain economic balance between the republics. Third, the end of the Cold War profoundly affected the special status Yugoslavia had held in Western priorities. It diminished the importance of Yugoslavia in American foreign policy, resulting in less favorable aid agreements and stricter IMF criteria.

As a result, the 1980s were not good times for Yugoslavs. Strict austerity measures were imposed, food subsidies ended, and savings quickly depleted as the currency devalued and inflation burgeoned. Overall unemployment reached an average of 14 percent in 1984, ranging from 0 percent in Slovenia to 23 percent in Bosnia and parts of Serbia.[7] This was particularly shocking in a nation accustomed to socialist subsidies, full employment, and well-stocked stores. By 1988 the inflation rate reached 200 percent, and then nearly 1,300 percent in 1989. GDP growth declined between 1986 and 1987, and after a slight rise into positive figures in 1988 plunged to nearly −15 percent by 1991.[8]

The National Bank, which had turned over substantial financial control to the republics starting in the 1970s, tried to reassert control over foreign exchange operations, allocations, and monetary authority. Republican politicians in the wealthier regions, however, sought to protect their economic and political positions by insisting on the right to control republican coffers. Even among the poorer republics, such as Bosnia-Herzegovina and Macedonia, support for the central state declined when it intruded on local matters. Of course, Slovenia and Croatia were the loudest opponents of reform and advocates of autonomy because they were also the richest and most Western-oriented republics. Unfortunately, a large Serbian minority lived in Croatia. Serbia was the most ardent advocate for strengthening the federal state, since local elites hoped to enhance its position and make Serbia the dominant republic within a recentralized federation.

The government effectively ceded all meaningful authority to the republics in November 1986 when it agreed to break all ties between the federal and republican budgets, and this soon translated into increased ethnic tensions. The process of economic decentralization initially led to a republican rather than national orientation for Yugoslav citizens. Political polarization thus occurred, pitting republican leaders and sentiment for independence against Serbian preferences for strengthening the central government. The enormous inflation rate and rising unemployment were used by local politicians to encourage popular sentiment against the state. The images of increasingly vocal and discontented populations agitating for radical reform throughout the Soviet Union and Eastern Europe increased Yugoslavs' disenchantment. While the federal government tried to concentrate on economic and political reform, republican leaders fanned ethnic nationalism in order to gain more leverage to oppose such reforms.

This was particularly true in Serbia, where the leader of the Serbian party, Milosevic, was bent on raising the status of his republic and consolidating a hold on the central state or, if that failed, incorporating all Serbs into a unified Greater Serbia. Milosevic was the first to make an explicitly nationalist appeal and in the late 1980s began encouraging Serb solidarity by recalling the Titoist system and its attempts to limit Serb power by dispersing the population throughout the country. Leaders first in Slovenia and then Croatia responded by portraying Serbia as the enemy of republican democracy and the republics as the guarantors of individual rights. The controversy thus shifted from specifically economic issues to the rhetoric of national exploitation and ethnic rights. At the same time, however, discrimination against and maltreatment of Serbs in other republics increased in response to Milosevic's rhetoric, defining the moral issue increasingly in terms of ethnic rather than individual rights. Milosevic became more aggressive in turn, expanding his appeal to include the protection of Serbs living outside the republic, and making corresponding revisions in the Serbian constitution. The opposition to recentralization in other republics led him to seek creation of a Greater Serbia and to draw links with historical nationalism, which attracted immense popular support. His recollections of glory and grievance ranged from the battlefields of Kosovo, the heart of the Serb empire in centuries past, to the partisan war fought during World

War II pitting Serbs against Croat guerrillas collaborating with the Nazis. Reclaiming Kosovo, which was a semiautonomous province inhabited by Albanians and Serbs, as a Serb possession was Milosevic's first call to arms. The aggressive stance of Serbia and its expatriates and their hints of territorial expansion set off a wave of declarations for state autonomy, which prompted similar declarations from minorities, particularly Serbs, living within those states. Minority populations in all republics began seeking territorial autonomy rather than protection of their civil rights, preferring to be in control of the rule making rather than lobbying for less discrimination.

When the wall crumbled in Berlin, so too did Yugoslavia's favored position with the West. The United States and Western institutions, such as the World Bank and IMF, lost interest in shoring up a shaky state that was no longer important with the end of the East-West rivalry. Aid decreased and loan requirements became increasingly harsh, further eroding the power of the state and encouraging republican politicians to strike out on their own. The rhetoric of "us versus them" increased in all republics, as local leaders based their appeal on protection of local ethnicities and local resources.

In November 1989 Slovenia asserted constitutional sovereignty over its borders by preventing the assembly of an association of minority Serbs and Montenegrins gathering to protest political and economic developments. The Serbian parliament responded by secretly approving a boycott of all Slovenian goods, prompting Slovenia to withhold its assessed share of the federal fund and send the funds instead directly to the provincial government. Slovenian delegates then walked out of the Extraordinary Congress of the League of Communists, held in January 1990, when they failed to gain support for their plans for moving the country toward a confederation of states. The Croatian leadership also became more assertive and led the move for adjournment when the Slovenes did not return. It was now apparent that no unifying authority existed and that the nation had disintegrated into competing authorities enjoying only regional legitimacy. Local leaders were determined to dissolve the Yugoslav federation since they anticipated better economic and power potential if they ruled their own states.[9]

The multiparty elections of November 1990 confirmed this and formed the point of no return for the country's dissolution. The elections took place in a country with no history or established structure of parliamentary democracy; in a political and legal vacuum, leaders resorted to symbols and personalities. Milosevic based his appeal on the slogan "all Serbs in one state,"[10] a threatening proposition to the other republics. The continuing economic crisis guaranteed that citizens would have to rely on their republics for social support, and thus favored representatives who promised protection at home and denial of resources to others. The new, nationalist-oriented governments in Slovenia and Croatia wasted no time, declaring sovereignty in July 1990 and proposing that Yugoslavia become a confederation of sovereign states.

The outcome of the elections in Bosnia was particularly important and drew the ethnic lines that led to war. The three major political parties were ethnically based, reflecting the population of the republic. They agreed to form a coalition government in order to defeat the other reformist parties, but only one party, the Muslim Party of Democratic Action (SDA), actually favored the territorial integrity of Bosnia. The Serb and Croat parties favored consolidating the positions of their patron republics. Following Milosevic's lead, the Serbs in particular strongly opposed Bosnian autonomy, and their intransigent position guaranteed that the power-sharing arrangement would not last.

The result of the rise of republican power was the complete breakdown in protection of minority rights. Ethnic discrimination appeared openly in all republics. Politicians rose to power by using ethnic stereotypes to simplify voters' choices, and carried this into their administrations, exploiting intolerance in order to consolidate their own positions. Defining the vote in terms of ethnic identity, the leaders also guaranteed that the confrontation would spill over republican borders, since sizable minority communities, particularly of Serbs, lived outside their home republic.

The spring of 1991 proved to be a critical point in Yugoslavia's crisis. The federal government still existed, but only in name. Urged by the Serbian leadership, it ordered the Yugoslav People's Army (JNA) onto the streets of Belgrade in March 1991 in response to a demonstration of opposition parties protesting Milosevic's control of the media. The JNA was perhaps the only federal institution still functioning, and claimed to be acting to protect the federal state. But as the country became defined by republics and the republics increasingly by ethnicity, the army's attempts to deny autonomy branded it as a tool of Serbian nationalism and reinforced the very divisions it sought to erase. Just days later, Serbs in the Croatian Krajina reacted to Croatia's intention to secede from Yugoslavia by declaring all Croatian laws not in accordance with the federal constitution void in their region, and announcing their own intention to secede from Croatia. Serbian paramilitary groups began operating in Krajina in April, and tensions escalated into fights between local Serb populations and Croatian police. On May 15 Serbia blocked the annual rotation of the chair of the state presidency to the Croatian representative on the grounds that he had based his platform on the goals of Croatian independence and Yugoslav dissolution. On May 19 the referendum on Croatian independence passed by 79 percent of the eligible electorate, although it was boycotted by the Krajina Serbs, who had voted seven days earlier to join the republic of Serbia.[11] Croatia and Slovenia announced their complete independence from Yugoslavia in June 1991.

The enfeebled Yugoslav government sent the Yugoslav army into Slovenia, ostensibly to protect Yugoslav territorial integrity. The war ended after ten days when the Slovenes gained victory through a Serb withdrawal. The situation in Croatia, which had a large Serb minority concentrated in the Krajina region, was markedly different. Milosevic was reported several times as saying that Slovenia was free to leave Yugoslavia but "Croatia, with its Serbian minority, must never leave."[12] Hostilities soon became open warfare between Croats and the Yugoslav army-assisted Krajina Serbs as nationalist rhetoric turned into wars over territory and the rights to self-determination. The war in Croatia lasted six months; it concluded when UN representative Cyrus Vance brokered a cease-fire in January 1992. No comprehensive political settlement was reached, however. Observers warned that without a settlement the conflict would spread to Bosnia-Herzegovina, where the magnitude of the destruction would be far greater.[13] Bosnia was the most ethnically mixed of the republics, composed of 44 percent Muslims, 31 percent Serbs, and 17 percent Croats, and both the Muslim and Croat communities felt threatened by the prospect of a national state ruled by Serbia.[14] Milosevic and Radovan Karadzic, leader of the Bosnian Serbs, had already declared an intention to annex territory rather than cede it to an independent Bosnia and lose the dream of Greater Serbia. Germany secured EC support to recognize the independence of Slovenia and Croatia on December 15, 1991, providing that the two republics submit requests for formal recognition by December 23. When they did and were recognized accordingly, Bosnia's declaration of independence became a foregone conclusion.

When the issue of independence was introduced in the Bosnian parliament, Serb delegates walked out. Shortly afterward they formed their own parliament and declared their intention to remain within Yugoslavia. Bosnian Croat regions in the west also declared autonomy as the Croat state of Herzeg-Bosna, and were incorporated into the Croat economy. The international community made one weak attempt to calm tensions in Bosnia when it chose Sarajevo as the headquarters for UNPROFOR, which was deployed to Croatia. UNPROFOR command was established in Sarajevo in March 1992, and the full deployment of 14,000 peacekeepers was authorized by Security Council Resolution 749 in April 1992 to enforce the cease-fire in Croatia.

German Chancellor Helmut Kohl had reasoned that recognition would deter Serbian aggression, since any moves into other republics would be defined under UN rules as trans-border aggression, and would bring the conflict to an end by making it an international affair that could lead to outside intervention. Instead, the isolated hostilities already taking place in

Bosnian towns intensified. The Bosnian government had lost all control over the eastern Serb and western Croat regions. It could not accept partition and felt it had no choice but to declare independence. A referendum on this issue passed overwhelmingly in February 1992. The election was boycotted by Bosnian Serbs, who declared their intention to maintain an independent republic connected to Serbia.

The time for international preventive action was in February–March 1992. At that time it was clear that the Bosnian Serbs would not accept an independent Bosnia, and just as clear that international recognition was only a matter of time. The cease-fire had taken effect in Croatia, so full attention could be turned to preventing similar violence in Bosnia. At this early date a preventive action could have deterred the Bosnian Serbs from their attack on Bosnia, since only the most rabid nationalists believed they had a legitimate claim to the territory they were demanding.[15] Once the violence hardened ethnic divisions, however, the conflict became much more difficult to stop.

International recognition of Bosnia came on April 5, 1992. Karadzic declared an independent Serb Republic of Bosnia and Herzegovina that same day. The war promptly exploded in Sarajevo, Mostar, and Bosanski Samac, creating a massive refugee crisis, widely documented genocide and mass rape, and a siege of Sarajevo, Bosnia's capital, that lasted for over 1,000 days.

Overview of the Conflict

Once a graceful and historic capital that considered itself Western, hosted the Olympics, and housed cultural riches, Sarajevo fell victim to relentless shelling and forced expulsion of Muslims and Croats from their homes. Around the country the story was the same—Bosnian Serbs, aided by former JNA forces, tried to secure the two-thirds of Bosnian territory the Serbs claimed as their own by means of military campaigns and ethnic cleansing. The JNA forces shortly disbanded, since the federal state no longer existed, but their artillery, weaponry, and approximately 80,000 troops who were Bosnian citizens became the new Bosnian Serb army, the territorial defense forces of the new Serb Republic of Bosnia and Herzegovina, led by a Bosnian Serb militant, General Ratko Mladic.[16] The international community responded by imposing a complete economic embargo on Serbia and Montenegro, now the Federal Republic of Yugoslavia, and seeking a peaceful, diplomatic solution.

UNPROFOR observers had been deployed to the Mostar region of Bosnia at the end of April, but were redeployed to Croatia as the fighting intensified in Bosnia. Two-thirds of the personnel at headquarters in Sarajevo were also withdrawn, leaving only 100 military personnel and civilian staff.[17] In early June the UN Security Council enlarged the operation's strength and mandate to include Bosnia. Units deployed to Sarajevo and initially concentrated on opening the airport to humanitarian supplies.

The UN embargo ruined the economy of Serbia but did not initially affect its support for Bosnian and Croatian Serbs. Large stockpiles of Yugoslav arms were available to the Serbians. Relief efforts helped the victims in Bosnia, but did little to prevent the creation of new refugees or stop the massacres and uprooting of entire communities. Diplomatic efforts could not find a compromise between Bosnian government (subsequently considered Muslim) insistence on maintaining the state's territorial integrity and Bosnian Serb insistence on creating their own independent state. The international community had little interest in taking forceful action, and the United States remained entirely distant from the early proceedings, calling it a European problem, which was in fact how the Europeans themselves characterized it.

Major humanitarian efforts began in June when UNPROFOR succeeded in opening Sarajevo airport, but the city itself continued under a state of siege. Serb forces also harassed relief convoys outside the city, and UN and American analysts estimated that only 25 percent of supplies were getting to the population.[18] In January 1993 the Vance-Owen Peace Plan was proposed, which declared Bosnia-Herzegovina a state of three constituent nations, each with the right of self-determination, and divided the country into nine cantons, three each for Serbs, Croats, and Muslims, plus Sarajevo. Overall it allocated 43 percent of the territory to the Bosnian Serbs, substantially less than the 70 percent they held militarily at the time of the negotiations, and not enough to entice them to sign. The plan's failure was a harbinger of things to come. The Bosnian Serbs wanted contiguous cantons, and more of them. Their strong military position made compromise unnecessary. This scenario would repeat itself several times over. The plan might have even encouraged ethnic cleansing, as it made clear that the international community did not want to recognize military conquests, and this led the Serbs to seek to populate Muslim regions with members of their own group.

Fighting continued throughout 1993. In April the tenuous Bosnian-Croat alliance collapsed, forcing the government to fight on two fronts when it was decidedly unsuccessful on one. The UN Security Council strengthened the no-fly zone over the country in April, patrolled by NATO, and the endless shelling of Srebrenica prompted the United Nations to declare it a safe area. (The no-fly zone was originally imposed by the Security Council in November 1992 but was not enforced until NATO's Operation Deny Flight began in April 1993.) The United Nations demanded the withdrawal of all Bosnian Serb units from the area and the cessation of all attacks, and deployed UNPROFOR troops to demilitarize the town. International opinion generally portrayed the Serbs as the perpetrators and the Muslims as their hapless victims, an image reinforced by news of Serb attempts to claim land by "cleansing" it of other groups. UN efforts were therefore mainly directed at protecting and aiding Muslim civilians. In practice the line between good and bad ethnic practice was somewhat ambiguous, even though the Serbs were clearly the most patent and aggressive perpetrators of ethnic cleansing. The fate of Srebrenica was illustrative of the tactics employed during the war—while Bosnian Serb forces shelled the citizens from without, local Muslim leaders prevented them from leaving for fear of losing the town if its Muslim population fled.

Srebrenica was attacked in April. Fighting in the southern and central regions intensified simultaneously, particularly with the movement of Muslim refugees into central Bosnia. In the west, Croatian militias and units of the Croatian army attempted to help Mate Boban, leader of Croatian Herzeg-Bosna, by their own ethnic cleansing. In May, Sarajevo and the predominantly Muslim towns of Tuzla, Zepa, Gorazde, and Bihac were also declared safe areas, but all of these regions remained under heavy pressure from Serb batteries throughout the year. UNPROFOR units were deployed to the safe areas, where they provided humanitarian aid but could do little to stop the Serb assaults. Croats and Muslims engaged in heavy fighting over the city of Mostar. Further attempts at diplomacy failed. An agreement between Tudjman and Milosevic and an EU proposal suggested various tripartite divisions of Bosnian territory, like the Vance-Owen plan, but met similar results. By the end of 1993 the United Nations estimated that between 140,000 and 250,000 people had been killed or were missing and over 4 million people had been displaced, including at least 2.25 million within Bosnia.[19]

The year 1994 opened with Serbia and Croatia, now in tenuous alliance, reviving plans discussed earlier by Milosevic and Tudjman to partition Bosnia-Herzegovina between them. The Bosnian government faced problems on all sides, since one of its erstwhile allies, Fikret Abdic, the Muslim leader in Bihac, had declared his area autonomous in November 1993 and reached an independent agreement with the Croats and Bosnian Serbs. The indiscriminate shelling of Sarajevo had previously hit civilian targets, including a soccer match and bread lines, but reached new lows in the eyes of the international community on February 5, 1994, when Serb artillery shelled a Sarajevo market, leaving 68 dead and 197 injured.[20] NATO immediately established a heavy-weapons exclusion zone around the city, declaring that within ten days there should be no weaponry remaining within a 20-kilometer radius. The Serbs complied but merely shifted their attentions elsewhere, and started pounding Gorazde in March and Bihac in November.

UN and EU diplomatic initiatives produced no results, and were replaced in April by a five-nation Contact Group composed of France, Germany, Russia, the United Kingdom, and the United States. Simultaneously, NATO became more aggressive in carrying out air strikes. By November the bluff and bluster of NATO and the Contact Group had worn thin, and Bosnian Serb forces engaged with government troops around Bihac trapped a force of UN peacekeepers, cut their supply lines, impeded fuel deliveries, and prevented all transit through Serb-held territory, threatening retaliation in response to further air strikes.[21] This tactic worked so well that five months later the Serbs were emboldened to remove their weapons from UN collection sites around Sarajevo and resume their siege. As the safe areas fell one by one, it became clear that NATO action led to Serb retaliation against UN peacekeepers, prompting the United Nations to declare publicly that it would not act forcefully to protect the safe areas, nor continue its operations in the country without the consent of all parties. The Bosnian Serbs responded to this invitation by barraging the safe areas and continuing their push westward.

Bosnian government fortunes improved slightly during 1994 with the signing of a cease-fire agreement with Croatia in February, and the subsequent peace agreements of March, which established a federation between the Bosnian state and Bosnian Croats and placed their two armies under unified command. The Bosnian Serbs were also given the option of joining, but their assembly in Pale naturally declined. Although the new Bosnian Federation rested on an uneasy political alliance, the joint military operations allowed it to gain back some of the Serbs' territorial booty. The marketplace bombing in February 1994 led NATO to threaten more aggressive air strikes, but in practice this proved difficult since Serb forces took UN troops hostage in retaliation.

The Contact Group proposed a plan in July that featured a 51 to 49 percent Muslim/Croat-Serb split of territory, but gave the Serbs a corridor between their declared republic in the east and the military stronghold of Banja Luka in the northwest, and provided for UN and EU administration of sensitive areas around Sarajevo and Gorazde. The plan was quickly rejected by the Pale assembly, which had no real incentive to give up its military gains, in spite of a provision linking rejection with the tightening of economic sanctions on Serbia. The Serbs still held a substantial majority of Bosnian territory and would not accept a minority share in the absence of meaningful reasons to compromise, a point that seemed lost on the West.

Pressure did come to bear from an unlikely quarter, however. Throughout the war, Milosevic had openly supported and sanctioned the activities of the Bosnian Serbs, but the cumulative effect of the UN-imposed sanctions on Belgrade and threats to tighten them had taken their toll. Milosevic sought relief, as the West had hoped he would, by pressuring Karadzic to accept a settlement. Serb authorities in the former Yugoslav capital now, for the first time, began to distance themselves from Karadzic, beginning a negative media campaign against him and closing their common border with Bosnia to all but trade in food and medicine in August. In September the Contact Group offered to ease the sanctions on Serbia in return for deployment of eighty-five international monitors along the Serb-Bosnian border. Serbia agreed to the deployment, but serious differences among the five contact nations prevented further action. The military situation began to unravel when Bosnian government forces attempted to expand their territory around the Bihac enclave but were turned back by an alliance of Bosnian and Croatian Serbs and the forces of Abdic.[22]

This last development proved particularly problematic, signaling the increased activity of Croatian Serbs in Bosnia and raising concern that the war could spread back into Croatia. Although NATO responded to their entry by bombing Ubdina airport in the Croatian Krajina, from which Serb planes used over Bihac had originated, the situation worsened substantially for both Bosnian and UN troops. The engagement of Croatian Serbs also made clear that problems in the Krajina and western Slavonia needed resolution. Two days later NATO sent another mission against targets in the Krajina and northwest Bosnia. The immediate result was the increasing harassment and detainment of UNPROFOR personnel by the Serbs. The lack of a political settlement in Croatia meant that Croatian Serbs were free to help their brethren in Bosnia, adding a western threat to the Bosnian Serb advance from the east. By December the UN command, concerned about troop safety, had asked NATO to suspend its patrols of the no-fly zone to avoid further problems.[23]

Still, UN forces were used by the Serbs as targets and shields. By this time it was clear that UNPROFOR was as much a hindrance as a help in resolving the problem. As a result, President Tudjman of Croatia demanded withdrawal of all UN troops in his country in January 1995. The UN forces in Croatia were subsequently restructured, but Tudjman urged more aggressive action, and Croatian government forces attacked Serbs in western Slavonia, a UN Protected Area, in May. The hesitancy, particularly of the United Nations, to take action even to protect the so-called safe areas, stemmed from what force commander General Sir Michael Rose described as an unwillingness to cross "the Mogadishu line," the tenuous boundary established in Somalia between peacekeeping and war.[24] The United Nations hoped to avoid the Somalia problem by remaining an entirely neutral presence, and sought to avoid any action clearly directed against a warring party, even when aggressive actions were directed against the United Nations.

The year 1994 represented continuing failure to resolve the conflict and stop the war, and the opening of 1995 was no better. The United Nations and NATO were still under attack and unable to significantly affect the conflict or protect its victims. Bosnian and Croat forces made little headway on the battlefield. The citizenry was still under barrage. The sanctions, though lessened, continued to cripple Serbia. Heavy fighting resumed around Tuzla in March and Sarajevo in May, where the Serbs removed their heavy weaponry from UN collection points, closed the airport, cut off all utilities, and blocked the transit of aid convoys. NATO initiated air strikes in response, but this led to the seizure of UN peacekeepers. The Serbs next seized Srebrenica, massacring 6,000 Muslim men and boys before moving on to attack other safe areas throughout the summer.[25] In light of the deteriorating situation, the United Nations restructured UNPROFOR, withdrawing it from all Serb-held territory and dividing it into three separate operations deployed in Croatia, Bosnia, and the former Yugoslav republic of Macedonia. Theater headquarters were shifted to Zagreb, and a 10,000-person Rapid Reaction Force (RRF) was deployed in Bosnia.

All of the safe areas except Gorazde had fallen by the end of June, when NATO declared that an attack on the last would be met with the use of force. There was little reason to think this threat more credible than the legion of those that had preceded it. With the restructuring of UNPROFOR, however, air strikes could be used more effectively because UN forces were less vulnerable to Serb retaliation. On August 28 the Serbs again shelled a Sarajevo marketplace, this time killing thirty-seven.[26] Two days later NATO began Operation Deliberate Force, a two-week air strike and bombing campaign directed against Serb targets. This operation stopped when the Serbs, once again, withdrew their heavy weapons from Sarajevo. At the operation's conclusion on September 14, its planes had flown 3,400 sorties, including 750 attack missions, and had secured the eastern section of the country.[27] Bosnian and Croatian forces had already been advancing from the west even prior to the NATO bombing, and their combined offensive threatened to change the military situation that had been holding for two years.

NATO's action, plus diplomatic pressure from all sides, including Milosevic's, finally brought the Bosnian Serbs to the negotiating table. Although the situation on the ground had not yet changed dramatically, Western resolve was now clearly focused on ending the conflict and using force to do so. The U.S.-sponsored Dayton negotiations began on November 1, 1995, bringing to a close forty-three months of fighting and resulting in a peace settlement that allocated 51 percent of the territory to the Federation of Bosnia and Herzegovina, the alliance of Muslims and Croats, and 49 percent to the Republika Srpska of the Bosnian Serbs. President Milosevic of Serbia accepted the plan on behalf of the Bosnian Serbs, though Nikola Koljevic, the senior Bosnian Serb present at the talks, refused to initial the agreement or attend the ceremony, and reportedly fainted when he heard the terms.[28] The Dayton Accord retained a single state, at least in theory, as demanded by the Bosnian government, but one composed of two entities. Sarajevo remained united and within federation territory, while Republika Srpska retained a corridor to Banja Luka. The central government was planned to operate by means of a rotating presidency and assignment of posts by nationality. The two republics retained independent armies and police forces. Coupled with the weakness of the central government, this last provision suggested that the plan created a de facto partition of Bosnia. The Dayton agreement also provided for separation and demilitarization of forces, democratic elections, and rehabilitation of civil infrastructure. The agreement's final provision was a 60,000-member NATO force to monitor and enforce the agreement. The Implementation Force (IFOR) deployed in December 1995, with a one-year engagement limit.[29] Its mandate has since been extended several times, most recently to continue the mission into 1999. The outbreak of fighting in Kosovo in late 1997 has renewed fears of spreading instability and helped ensure NATO's continued commitment in Bosnia.

The bulk of IFOR's troops were supplied by the United States, France, and the United Kingdom, with the remainder coming from twenty-one other countries. Its role was strictly military. The civil side of the Dayton settlement was the responsibility of an EU envoy. The initial separation and demobilization of forces was successful, but IFOR has been less successful in dealing with the refugee problem and its destabilizing effects, particularly in light of resistance among local Serb populations to the return of Muslims, and vice versa. As the operation's exit date approached, it became clear that withdrawal would result in a resumption of violence, since so many political and security problems remained unsolved. Accordingly, a reduced force was authorized to remain in Bosnia. Composed of approximately 36,000 troops (30,000 NATO troops and 6,000 non-NATO troops), the Stabilization Force (SFOR) still faces great animosity among Serbs, Croats, and Muslims, and a lack of cooperation in meeting the terms of the Dayton agreement. The problems that caused the war have not entirely been solved. The conflict remains simmering, ready to erupt if NATO forces leave before stability is achieved.

Costs of the Conflict to International Actors

The costs of the conflict have been horrendous, and not only for the local population. There have been substantial military, humanitarian, rehabilitation, and other economic costs paid by international organizations and individual countries. If anything, the following understate the real, but not fully commensurable, costs.

Military Costs

The military costs of the Bosnian conflict to outside powers have been substantial. Including the projected costs of SFOR, they will total approximately $19 billion. UNPROFOR was deployed in Bosnia in June 1992 with military, police, and civilian components, and was charged with opening Sarajevo airport for humanitarian purposes, demilitarization of selected areas, and protection of residents. Hindsight makes clear that even this limited mandate was unattainable without significantly different rules of engagement, but the force retained the same mandate until December 1995, when it was relieved by IFOR. UNPROFOR began with a strength of 9,700 in 1992, which had increased to 40,000 troops by the start of 1994.[30] Its expenses reflect this buildup, since in 1992 it cost only $250 million, but in its last three years the expenses had escalated to well over $1 billion per year (see table 2.1).

UNPROFOR was initially created to monitor the cease-fire in Croatia; its first deployment in Bosnia came in June 1992. This analysis counts its total expenses for 1992 only from June to December. From that point on, its costs include the portion of the force deployed in Croatia, since Croatian Serbs were active in the western region of Bosnia and provided airstrips and logistical support for Bosnian Serbs operating in that area as well. The total estimated cost of UNPROFOR operations comes to $4.8 billion. It is not entirely clear whether the costs of its companion operations, Operation Deny Flight and Operation Sharp Guard, to enforce the no-fly zone and the arms embargo, respectively, are included in this total.[31] However, at least a portion of their costs were probably paid by NATO and the participating nations.

TABLE 2.1
Bosnia: UNPROFOR Costs by Year ($U.S. Millions)

Year	Cost
1992	125
1993	1,124
1994	1,900
1995	1,700
TOTAL	**4,849**

Sources: International Institute for Strategic Studies, *The Military Balance, 1993–1997* (London: Oxford University Press). UNDPI, *Information Notes, United Nations Peacekeeping* (New York: United Nations, 1994). Angela Burke and Gordon Macdonald, "The Former Yogoslavia Conflict," in *The True Cost of Conflict: Seven Recent Wars and Their Effects on Society,* ed. Michael Cranna (New York: New Press, 1994).

This would be expensive enough, but it is not the end of the story. The 60,000-strong NATO force that took over in December 1995 cost $5 billion through the end of 1996. IFOR was implemented with a fixed exit date of December 1996, but it became clear that sticking to this timetable would seriously jeopardize the prospects for peace in the region. In November 1996 the United States announced its commitment to participate in SFOR, the mandate for which was extended into 1999. SFOR cost $4 billion in 1997 and can be expected to incur the same cost through 1998.[32]

In addition, three UN operations previously part of UNPROFOR continued to operate independently throughout 1996. The United Nations Preventive Deployment Force (UNPREDEP), United Nations Mission in Bosnia and Herzegovina (UNMIBH), and United Nations Transitional Administration for Eastern Slavonia, Baranja and Western Sirmium (UNTAES) cost $50 million, $163 million, and $292 million, respectively, for the year. These missions were continued through 1997. The two missions not operating directly in Bosnia are included in the total costs because the threat of war expanding to other republics made their operation necessary. UNTAES in particular is closely connected to the Bosnian conflict. Croatian Serbs from eastern and western Slavonia were active in fighting around the Bihac pocket in Bosnia and, as noted earlier, provided bases in Croatia for Bosnian Serb aircraft.

A mission operating under the aegis of the European Union was also active in Bosnia. The Mission of the International Conference on the Former Yugoslavia consisted of 178 military observers operating on the border between Serbia and Bosnia, and cost approximately $3.9 million per year. This mission was established in September 1994 and operated through 1996, for a total cost of $9.1 million.[33] Personnel costs and contributions of in-kind equipment were borne by the participating countries, making this figure an underestimation of the final costs. The total costs of military operations are summarized in table 2.2.

The total cost of military operations through the end of 1996 comes to $10.4 billion. Eight billion dollars should be added to account for the cost of SFOR through 1998, since that force's presence and mandate is no longer in doubt. Another $696 million will likely be added if, as expected, the UN missions also continue their presence in connection with SFOR. This means that military operations alone will have cost the international community $19 billion in relation to the Bosnian conflict. The irony of course is that from 1992 to 1995 the UN forces on the ground, while expensive, were incapable of bringing the conflict to an end.

Humanitarian Costs

The United Nations High Commissioner for Refugees (UNHCR) has been the coordinating organization in the humanitarian effort to feed, pro-

TABLE 2.2
Bosnia: Military Costs ($U.S. Millions)

UNPROFOR	4,849
IFOR	5,000
UNPREDEP	50
UNMIBH	163
UNTAES	292
ICFY	9
Total through 1996	**10,363**
SFOR (est. through 1998)	8,000
UN missions	696
Total through 1998 (est.)	**19,059**

Sources: International Institute for Strategic Studies, *The Military Balance 1994–95 and 1996–97* (London: Oxford University Press). Stockholm International Peace Research Institute, *SIPRI Yearbook 1997* (Oxford: Oxford University Press, 1997). United Nations, *Information Notes, United Nations Peace-Keeping* (New York: United Nations, 1994), 104–8. UNDPI, *The Blue Helmets: A Review of United Nations Peace-keeping,* 3rd ed. (New York: United Nations, 1996).

tect, and aid refugees and victims of the conflict. It is the point agency for the aid operation, including the costs to the World Health Organization (WHO), World Food Programme (WFP), and United Nations Children's Fund (UNICEF), among others, in its coordinated appeals. Through the first half of 1995, $3.2 billion was channeled through UNHCR, providing for food, water, and medicine for over 2 million affected citizens.[34] Half of Bosnia's population was the beneficiary of humanitarian assistance. The costs of aid declined somewhat in 1995 as a result of NATO's increased involvement and the move toward peace, but costs for the remainder of 1995 and 1996 were estimated at a minimum of $550 million.[35] At the end of 1995, UNHCR officials estimated that $500 million would be needed through 1997 for repatriation efforts alone.[36] This program has proven even more difficult than anticipated, however. Local officials remained successful through 1996 at blocking attempted returns, bringing efforts to a standstill.

Substantial costs have also been borne by nearby countries, where hundreds of thousands of Bosnians have fled. Germany plays host to almost half of the 700,000 Bosnian refugees in Europe, and spent $51 million for refugee assistance in 1992. Since then it has spent an estimated $2.5 billion per year in assistance and repatriation programs.[37] Since 1993, that amounts to $10 billion. Even if we exclude 1996 on the grounds that the peace agreement late in 1995, and subsequent IFOR deployment, substantially calmed the refugee situation and allowed for more efficient repatriation, Germany's costs still come to $7.5 billion. Private and nongovernmental organizations have also been active in the area, spending a combined total of at least $200 million through 1995.[38] The humanitarian costs are summarized in table 2.3.

This is a staggering sum, particularly because it underestimates some costs and does not account for the costs borne by Hungary—for which figures are not available—host to the second-largest group of Bosnian refugees, or nations formerly part of Yugoslavia, such as Croatia and Serbia, which have substantial numbers to deal with as well.

Other Direct Economic Costs

The estimated economic damage of the war to Bosnia is $60 billion.[39] Theoretically, this is Bosnia's problem. In practice, the international community will ultimately have to pay to help rebuild Bosnia's economy. A World Bank/IMF assessment in 1996 predicted that $5–$6 billion worth of external financing would be necessary over the next three years for rehabilitation, including such projects as rebuilding roads and redevelopment of the industrial sector.[40] This figures does not include any humanitarian aid. The Bosnian government estimates its own needs at $47.9 billion, which includes servicing of its foreign debt, making up the balance of payments deficit, and rebuilding all sectors of the economy and civil infrastructure.[41]

The project facing the international community is nothing short of rebuilding an entire country. By the end of 1995, 45 percent of all industrial plants and 75 percent of oil refineries in Bosnia had been destroyed. The country's entire transportation system was damaged. Electric generating capacity was 20 percent of its prewar level. Some 33 percent of all health facilities and 50 percent of all schools had been destroyed. The Muslim

TABLE 2.3
Bosnia: Humanitarian Costs ($U.S. Millions)

UNHCR (through 1996)	3,786
UNHCR (repatriation)	500
Private organizations	200
National hosts	7,500
TOTAL	**11,986**

Sources: "UN Chief Eager over Peace Plan," cited December 1995, available from www.nando.net/newsroom/nt/1204yugo33/html. "Thin Hope for Bosnian Refugees in Peace Planning," Reuters Information Service cited December 9, 1995, available from www.nando.net. "Land of Slaughter," *Time* (June 8, 1992). "War Refugees Panicked by German Moves to Send Them Back," Associated Press, cited January 12, 1996, available from www.nando.net. American Council for Voluntary International Action, "Humanitarian Efforts in Bosnia," available from www.interaction.org.

areas operated at only 5 percent of their prewar production capacity. Croat areas were productive by comparison, but still operated at only 15 percent of prewar levels.[42]

The World Bank has already committed $6 billion to be paid over three years, with the United States agreeing to shoulder 10 percent of the burden. By the end of 1996 alone, $1.8 billion had been paid for projects already begun or earmarked to start in 1997, with the European Bank for Reconstruction and Development (EBRD) funding projects totaling an additional $282 million, and the European Union adding $78.1 million.[43] A total of $2.2 billion has therefore already been spent. Assuming that the European Bank or other sources do not give any more reconstruction aid independently, which is unlikely, the costs will come to $6.4 billion (see table 2.4).

The tasks are difficult, however, and are likely to require more funds. The goals for 1997 include establishing the economic, financial, and political institutions necessary to integrate the Bosnian Federation and Republika Srpska. This means long-term rehabilitation programs that must include creation of jobs, revitalization of the economy, and reduction of the external debt in order to be successful.

Economic Opportunity Costs

The disastrous efforts of the war on Bosnia's economy had significant but largely immeasurable implications for trade throughout the region. In 1991 the country had annual exports of $2 billion and imports of $1.7 billion. At the end of 1995 Bosnia's imports were $700 million, a relatively robust 41 percent of the previous total, but its exports had slipped to less than $200 million, 10 percent of their prewar level.[44] This affected the

TABLE 2.4
Bosnia: Economic Costs ($U.S. Millions)

World Bank	6,000
EBRD	282
EU	78
TOTAL	**6,360**

Sources: U.S. State Department, *Fact Sheet,* prepared by the Bureau of European and Canadian Affairs, released by the Department of Public Information. "Implementing the Dayton Peace Agreement: The Contribution of the U.S. and International Community to Economic Revitalization, cited August 12, 1996, available from www.state.gov/www/current/bosnia/bosnia_economic_recovery.html. Central and Eastern Europe Business Information Center, "Summary of Multilateral Reconstruction Programs for Bosnia and Herzegovina," available from www.itaiep.doc/ceebic/balkan/opps/multi2.html. "Donors Pledge $1.23 Billion to Help Rebuild Bosnia," available from www.europa.eu.int.

high-export industries of paper, timber, and furniture, and forced its trading partners, mainly Germany and the former republics of Yugoslavia, to redirect their trade and find new providers for those goods.

Greece had to redirect the 20 percent of its exports that had previously gone through Yugoslavia, mainly Serbia and Macedonia, because of the embargo imposed on those two republics.[45] Romania was boldest in fixing a price tag, claiming that it lost at least $7 billion in trade due to the sanctions imposed on Serbia and, along with Bulgaria, demanding direct compensation for lost trade revenue.[46] Slovakia, Hungary, and Ukraine have similarly demanded preferential treatment in contracting and supplying reconstruction to offset financial losses resulting from the sanctions.[47] During 1995 Croatia experienced a contraction of exports due to military campaigns in the summer and autumn affecting the Krajina and western Bosnia. Imports expanded throughout the region at the same time, leading to an increased trade imbalance.[48] A very conservative estimate, starting from Romania's expected loss, suggests that Bosnia's neighbors lost $10–$14 billion worth of trade revenue due to the conflict.

Since the signing of the Dayton Accord, there has been a big push to integrate regional economies and promote public and private investment. This sort of business and economic activity was retarded by the war for four years. Any estimation of its financial gains in the absence of war would be entirely speculative, but it is reasonable to suggest that many such opportunities would have been tried with potentially significant returns. Further, the shaky economies of the region, notably Bulgaria and Romania, suffered from the inability to boost trade or business in part because of the crippling effects of sanctions on trade and the instability caused by the war in the region as whole. The onset of peace is expected to significantly improve their prospects for economic success.[49]

Although IFOR and SFOR were expected to provide an employment bonanza and pump up to $7 million into the Bosnian economy through their presence, this hardly offsets the costs of the conflict in potential income, business, and investment opportunities.[50] Although the price tag is unknown, these losses constitute an important cost of the war.

Additional Costs to Individual Nations

The American portion of the war's cost burden has been substantial. Between 1992 and 1996 United States gave $1 billion in humanitarian assistance, plus $587 million in policing, demining, and economic assistance.[51] The government estimated that during FY1996 it would spend $550 million in support of the civilian implementation of the Dayton Accord, including reconstruction assistance and electoral organization.[52] In 1997 it expected to spend $470 million for civilian implementation, plus $120 million in humanitarian aid.[53] It also spent an estimated $100 million training and equipping the Bosnian Federation with defense articles and services.[54] This means that the U.S. government has paid $2.8 billion for aid and assistance to Bosnia outside of its contributions to UN- and NATO-related operations and projects. In all cases these figures represent costs that would not have otherwise been incurred.

The largest consistent individual aid donor behind the United States was Germany, which had already contributed over $1 billion worth of aid through the Development Assistance Committee by the end of 1994. Italy, Austria, and the Netherlands were also major contributors, and the United Kingdom contributed approximately $200 million in bilateral aid, distinct from its contributions made through the United Nations and European Union.[55] In March 1996 Japan joined these nations as an individual contributor, providing a grant-in-aid of approximately $24.1 million to Bosnia.[56] Contributing nations therefore spent over $6 billion independently of the costs to international organizations. These costs were primarily targeted to emergency relief and rehabilitation of the country, and are summarized in table 2.5.

Total Costs

The total measurable cost to the international community of the Bosnian conflict has been therefore $53.7 billion. The costs are summarized

TABLE 2.5
Bosnia: Costs to Individual Nations ($U.S. Millions)

U.S.	2,800
Germany	2,100
Austria	524
Italy	320
Netherlands	312
U.K.	200
Japan	24
TOTAL	**6,280**

Sources: FY96-Funded Economic Development and Humanitarian Assistance for Bosnia-Herzegovina, available from www.itaiep.doc.gov/ceebic/balkan/aid.htm. U.S. State Department, *Fact Sheet,* cited November 11, 1996, available from dosfan.lib.uic.edu/www/current/bosnia/bosnia_economic_recovery.html. White House Fact Sheet, *Training and Equipping the Bosnian Federation,* released by the White House July 9, 1996, and distributed by the Bureau of Public Affairs, cited July 12, 1996, available from www.state.gov/www/current/bosnia/iforrole.html. *Japan's Office of Development Assistance, ODA Annual Report 1995* (Tokyo: Association for the Promotion of International Cooperation), 494. "UK Bilateral Humanitarian Aid for the Former Yugoslavia," available from www.oneworld.org/oda/oda_yugo.html. "Emergency Aid for Refugees, Internally Displaced Persons and Afflicted Persons in the Former Yugoslavia," available from www.nttls.co.jp/infomofa/press/release/emgcy_aid.html.

in table 2.6. This figure underestimates the true cost of the conflict to the international community. Some direct costs are not available, such as the expense of refugees in Hungary or Austria, the other main host countries. Many personnel and equipment costs borne directly by contributing nations cannot be accurately quantified. Nor can the many indirect costs, such as the loss of business and investment opportunities. Although such effects of the war are to a large degree speculative, potential trade and business revenues were certainly lost when war ravaged the country and affected the entire region.

Estimated Costs of Preventive Action

Preventive action could have been taken in January–March 1992, after the cease-fire had been imposed in Croatia but before Serbs began their offensive in Bosnia. At this early date the war was waged primarily by armed thugs who took advantage of areas where civil order had collapsed and who sought to enforce their own control. Estimates on the size of the force needed vary. The Pentagon claimed it would have needed several hundred thousand troops, but this is a massive estimate suited more to intervention after violence had broken out. Early in 1992 the size of local paramilitary forces was still remarkably small, and they were scattered throughout the country in uncoordinated and locally based groups.[57] These groups were successful in creating chaos mainly because they were the biggest bullies around, but they were weak on discipline, motivation, and most critically, popular support. Had they been faced with an organized, Western military force, "their most likely reaction would be to flee."[58]

Fifty thousand troops is a more reasonable estimate for a preventive operation. The force would have had to be a well-armed, well-disciplined, and offensively capable operation, but probably would have been highly successful in controlling the violence. Much like the eventual NATO force, it would have been composed mainly of infantry battalions with substantial logistical and communications support. Once it gained control of local

TABLE 2.6
Bosnia: Total International Costs of Conflict ($U.S. Billions)

Military	19.06
Humanitarian	11.98
Economic (direct)	6.36
Economic (opportunity)	10.00
Individual nations	6.28
TOTAL	**53.68**

areas and forced the criminal bands to demobilize, it could have been gradually withdrawn to leave only a disciplined police force.

Given the controversy surrounding this conflict and how to handle it, however, we must consider the financial aspects of a larger force as well. This section will present an analysis of two hypothetical operations—the massive, Pentagon-style force as well as a smaller, purely preventive operation. In either case the force would have been composed mainly of infantry, with some air support.

The war in Croatia was concluded in early January 1992, and demonstrated the passions attendant upon the independence of the constituent republics. The greater mix of ethnicities in Bosnia suggested that violence there would be worse. The Bosnian Serbs, backed by Milosevic, had declared their intention to thwart Bosnian independence but as yet had made no concerted attack on Muslims or attempts to gain territory. Violent flare-ups, particularly around Sarajevo, underscored the potential problem, but these incidents were as yet uncoordinated. Troops needed to be installed at this point, to separate the disgruntled parties and make clear to all who dreamed of revanchism that it would not be tolerated.

Pentagon officials estimated in early 1993 that 300,000 troops were necessary to achieve peace.[59] This proposal was based on the Powell doctrine of massive force. The estimate also came after the fighting had started and the Serbs had made substantial territorial gains, and thus represents a somewhat higher number than would have been required in early 1992, before the violence. Because the eventual IFOR unit was also composed primarily of infantry battalions, its costs will be used as a starting point. This probably places the estimate a bit high, however, since a preventive force would not have had to engage in the withdrawal and demobilization of Bosnian Serb forces that IFOR eventually did.

A preventive force of 200,000 troops, installed in February 1992, before fighting began, would have operated at a cost of approximately $16.5 billion per year.[60] Faced with a battle-ready international force, it seems highly unlikely that the Bosnian Serbs would have attacked Sarajevo and attempted to move westward, particularly since Milosevic's own complicity would have been deterred by the potential of engaging a resolute international force. Milosevic was the key instigator of the Bosnian Serbs' territorial conquest, and their most important source of political support and military supplies. By neutralizing his goals for Greater Serbia, much of the violence could have been avoided.

In all likelihood the force would have had to operate for several years, though not at such massive strength. Assuming an operation lasting four years, with force size being reduced by 50 percent over the first three years and maintained at 50,000 between years three and four, the cost of a massive preventive operation would be approximately $33.3 billion. Though it is uncertain how long a preventive force would have needed to operate, four years seems enough time to calm the security situation and create diplomatic solutions, particularly since in early 1992 the violence was instigated by criminal extremists. A major sticking point in the early diplomatic attempts to gain peace was the disbursement of territory and the populations who called it home. Acting before the majority of land was seized by the Serbs, and Muslims were forcibly driven from their homes and slaughtered, an international intervention force would have created the possibility for compromise on all sides. Furthermore, it would have forced Milosevic to alter his plans for territorial expansion. Without his patronage the Bosnian Serbs would have been much less aggressive, much less well equipped militarily, and more amenable to compromise and dispute settlement.

But it is quite likely that a smaller force would have been sufficient to deter the Bosnian Serbs and Milosevic's complicity. A 50,000-member force, deployed in February 1992, would have demonstrated Western resolve, shown that the lesson of Croatia had been learned, and prevented the Bosnian Serbs' offensive. Zimmermann and others suggest that if the West had pushed back when the Serbs first pushed, the Bosnian violence could have been avoided. The Bosnian Serb army was composed of untrained irregulars who knew they had no right to Bosnian land, and who respected American military power.[61] A much smaller operation than that envisioned by the Pentagon might then have been successful in preventing a tremendous amount of violence. Even though smaller, however, this force would have needed offensive capabilities and a mandate authorizing their use. While the sheer size of a 200,000-member force might itself have been a deterrent, a smaller force would have needed a mandate allowing it to actively engage and demobilize local warlords and gangs. This hypothetical force should have been composed of infantry battalions with air and logistical support. Although resistance would have been sporadic and regional, to be successful this smaller force would have needed the capability to actively engage local leaders and reimpose civil order, particularly in rural areas.

The critical point here is the early aspect of the proposed intervention. If action is actually taken before violence erupts, the prospects for using a smaller force more successfully increase markedly. The months of January to March 1992 were the West's window of opportunity. Preventive action taken during this period, *before* mass violence broke out, could have been achieved with a determined and well-equipped midsize force. The pessimistic predictions that only a massive force installed over a long period of time, perhaps as long as a decade, could have stopped the violence assumes that intervention occurs after the fighting has already begun. The central presumption of this study is that preventive action should take place before the violence starts. If it does, not only will the financial burden be smaller but a smaller force can be used with great success.

Based on the UN operation in Somalia, which cost $862 million per year for 15,000 troops, this smaller mission would have cost approximately $2.6 billion per year.[62] This is slightly less than half the cost of IFOR, which was composed of 60,000 troops but operated in a much different atmosphere. By the time of IFOR's entry in December 1995, the situation was one of generalized violence, massive social dislocation, and ethnic hatreds based in nearly four years of vicious war. A preventive operation deployed before the war would have encountered a very different situation, where violence was instigated by geographically separated and uncoordinated extremists and had not yet gripped the entire population or devastated the entire country. Predicting a four-year operation, as in the larger force analyzed above, the total cost of preventive action would have been $10.8 billion. Again, it must be stressed that this smaller force would likely have been highly effective at preventing the violence. The Pentagon's estimate was made after fighting had already begun, and officials present in Yugoslavia at the time felt even limited force would have proven Western resolve. Thus, early action would have also been highly cost-effective while preventing tremendous destruction of property and lives.

Conclusions

Taking the estimates for a preventive force at four years, we can conclude that the savings of such an action to the international community would have been between $20.4 billion and $43.4 billion. A large-scale preventive force would have cost approximately $33 billion for four years. A much smaller force could have been used just as effectively if deployed early, and would have cost only $10.8 billion for the same time frame. The conflict actually cost the international community $53.7 billion. The costs of the war are undoubtedly higher, particularly when taking into account the effort it will take to rehabilitate Bosnia's economy, provide services such as roads and electricity, and return displaced persons to their homes.

Bosnia is a case particularly sensitive to the argument that the numbers would have come out as, at best, a wash, because of the potential for a drawn-out, Vietnam-like international military commitment. It is critical, however, to recall the central premise of this study, that preventive action should take place *before* the outbreak of violence. The hypothetical intervention forces discussed here are predicated on the assumption that intervention should have occurred before the outbreak of full-scale violence and the hysteria of mass nationalism. Early in 1992 the realm of violence was inhabited by criminals, thugs, and extremists operating on the basis of opportunism rather than ideological commitment. This was before the Serbian practice of ethnic cleansing led to a cycle of violence, retribution, and mass hatred. A disciplined, well-armed Western force operating under robust rules of engagement would have been able to control the local warlords through police action rather than all-out war. Indeed, some suggest that the task would have been even easier, since the gangs, defined by cowardice rather than commitment, would have probably fled when faced with an international military force.[63] Preventive action would have created financial savings—how big is dependent on the size of the force envisioned.

The arguments against early action in Bosnia were that the terrain was "forbidding," making a high-tech war impossible. One NATO commander said the fight would be "eyeball to eyeball down in the mud."[64] But preventive action could have been taken before the fighting began, saving money as well as a country. Furthermore, the international community pays the costs, whether sooner or later. Not only would preventive action have saved money, but what was spent would have been used for better purposes than the $48 billion spent on the conflict so far.

Even now, with Bosnia's future still somewhat unresolved, there is a tendency to believe that the international community could have done little to alter the violence endemic to that area. But any conscientious policymaker must believe that things could always be done better, and recent developments suggest that the international community was at least partly successful. The new prime minister of Republika Srpska, Milorad Dodic, is a moderate who spoke out against Karadzic during the war. He is enforcing implementation of the Dayton Accord, has moved the government from Pale to Banja Luka, and champions economic reform and revitalization as the means to peace. Although tensions remain high, Dodic's policies provide real hope for stability.[65] The September 1998 elections brought mixed results, with success for moderates locally, but hard-line Nikola Poplasen, no champion of an ethnically mixed state, was elected Srpska's president. It remains unclear whether he will actively hinder the implementation of the Dayton Accord. President George Bush, enjoying the euphoria of the Cold War's end, preferred not to take on any difficult problems. European nations sought to establish their own regional control over crises, but could do little without an American commitment, financially and militarily. Early action would have been cost-effective and vastly more constructive, since it would have prevented the tragic and devastating effects to the country and its citizens that are now proving so expensive, and perhaps allowed for economic revitalization and strengthening of the new nation.[66] Instead, the world must rebuild from the bottom up. No one knows what will result, or how this generation of Bosnians—Serbs, Croats, and Muslims alike—will rebound from the experiences of their independence.

3

Rwanda

Andrea Kathryn Talentino

Case Preview

On April 6, 1994, Presidents Juvenal Habyarimana of Rwanda and Cyprien Ntaryamira of Burundi were killed when their airplane was shot down by a rocket. This sparked a resumption of the civil war between the Hutu-dominated Rwandan Government Forces (RGA) and the rebel Tutsi Rwandan Patriotic Front (RPF). The war had been going on since 1990 but had been suspended by a peace agreement in the fall of 1993. The plane crash also provided the catalyst for a spree of civilian massacres that claimed over 800,000 lives and displaced 3 million people, 2 million of whom fled across international borders. The result was a humanitarian crisis of a magnitude unparalleled since World War II. The existing but shaky government disintegrated within two days, and the self-proclaimed interim government lasted few more before it moved to Gitarama, leaving the capital of Kigali to be divided among roving bands of RGA, RPF, and assorted civilian militias. The civilian genocide quickly eclipsed the civil war in its destructive force, sweeping men, women, and children into a fight with little rationale but one clear divide—Hutu versus Tutsi. The speed of the crisis proved almost as overwhelming as its savagery, as neighboring Burundi, Zaire, and Tanzania were flooded with refugees, numbering in the hundred thousands, sometimes in the space of a single day. The hastily erected refugee camps could not contain the scope of the tragedy and provided little sanctuary; while massacres continued outside the camps, cholera, dysentery, and malnutrition formed the enemy within, resulting in 1,000 deaths per day at one camp, and the rate of one death per minute by the end of July.[1]

The international community responded to events in Rwanda by withdrawing most of the United Nations Assistance Mission for Rwanda (UNAMIR), a force established in October 1993 to help implement the terms of the Arusha Peace Accord, the agreement that had led to the reprieve in the civil war, and provided a secure environment for the installation of the interim government. By late April 1994, UNAMIR was reduced to almost 12 percent of its previous strength due to the unstable security environment and increasing vulnerability of UN personnel, leaving only 270 military personnel in Kigali "to monitor and report on the changing situation."[2] Humanitarian workers were initially evacuated as well, but returned when the flood of refugees to surrounding countries threatened another crisis if relief was not provided quickly. The United Nations High Commissioner for Refugees (UNHCR), World Food Programme (WFP), Red Cross, and other aid organizations rushed to the scene and began establishing refugee camps and providing food, water, and medicine to the displaced. The UN Security Council soon authorized rebuilding the initial operation into UNAMIR II, a force of approximately 5,000 troops to provide humanitarian aid, but logistical problems delayed its deployment for several months. France filled the breach by spearheading Operation Turquoise, which created a safe zone in southwest Rwanda designed to protect threatened civilians and provide security so humanitarian aid agencies could operate. The United States also contributed humanitarian personnel and supplies through Operation Support Hope.

The resumption of the civil war in Rwanda was relatively short lived, as was the civilian genocide, but together they led to enormous costs for both the international community and surrounding region. The cost to outside nations of the chaos and violence that began in April 1994 is approximately $4.5 billion. The majority of these costs reflect the human toll of the civilian genocide, which caused populations to flee and burdened the entire region. The $4.5 billion includes the direct costs of UNAMIR II and other military missions aimed at providing humanitarian aid, the costs of rehabilitation since the cessation of hostilities, and the ongoing costs of feeding and protecting refugees and maintaining the camps. It includes the cost of operations only since April 1994, omitting the cost of UNAMIR I and aid programs begun prior to those hostilities. The humanitarian costs have been by far the most burdensome and long lasting, reaching $1.7 billion through the end of 1996 and paying for, literally, millions of gallons of water, thousands of metric tons of food, and hundreds of metric tons of medical supplies and equipment. The mass of refugees has also strained economies and exacerbated instability in Zaire and Burundi. Though not currently directly measurable, these effects will have financial consequences over the long term. Chronic political instability in the region has severely hindered the UNHCR's repatriation efforts, and the refugee camps have had environmental consequences that may harm agriculture in the area.

These costs, particularly those connected to the refugee crisis, could have been avoided if the international community had taken preventive action in late March and early April 1994. The purpose of this chapter is both to describe events in Rwanda and to identify where international action could have been taken to alter their consequences. It is clear that even after the plane crash, and as late as the last week in April, international intervention could have prevented the tragic violence that characterized the next three months. Even more critically, UN personnel knew prior to April that the security situation was rapidly deteriorating and that the problem was no longer simply the civil war but also the organization of extremist paramilitary groups. February was a violent month, with intense fighting in Kigali demonstrating the unstable situation. The UNAMIR force commander received warnings in January concerning preparations being undertaken by independent militias and the existence of arms caches. Despite his urging, the mission's mandate was not adapted to fit the deteriorating security situation. Just days into the crisis in April, the interim government of Rwanda requested an expanded UNAMIR presence, and the African Group at the United Nations urged a more effective mandate. UN Secretary General Boutros Boutros-Ghali advocated an immediate and massive reinforcement of UNAMIR, accompanied by a mandate change allowing it to restore law and order and coerce opposing forces into a cease-fire. Thus from mid-March through mid-April a clear chance existed for international action that could have entirely prevented, or at the very least substantially limited and controlled, the violence. Instead, the international community opted to reduce the force and limit its activities primarily to observer duty, saving short-term military costs but ensuring long-term humanitarian ones.

One UN official said that a few hundred paratroopers dropped into the disturbance in April and allowed to use force could have solved the problem and prevented the initial unrest from becoming all-out war.[3] More likely, the enhancement of UNAMIR would have provided the most effective and preventive solution if undertaken in mid to late March. Major General Romeo Dallaire, commander of UNAMIR, commented later that with only 5,000 troops and an expansive mandate he could have prevented most of the killing.[4] This is particularly true because the worst violence was caused by untrained, irregular civilian militias motivated by hatred rather than a clear political objective. Preventing their actions would have entailed a small enlargement in force size and a dramatic increase in capability, allowing UNAMIR to bring the rogue elements among the citizenry under control and maintain a secure environment.

A comparison with other missions operating under expansive mandates suggests that the costs of a forceful deployment to Rwanda would have been approximately $500 million per year. The best parallel is the UN operation in Mozambique, which involved 4,000 troops and 1,000 police monitors and observers, operating under an active mandate encompassing military, political, and humanitarian duties. It cost just under $300 million per year and provides a good baseline for comparison since many of these same functions were necessary in order to solve the problems in Rwanda that led to the violence.[5] The Mozambique operation had to deal with irregular civilian forces and address the underlying political problems that caused the civil war. Both these functions would have been critical in Rwanda as well, in order to provide a lasting preventive effect.

Even so, preventive action would have been cheaper for the international community than the cost of the crisis as it unfolded. The total measurable costs of the conflict are $4.5 billion, and do not include the enduring effects on regional economies, production, and stability. A preventive operation in Rwanda would have required a slight increase in troop strength and a significant increase in offensive capability, judging by General Dallaire's estimations, bringing the cost to approximately $500 million per year. Even if we assume that the rigors of quelling unrest and rebuilding stable political structures would require two years of effort at the highest troop and financial levels, certainly an overestimation if action was taken before the violence broke out, and a third year at reduced strength, the international community would have saved a substantial amount of money. In fact, the $1.3 billion estimated cost of preventive action is less than the $1.7 billion the international community spent feeding and caring for refugees.

Origins of the Conflict

Conflict in Rwanda has its origins in the ethnic struggles that accompanied the drive to independence. The population is 85 percent Hutu and 14 percent Tutsi, but the latter were favored in the educational system and civil administration under Belgian colonial rule. The principle of majority rule that characterized decolonization thus posed a major threat to the Tutsi and a great opportunity to the Hutu political movement, and was opposed by the Mwami, the traditional Tutsi leader of the country. Not surprisingly, violence accompanied the Hutu rise to power. With administrative help from Belgium, the departing colonial trustee, the Hutu staged a revolution from 1959 to 1961 that abolished the monarchy and ended Tutsi domination. Tutsi fortunes were sealed in September 1961 when a referendum and elections handed 80 percent of the legislative seats to Hutu-led parties.

This electoral victory started a cycle of violence and exodus, and by the arrival of independence in 1962, 120,000 Tutsi had fled to neighboring states.[6] These groups immediately began organizing and staging military attacks against Hutu and government targets across the border in Rwanda, leading each time to retaliatory killings of Tutsi and creating more refugees, making the cycle complete. Ethnic divisions were further reinforced when Habyarimana, a Hutu, seized power in 1973 and established a single-party government, ruled by the Mouvement révolutionnaire national pour le développement (MRND), which instituted a strict quota system allocating jobs and resources according to "ethnic proportions."[7] Under this system, the Tutsi minority received a 10 percent allotment.

By the end of the 1980s nearly half of the Tutsi population had become refugees, and issues of repatriation and resettlement posed an ongoing problem. President Habyarimana repeatedly took the position that population pressures and economic imperatives prevented accommodation of large numbers of refugees, and only allowed the return of those who could prove they would be self-supporting. The sharp decline in 1987 in the price of coffee, the country's main export, combined with drought and a rising population led to an increasingly serious economic situation that continued to worsen despite international aid. Ethnic and regional tensions remained high as a result. The price of tin, Rwanda's second-largest export, began to drop at the same time, and the political stability of the regime reflected the curve of the country's exports. Foreign aid became the only source of support for political elites, and the increasing competition to control its use led to internal power struggles. Cooperative agreements between competing clans broke down as resources shrank.[8]

In 1988 Tutsi refugees in Uganda, along with some moderate Hutu, founded the Rwandan Patriotic Front (RPF), proclaiming themselves a political and military movement dedicated to returning refugees to their rightful land and reforming the government so as to allow ethnic power sharing. By 1989 the Rwandan budget had decreased by 40 percent, mainly in social services. Rapid population growth continued and the food supply was increasingly insufficient. A structural adjustment program initiated by the World Bank in 1990 resulted in a 40 percent devaluation of the currency, weakening the already struggling economy.[9] GDP per capita was declining steadily, the real growth rate was in negative figures, and the country's external debt was growing.[10]

Expressions of discontent with the government rose within Rwanda, increasing the pressures for change. President Habyarimana agreed in July 1990 to accept multiparty rule, but in October 1990 the RPF launched its first attack, advancing across the Ugandan border with 7,000 men. The war between the RPF and government forces had begun, and it is here that the contemporary crisis really begins. The refugee situation transformed an ethnic-based feud into a protracted guerrilla conflict. One of the most critical developments to come out of the October attack was the creation of the civilian militias, which would play a large role in the events of 1994.

Discussions between the government and RPF began almost immediately, as did a string of cease-fire agreements and subsequent violations. The Arusha peace talks began in 1992, sponsored by Tanzania and the Organization of African Unity (OAU). The first round established a cease-fire and a buffer zone between RPF-held territory and the rest of Rwanda, to be monitored by OAU observers. Through the remainder of that year and into the next, agreement was reached on all major issues, and accords were signed on the rule of law and power sharing by January 1993. Hostilities erupted once again in February, however, when the RPF responded to the massacre of Tutsi in the northwest and alleged human rights violations by the government by seizing territory in the buffer zone. The Arusha talks were suspended, fighting continued along the Rwanda-Uganda border, and the refugee and displaced persons situation became more acute.

In May 1993, at the request of both the Rwandan and Ugandan governments, the United Nations dispatched an observer mission, the United Nations Observer Mission Uganda-Rwanda (UNOMUR), to their common border to prevent incursions across the buffer zone. Its primary task was to verify that no weapons or ammunition crossed the border into Rwanda. The Arusha talks reconvened in March and were concluded on August 4, 1993, with the signing of a comprehensive peace agreement calling for a democratically elected government, repatriation of refugees, integration of the armed forces, and establishment of a broadly inclusive transitional government. The parties to the talks also called for a neutral international force to help implement and monitor the agreement, and the United Nations supplied this in the form of UNAMIR, which began its tour of duty in October 1993.

Simultaneously, however, the situation continued to simmer just below the boiling point. Militants within the government were not eager to join any power-sharing agreement and sought to turn sentiment against the Tutsi. The MRND and Hutu-supremacist Coalition pour la défense de la république (CDR) had each formed a militia, the Interahamwe and Impuzamugambi, respectively, which were being trained and armed by government forces in special camps throughout 1993.[11] CDR-sponsored radio broadcasts inflamed popular sensibility by suggesting that the Tutsi opposition wanted to revive its colonial-era dominance, and claiming that UNAMIR was working in league with the RPF to oust Hutu leaders. The Special Rapporteur dispatched by the United Nations reported that official government propaganda deliberately branded all Tutsi as RPF accomplices and moderate Hutu as traitors. Rumor ran rampant and was being manipulated by those who "continued to fuel ethnic hatred in order to cling to power." He also described the situation, particularly the plight of the many displaced persons, as "nothing short of a time bomb with potentially tragic consequences."[12]

At the time such warnings could pass unheeded, since, in spite of delays installing the transition government and deploying the UN mission, the cease-fire agreement between the RGA and RPF, though fragile, held steady. The growing problem was no longer civil war, however, but civilian hatreds. The original target date for installation of the transition government, September 10, could not be met, primarily because UNAMIR did not get off the ground quickly and a large portion of the Arusha agreements rested on the assumption that it would secure the conditions that would allow for the peaceful installation of the government. This first phase, expected to last approximately ninety days, commenced on October 22, 1993. Immediate complications arose, however, due to events in neighboring Burundi where a military coup, on October 21, drove 375,000 Hutu refugees into Rwanda. The two countries thus represented each other's mirror image—Hutu fled to Rwanda from Tutsi-led Burundi while Tutsi fled to Burundi from Hutu-led Rwanda—increasing regional instability and the potential for violent outbreaks. Armed and dangerous civilian militias operated in the northern demilitarized zone (DMZ), ruthlessly targeting other civilians and practicing vigilante justice against Tutsi, substantially complicating the security situation.

In spite of these sideshows, the two main Rwandan belligerents continued to cooperate by reconfirming in December their commitment to the Arusha Accord and pledging to complete the establishment of the transition government by the end of the year. The end of the year came and went, and still no government took control. President Habyarimana was sworn in on January 5, 1994, but without any supporting cast, as agreement could not be reached on the list of members for the government ministries and the National Assembly. Instability spread in Kigali. Arms and ammunition continued to be imported via the airport, in direct contradiction of the Arusha Accord. The UNAMIR commander heard reports of a Hutu militia stockpiling weapons and plotting to kill large numbers of Tutsi in the capital. When he suggested that UNAMIR mount a military operation to capture the arms caches, he was informed by the UN Department of Peacekeeping Operations that such actions exceeded his mandate. His mission was intended only to contribute to the security of Kigali within the context of a weapons-free zone established by the warring parties.[13]

UNAMIR was subsequently allowed to assist government authorities in illegal arms recovery operations, thereby helping to stabilize the security situation. Nonetheless, February was marked by violent incidents, including the assassination of two political leaders and the ambush of an RPF convoy accompanied by UNAMIR forces. The government imposed a curfew on Kigali and other major cities, but still operated at only partial strength since agreement on the membership of its governing bodies remained elusive. An attempt to install the government at the end of February failed when the involved political parties boycotted, claiming Habyarimana had imposed unilateral solutions that masked disagreement among Hutu leaders. It was at this point, from mid-March through the first week in April, that international action could have been taken to prevent the outbreak of conflict. Violence was increasing, the militias were known to be organizing, and repeated attempts to install the complete government had failed. The potential for large-scale violence was clear, and UN troops were already in the country. The international community did nothing, however, a choice with tragic and costly effects.

At the end of March the names of the proposed ministers and deputies were announced, but planned ceremonies were again canceled. By March 30 the government was still not installed, and mining of roads, violent demonstrations, and assaults on citizens characterized Rwandan life. Earlier that month the Belgian foreign minister had expressed concern over the operation of civilian militias and warned "that a prolongation of the current political deadlock could result in an irreversible explosion of violence."[14] The lingering effects of drought, economic decline, and the huge number of displaced persons contributed to an already tense situation, and strained any capacities the state still retained to provide for its citizens. On April 5 the Security Council renewed UNAMIR's mandate for four months, but made it subject to review if the transition government was not installed within six weeks.

Overview of the Conflict

The Security Council's vote was immediately overtaken by events. The shoot-down the following day led to a complete breakdown of authority and an explosion of civilian violence that only forceful, armed action could have stopped. The presidents were returning from a one-day meeting in Dar es Salaam called to discuss solutions to the political and security problems of their countries. Though not entirely proven, responsibility for the shoot-down is widely attributed to Hutu extremists, a twelve-man group known as the "social commission," who purportedly planned the crisis and resultant genocide to preempt any form of power sharing with the Tutsi.[15] The immediate result of the plane crash at Kigali airport was a firestorm of civilian violence, though not initially resumption of the civil war. Instead, members of the Presidential Guard, acting in collaboration with the Hutu militias, immediately began killing Tutsi and Hutu members of the opposition. Hutu militia manned roadblocks erected all around Kigali within thirty minutes of the plane crash, where identity cards were checked and all Tutsi separated and killed. Members of the army, militiamen, and armed civilians went from house to house using prepared lists and maps to identify and locate Tutsi victims.

As the violence continued, it became more evident that it was not a spontaneous uprising but a preplanned assault on Tutsi and Hutu moderates. It was also clear that the civilian fury was distinct from the civil war. Radio broadcasts encouraged the elimination of Tutsi, and blamed the RPF and its Hutu collaborators for the shoot-down. The earliest roadblocks were erected even before the announcement of the plane crash.[16] Among the first to be killed were the prime minister and president of the supreme court, followed by other opposition leaders, intellectuals, professionals, and businessmen. The worst perpetrators were the Interahamwe and Impuzamugambi militias, who cultivated a virulently anti-Tutsi frenzy and coerced other civilians into joining their rampage.[17]

The RPF took advantage of the chaos to resume its activities, breaking the cease-fire in place since August 1993. It also jumped into the civilian melee in an attempt to save Tutsi from slaughter. The resumption of the civil war was a separate process of violence, however, distinct from the civilian massacres. RPF troops cantoned in Kigali broke out of their barracks and engaged RGA troops, while units stationed in the DMZ moved south toward the capital. By the end of the month the RPF controlled the northeastern sector of the country. The government, such as it was, collapsed, and its more moderate members were killed. The two distinct manifestations of the violence could be seen most clearly outside the capital, where civilian mayhem and civil war continued in different areas. The south and west witnessed the worst massacres but little fighting, while Kigali and its surrounding regions fell prey to both forms of violence. By the end of the week the death toll was estimated at 20,000, and reached ten times higher by the end of the month.[18]

Events in the western province of Kibuye demonstrated the disjunction between the civil war and civilian massacres and the extent to which the latter operated by plan. Kibuye had seen no previous fighting, but contained the country's highest concentration of Tutsi—40 percent of the population as compared to 15 percent elsewhere. Hutu officials visited Kibuye in early April to enlist the aid of local officials, who then distributed guns and placed a reward of $1 on every Tutsi head. Hutu were told to "get to work" and "clear the bush"—euphemisms for massacre. Panicked Tutsi sought sanctuary in the local church and soccer stadium but were gunned down, smoked out, and killed. By the end of April only 7 percent of Kibuye's Tutsi population had survived.[19]

The UNAMIR force attempted to provide protection and humanitarian supplies to civilians seeking refuge from the violence. Its task was complicated by the fact that it was not perceived as impartial, containing among its members citizens of the former colonial powers France and Belgium. Ten Belgian members assigned to protect the prime minister were killed when militiamen assaulted her home in some of the earliest fighting. UN headquarters in Kigali was shelled and its vehicles used as targets. With the exception of the Red Cross, humanitarian aid workers were evacuated. UN forces were withdrawn from the DMZ and border regions and concentrated in Kigali, where they attempted to provide protection and assist in the evacuations. It is generally believed that at least 800,000 people were killed by the end of July.[20]

The speed of events contributed to the problem, since the onset of anarchy prevented attempts to bring the rogue elements among the citizenry under control. On April 8 several extremist members of the former government regrouped and attempted to install an interim government, but its inability to restore authority and the intensified fighting between RPF and RGA units forced it to flee the capital four days later and establish itself in Gitarama, 40 kilometers to the southwest. On that same day, April 12, the government of Belgium decided to withdraw its forces from UNAMIR because of the volatile situation and the inability of the force to protect even its own safety. With the Belgian forces representing the third-largest contingent to the mission and possessing critical heavy weaponry and communications capacity, the Belgian withdrawal severely crippled UNAMIR's capacity to act.

Before the Belgian redeployment, UNAMIR consisted of approximately 2,500 military personnel. Its task was to monitor the DMZ, assist in providing security in Kigali, and ensure that preparations for disengagement, demobilization, and integration were taking place.[21] The force commander requested new rules of engagement in early April allowing for the protection of civilians, but was rejected. Without a revised mandate and more troops, UNAMIR could do little to stop the violence. Anticipating that the Belgian withdrawal would effectively paralyze UNAMIR's enforcement capabilities and perhaps even jeopardize its ability to engage in self-defense, the Security Council reduced the force to 270 personnel charged with acting as an intermediary in securing a cease-fire and monitoring the situation. Although within a matter of weeks it authorized a beefed-up force of 5,500 to protect civilians and relief operations, by the end of June fewer than 400 members were on the ground.

Meanwhile, the interim government expressed its willingness to establish a cease-fire and start working toward peace under the structure of the

Arusha Accord. RPF forces held it directly responsible for the massacres, however, and refused to negotiate. Fighting continued among government and rebel forces, civilians and militias. By the end of April the picture was, by any standards, horrific. Large-scale massacres and tortures occurred throughout the country, carried out by means of machetes, axes, and clubs. Women were raped. Men and women—young and old—were subject to torture, maiming, and degradation. Bodies choked the rivers and spilled over waterfalls. The capital consisted of two sectors, one RGA and one RPF, with only artillery and mortar fire flowing between them. Hundreds of thousands fled. By the end of April there were 1.5 million persons displaced within Rwanda, and approximately 500,000 seeking sanctuary across its borders.[22] By the end of May the country was divided—the RGA held the west and south with a stronghold in the Gisenyi-Ruhengeri region in the northwest, and the RPF held the north and east and was strengthening its hold on Kigali, from which Hutu refugees now streamed in an attempt to reach Hutu-held Gitarama to the west. The radio, not in Tutsi hands, encouraged Hutu to flee. Panic reigned as both groups did all they could to instill hatred and encourage mayhem against the other side.

The UN Security Council authorized the expanded UNAMIR II force in May but logistical difficulties hampered its deployment, prompting France to launch a unilateral initiative to deal with the tragedy. Though its history of support for the Habyarimana regime made the operation somewhat controversial, it was a strictly humanitarian effort, authorized by the United Nations. Operation Turquoise commenced on June 23 with the participation of assorted African nations acting under French command and control. The operation consisted of 3,000 troops who operated in the south and west of the country, protecting Tutsi civilians and attempting to prevent the flight of Hutu refugees panicked by the imminent RPF victory. The safe zone it established was soon inundated by civilians, leading the force to also undertake the distribution of humanitarian aid. Despite various threats from the RPF, the mission operated successfully.

Fighting remained intense in the south and north throughout the summer, sending enormous numbers of refugees into Zaire. On July 4, 1994, the RPF took sole control of Kigali, and one day later captured the country's second-largest city, Butare. By July 14 it had captured the stronghold at Ruhengeri, forcing the RGA into a small pocket of territory in the northwest. Its victory led to the largest population movement ever recorded by the United Nations when 250,000 refugees crossed into Tanzania in a single 24-hour period, and 1 million Hutu crossed into Goma, Zaire, within three days, sometimes at the rate of up to 500 per minute.[23] Cease-fire negotiations failed and the RPF continued its advance while panicked civilians continued their flight. By the end of the conflict, 2.25 million Rwandans had sought refuge in Burundi, Tanzania, and Zaire.[24]

The United States launched its own humanitarian effort in July, Operation Support Hope, operating water purification plants and airlifting aid from Uganda and Kigali. At its height this force involved over 2,000 troops. The United Nations, Australia, and Canada also sent engineers and medics to set up "way stations" to encourage the refugees to return home. Tutsi refugees returned happily, but the massive numbers filling the camps consisted mainly of Hutu, who feared reprisal at home from the new government and within the camps themselves from the former army and militia members who had fled with them. The control the militias exerted over the camps, where they took advantage of aid supplies to regroup and retrain while terrorizing the population, remains an enduring problem for the future of stability in Rwanda as well as its neighbors.

By mid-July the RPF had reached the Zairian border and, now controlling the entire country, declared a unilateral cease-fire. On July 19 it installed an inclusive Government of National Unity, intended to operate for five years. All parties to the Arusha Accord received representation in the new government, with the exception of the former ruling party, the MRND, and the virulently anti-Tutsi party, the CDR. This brought the civil war effectively to an end, and, with the flight of former RGA forces and Hutu militia members into Zaire, the military conflict within Rwanda itself ceased. The new president, Pasteur Bizimungu, immediately invited the return of all refugees who wished, but with the fear of Tutsi reprisals still dominant, few took advantage of his offer.

The RPF victory thus marked the end of the civil conflict and the civilian massacres but had no effect on the desperate humanitarian situation they had spawned. The resources available to the international operations and aid agencies functioning in the area fell far short of the demand. UNAMIR was still not fully deployed. UNICEF reported a malnutrition rate of 15 percent among children.[25] Cholera, dysentery, and other diseases haunted the camps established in Zaire and Burundi. The largest camp, at Goma, Zaire, alone required 600 metric tons of food and 1 million gallons of purified water per day.[26] While the official conflict ended, the war against death and despair continued, waged now by aid workers who faced problems far beyond their capacity to solve.

In late 1996 hundreds of thousands of the refugees returned home to Rwanda, pushed by increasing instability and ethnic strife in Zaire. A Tutsi rebellion there has been supported by Rwanda, and the rebels now control the eastern section of the country as far west as Kisangani. The conflict in Zaire raised concerns that Hutu-Tutsi animosities might break out again in the region as a whole, involving neighboring Burundi, Rwanda, and perhaps even Uganda in a new spate of civilian massacres.

Costs of Conflict to International Actors

The costs of the conflict to the local Rwandan population were of course enormous. But outside actors also paid a significant price, through costly military operation, humanitarian aid, and the involvement of international organizations and other contributing states. In addition to the direct costs of rehabilitation, there were significant but immeasurable economic costs, such as the negative effects of the refugee camps on agricultural production. The total figure presented below underestimates these and other costs, since the presence of intangible factors makes a completely comprehensive accounting difficult.

Military Costs

The military costs of the Rwandan conflict to outside powers have been relatively small—the violence was short lived and the international community did little about it (see table 3.1). Military actions were taken for solely humanitarian purposes and, as the record shows, when the going got tough, international forces pulled out. From the outbreak of fresh hostilities in April 1994 through the end of 1995, the United Nations spent $449.7 million on military deployment and observer missions. Several countries also sent military units to provide support for aid organizations, but it is not entirely clear whether they operated as part of UNAMIR or as independent operations.[27] The UN's Operation Gabriel and the engineer and medical contingents sent by Australia and Canada fall into this category. In order to avoid double counting they will be subsumed in UNAMIR costs.

Humanitarian Costs

From the start of the crisis in 1994 through December 1995, the total cost of humanitarian and refugee aid, paid through UN agencies, was

TABLE 3.1
Rwanda: UN Military Operations ($U.S. Millions)

UNAMIR/UNAMIR II	419.6
UNOMUR	8.5
International Tribunal	19.0
UN Office in Rwanda, established 1/95	2.6
TOTAL	**449.7**

Sources: UNDPI, *The United Nations and Rwanda, 1993–1996* (New York: United Nations, 1996), 368–520. United Nations, *Information Notes, United Nations Peace-keeping* (New York: United Nations, 1995), 235. International Institute of Strategic Studies, *The Military Balance 1994–1995* (London: Oxford University Press, 1995), 272.

$1.35 billion, funding the activities of the UNHCR, WFP, Food and Agriculture Organization (FAO), United Nations Children's Fund (UNICEF), the World Health Organization (WHO), and other UN agencies (see table 3.2). UNHCR and WFP received 85 percent of the total UN allocations.[28] The UN figure does not include the costs paid by nongovernmental agencies such as the Red Cross and Médecins sans Frontières, which also operated in the area. Some of these costs, particularly those to the American Red Cross and the Cooperative for Assistance and Relief Everywhere (CARE), are accounted for in the direct cost total to the U.S. government, as is Operation Support Hope, a humanitarian effort of the U.S. government.

Of the total, approximately $584.5 million was spent directly in Rwanda, while the remainder paid for spillover problems in the surrounding region, particularly the refugee camps in Zaire, Burundi, Uganda, and Tanzania.[29] Efforts by the UNHCR to repatriate refugees have not been successful, and the camps are still operating. Recent estimates place their collective cost at $1 million per day.[30] This adds an additional humanitarian cost of approximately $330 million through November 1996. The $1-million-per-day sum dropped substantially after that month, when instability in Zaire and the subsequent promise of an international force led thousands of refugees to return to Rwanda.

Other Direct Economic Costs

Rwanda's economy, always fragile, suffered further during the conflict, leaving it with a GDP of $7.9 billion, $950 per capita.[31] The growth rate had been negative since 1993, as had its industrial production growth rate, which accounted for only 17 percent of GDP.[32] Its exports declined from a rate of $118 million in 1990 to just $44 million in 1995, a drop of over 60 percent, affecting its main trading partners of France, Germany, Bel-

TABLE 3.2
Rwanda: Humanitarian Costs ($U.S. Millions)

UNHCR	557.4
WFP	615.8
UNICEF	103.8
FAO, WHO, UNESCO, International Organization for Migration, Department of Humanitarian Affairs	180.0
Camps, January–November 1996	330.0
TOTAL	**1,787.0**

Sources: John Borton, "Study Three: Humanitarian Aid and its Effects," *Journal of Humanitarian Assistance,* available on the Web at 131.111.106.147. UNDPI, *The United Nations and Rwanda 1993–1996* (New York: United Nations, 1996). "Aid Workers Flee after Rebels Take Zairian City," *Los Angeles Times* (November 3, 1996), A1.

gium, the United Kingdom, and the United States, and primarily the commodities of tea and coffee.[33] Imports stayed relatively steady during that span, but the country's external debt jumped from $645 million in 1990 to $873 million in 1995, representing in part the sums poured in to stem the effects of war.[34]

The international community committed $878.5 million of economic aid to Rwanda to be dispensed through the United Nations, with the World Bank, European Union, United States, UN Development Programme, and Germany as the highest donors (see table 3.3)[35] Pledges reached $1.2 billion, but as of 1996 only the $878 million had been received. These funds went to rebuilding the infrastructure of the country, reactivating the judiciary, undertaking basic sanitation and transportation projects, and rehabilitating what little industry the country possessed. Members of the Organization for Economic Cooperation and Development (OECD) also provided $655.5 million in bilateral aid, a 95 percent increase from their aid level in 1993.[36]

Rwanda's neighbors, who have borne the brunt of the refugee problem, have paid significant costs as a result, though reliable figures cannot be obtained. Zaire (now the Democratic Republic of the Congo), Burundi, Uganda, and Tanzania have all been affected and must cope with not only the immediate financial consequences, but also with problems of disease and overpopulation that accompany the influx of refugees. Despite its vast mineral wealth, the Democratic Republic of the Congo continues to be plagued by high inflation and a negative industrial production growth rate. Burundi, the second-largest refugee host, experienced similar problems. In 1990 it posted modest inflation and a respectable growth rate, 4.4 percent and 5.1 percent respectively, but by 1995 it too had a negative growth rate and 10 percent inflation.[37] While the Rwandan conflict is not entirely to blame for anemic regional economies, the mass migrations it created have made economic progress more difficult in the host countries. Total cost to these countries can be roughly estimated at $150–$200 million.[38]

TABLE 3.3
Rwanda: Economic Aid ($U.S. Millions)

UN contributions	878.5
Bilateral contributions by OECD members	655.5
Regional economic cost	150.0
TOTAL	**1,684.0**

Sources: UNDPI, *The United Nations and Rwanda 1993–1996* (New York: United Nations, 1996), 607–55. OECD Development Assistance Committee, *Annual Report* (Paris: OECD, 1996), A65. www.africanews.org/ciaworldfactbook/1996.

Economic Opportunity Costs

Due to Rwanda's woeful economic state prior to the outbreak of violence, the civil war probably did not disrupt potentially lucrative business or trade ventures. There are, however, numerous costs that cannot be quantified, particularly the devastating environmental effects caused by the mass relocation of citizens. The areas around the major refugee camps have been subject to deforestation and erosion, which will likely cause a decline in agricultural production, a particular concern around the Goma region in Zaire. Goma was also previously a lakeside resort for tourists and close to an important tourist attraction, the mountain gorillas.[39] Zaire lost direct tourist revenue and stands to lose agricultural production. This is particularly harmful in a country whose own political instability has been exacerbated by the refugee crisis. Its shaky economy boasts 40 percent inflation, a GNP per capita of $440, and an industrial production growth rate of −20 percent.[40] It needs all the revenue it can get.

Ironically, areas near the camps were able to reap at least a short-term benefit. Local farmers took advantage of the sudden influx of cheap labor. Benako camp in Tanzania became the country's second-largest city, offering business opportunities for Tanzanians who sold products at the markets and hired out cars to journalists.[41] Mugunga camp in Zaire grew to include 111 restaurants, 756 bars, and 3 movie houses.[42] But local populations were poorly compensated for the long-term, detrimental effects of the camps on their assets, livelihood, and environment, and in some cases had fewer goods and services available than those within the camps.[43] Moreover, as the camps have closed or shifted locations, the disruptions have continued in the local economies, contributing to the regional instability.

Additional Costs to Individual Nations

Along with the funds channeled through international agencies, several major powers incurred additional costs through activities of their own independent agencies (see table 3.4). France and a handful of African nations spent a total of $212 million to fund Operation Turquoise.[44] Though authorized by the UN Security Council, the cost of this action was borne entirely by the contributing nations, with France bearing the lion's share. Outside of this operation only Belgium listed Rwanda among its top fifteen aid recipients for 1994. It contributed 4.2 percent of its Overseas Development Assistance (ODA) total, approximately $28.9 million.[45]

For FY1994/95 the U.S. government spent $490.49 million on the Rwandan crisis, independent of its contributions to UN operations or programs of other international agencies. This figure included disaster assis-

TABLE 3.4
Rwanda: Costs to Individual Nations ($U.S. Millions)

France (Operation Turquoise)	212.00
United States	490.49
Belgium	28.89
TOTAL	**731.38**

Sources: Stockholm International Peace Research Institute, *SIPRI Yearbook 1996* (Oxford: Oxford University Press, 1996), 89. OECD Development Assistance Committee, *Annual Report* (Paris: OECD, 1996), A65. U.S. Agency for International Development, Office of U.S. Foreign Disaster Assistance, Situation Report #6, FY95 (July 24, 1995).

tance channeled through agencies such as CARE and the American Red Cross, as well as at least $30 million spent by the Department of Defense for Operation Support Hope. Of the total, approximately $230 million went toward addressing the regional humanitarian problem, with the remainder being spent directly in Rwanda.[46]

Total Costs

The total measurable cost to the international community of the Rwanda crisis was $4.5 billion. Three months of military conflict thus cost nearly $1.25 billion each month when the enduring economic, humanitarian, and rehabilitation costs are taken into account. The costs are summarized in table 3.5.

Estimated Costs of Preventive Action

Would preventive action have been any cheaper? Even if it had entailed a force encompassing both civil and military duties, the answer is yes. A preventive operation could have been launched in September 1993, after the Arusha peace agreements had been signed but while the situation was still clearly unstable. Even more critically, international intervention could have

TABLE 3.5
Rwanda: Total International Costs of Conflict ($U.S. Millions)

Military	449.7
Humanitarian	1,787.0
Economic	1,533.0
Individual nations	731.4
TOTAL	**4,501.1**

occurred in March 1994, when it became clear that the lack of a stable government and the deteriorating security situation could have severe consequences. Only the presidency was functioning, despite a year's worth of efforts to install the legislature and ministries, and the existence of the civilian militias was known at this time. A window of opportunity existed from early March through approximately April 21, which was when the conflict spread significantly beyond Kigali. Even in the first few weeks of the violence, action could have been taken to bring the militias under control and essentially quarantine the violence in the capital. The potential for violence was very clear from early March through the plane crash in April, but it was equally clear that it could have been stopped with even a relatively small preventive force. As late as April 7, 1994, one day after the eruption of the civilian violence, UNAMIR Force Commander General Dallaire requested more troops and more forceful rules of engagement from the secretary general. His request was rejected, and UNAMIR was restricted to protecting the modest number of citizens who sought shelter in areas under its control.[47]

General Dallaire believes that regardless of the opposition faced, an international force could have prevented the mass killing. In the worst case scenario both RPF and RGA units would have opposed the international troops, which would have had to make a forced entry by air and been prepared for immediate offensive combat operations. In the face of less organized and more sporadic opposition, a buildup of the existing UNAMIR forces in both troop levels and enforcement capacity would have been sufficient. General Dallaire argues that given the type of fighting even through the first two weeks in April, the intervention force would have encountered only periodic interference from small units rather than whole-scale opposition by both the RGA and RPF. Particularly since the early violence was perpetrated by the militias, a preventive operation could have been successfully undertaken by an expanded UNAMIR force operating in a phased combat operation.[48]

In addition, given the intransigent political and security problems afflicting the country, any preventive force would have needed a civil rehabilitation component in addition to its military mandate. The first necessity was certainly stopping the violence and controlling the militias, but simply separating combatants, even if it included forceful disarmament, would not be enough—an effective operation would also need to address the shaky political situation and create mechanisms for its resolution. Failure to do so would merely defer the problems to a later time. An effective preventive operation would thus have had to include both the combat-ready brigades envisioned by General Dallaire and a political component aimed at assisting in the construction of a more stable and broadly representative government.

The United Nations Operation in Mozambique (ONUMOZ) provides a good cost comparison for a hypothetical preventive operation in Rwanda. ONUMOZ was composed of 4,000 troops and 1,000 monitors, and cost approximately $294 million per year.[49] Its mandate included political, military, electoral, and humanitarian elements, and entailed monitoring a cease-fire; separation, demobilization, and cantonment of forces; disbanding of private, irregular armed groups; monitoring of legislative and presidential elections; disbursement of humanitarian aid; and protection and repatriation of displaced persons.

All of these duties were also required in Rwanda. The crisis was caused by long-standing political problems that had to be solved in order to achieve any long-term suppression of violence. The first order of business would have been disarming and disbanding the militias, as General Dallaire envisioned. This would have prevented a great deal of the violence, since it was Hutu extremists and not the RPF that created the initial problems. Once disaffected groups among the citizenry were neutralized, the force could have turned to resolving the political situation. The estimates of the secretary general at the time suggest that a much larger force than that used in Mozambique would have been needed, at least initially. However, General Dallaire argues that 5,000 well-armed troops with robust rules of engagement would have been sufficient. He has since described a force composed of five battalions of infantry working in a six-phase plan to gain control of the country. Three battalions would have arrived by air, landing in Kigali, while two advanced south from Uganda. The offensive capabilities of this force would have raised the cost over that of other, less military-oriented interventions. Using both ONUMOZ and the costs of the Implementation Force (IFOR) in Bosnia as guidelines, however, the force would not have cost over $500 million per year.[50]

Even this seems to be a high estimate, since in March 1994 the greatest threat to security came from the militias. RPF and RGA forces had already been separated and cantoned. Disbanding of the militias would have been the highest priority, but could likely have been completed in less than one year with a determined force. General Dallaire believes that a properly equipped force that advertised its mission would have had no difficulty in controlling the violence, even if it acted as late as mid-April 1994.[51] His comments about the possibility of prevention reveal two critical aspects of the crisis in Rwanda. First, military personnel in Rwanda understood the precarious situation and the likelihood of violence several weeks before the plane crash. Second, they conveyed their concerns and recommendations for how the crisis could be avoided to the United Nations. The United Nations chose to scale down the UNAMIR operation rather than increase its capability, thereby condemning half a million Rwandans. The problem was not lack of information or lack of military options. What could happen and how it could be prevented were well known. By not acting, the members of the Security Council simply assured themselves of a greater financial burden and the stigma of moral failure.

The full political and electoral goals of the international force could not be achieved in one year, however, particularly since the first months would have been preoccupied with military factors. At least one and possibly two more years would have been necessary to complete the task. The international force probably should have been expected to operate for two years at full strength and a cost of $500 million per year, followed by a final year in which it concentrated primarily on political and humanitarian issues, with half the personnel and a less offensive mandate, at a cost of about $300 million. The time frame is entirely consistent with ONUMOZ, which operated for approximately three years. The UN operation in Cambodia also had a similar, wide-ranging mandate, and completed its tasks in slightly less than three years. This brings the total cost of comprehensive preventive action, addressing both the military and political problems of Rwanda, to $1.3 billion over three years.

Conclusions

Rwanda presents a powerful argument for the utility of preventive intervention. Particularly in light of General Dallaire's position, there is very little ground for arguing that intervention would have been as costly as the conflict. The violence unleashed in April 1994 had costs far greater than the costs of the effort necessary to prevent it. The possibility of violence and the identities of the probable instigators were known at least one month before the crisis began. Military commanders present in Rwanda believed they could prevent the chaos by neutralizing the militias, and believed they could do so even in early April, after violence had broken out but before it spread beyond Kigali. The costs of the hypothetical force discussed above are thus an overestimation, since they envision an offensive-capable force operating for two full years. At the very least, preventive action in Rwanda could have saved $3.2 billion.

The total cost of the crisis to the international community was $4.5 billion, mainly in the form of humanitarian aid. Preventive action might have cost $1.3 billion. The savings are particularly large in this case because the military conflict itself was very short, but its consequences were both very expensive and quite long lasting. The immediate security problems that led to the crisis could have been dealt with relatively quickly if the international community had been willing to use force at the outset of the conflict. Officials present in the country asked for troops and an active mandate to prevent the civilian violence, but were denied. Failure to take action led not only to a civilian tragedy, but to much higher costs incurred trying to cope with it.

What is more, the preventive action postulated here would have addressed not only the immediate military situation but the underlying political crisis that created it. Action was never taken to stop the violence, merely to feed and house the thousands who fled from it. Rwanda requires economic and political restructuring in order to become stable. The $4.5 billion paid by the international community has stanched the latest humanitarian crisis, but has done nothing to solve the problems that caused it or prevent another outbreak of violence. Thus, the question is not only how much could have been saved, but how much might still have to be paid in the future? Preventive action could have saved over $3 billion in 1994 and quite possibly prevented further outbreaks, for additional savings. Instead, the international community spent those $3 billion trying to feed and protect civilians while doing nothing about the causes of their suffering or displacement. Each day that refugees cannot go home represents more costs, and increases the possibility of future conflict.

4

Somalia

Mike Blakley

Case Preview

STATE COLLAPSE AND DROUGHT in 1989–90 brought millions of Somalis to the brink of starvation. Without a local government interested in their welfare or able to forestall the humanitarian crisis, hundreds of thousands of Somalis left their homes for neighboring states and other areas within Somalia in search of food and water. Rival clans fought on the city streets and in the countryside for power and food, worsening the refugee problem and deepening the economic crisis. International refugee relief efforts, begun by private charities and later aided by the United Nations and Western nations, eventually yielded to an ill-fated nation-building project led by American forces. On March 3, 1995, all foreign troops were withdrawn after failing to capture Mohammed Farah Aideed, the leader of the most important Somali faction. Those forces also were unable to create an economic and political infrastructure capable of averting a future crisis. After the U.S. withdrawal, few Somalis were in danger of starvation, but this was not due to effective state building or foreign-assisted political development. It stemmed, rather, from better weather and improved prices for Somalia's primary export, livestock.

The Somali case serves as an object lesson in the need for planning and goal setting before international interventions occur. Political leaders must also ensure that relevant objectives can be met by the forces committed.

The case demonstrates the need for effective cooperation between international actors; proper coordination in Somalia could have saved lives and money. It also demonstrates the enormous economic cost of internal conflict to the international community, even in an isolated place such as Somalia. These costs would have been reduced if intervention had occurred earlier in the crisis, but the costs in human and economic terms were insufficient to spur early intervention. The international community and the United States in particular need a greater awareness of the remedies that might have been applied early. The total cost of the Somalia crisis to the United Nations, the United States, and the rest of the international community exceeded $7 billion.[1] About 50 percent of this was spent directly by the United States, 40 percent by the United Nations through its peacekeeping budget, and 10 percent by other nations and nongovernmental organizations (NGOs). This estimate is an extremely conservative one and understates the total cost. It includes only direct expenses and not regional losses due to economic disruption. The estimate also does not include the substantial cost borne by NGOs for famine relief, economic development, and refugee resettlement.

There were two occasions when more cost-effective preemptive action could have averted the crisis and much of the expense that was ultimately incurred. The first conflict prevention point was in 1989, and the second was in mid-1991. In 1989, Western economic and military aid to Somalia stopped.[2] The U.S. government expressed a desire to spend less on foreign affairs and was dismayed over increasing human rights violations by the Siad Barre regime. While there were human rights violations, the regime in power had been supported by the United States for many years as part of its Cold War strategy in East Africa.[3] American aid to Somalia had averaged $20–$50 million per year and peaked at $100 million in 1986. This aid, though small by Western standards, was sufficient for the regime to maintain internal order and allow Somalia to function as a political unit.[4] The money produced balance in a subsistence economy and helped keep the peace. Even as late as 1987, a consortium of Western donors was considering funding a long-term, large-scale rural electrification scheme based on the construction of a hydroelectric power station near the town of Bardera. The sudden and unexpected withdrawal of foreign aid and foreign investment in 1989 triggered the collapse of the Somali government. The aid had supported the power of one man and his clan, and its withdrawal led to a fight for independence from his regime.[5] Resources that might have bought or produced food were diverted to a power struggle just as foreign aid of any type disappeared. Chaos and starvation were the result. By simply continuing the relatively small amount of aid and changing its character from military support to sustainable economic development aid, the international community could have at least maintained the status quo and averted a humanitarian and financial disaster. While paying leaders to maintain order may seem like a misguided policy, the United Nations in fact frequently compensated rival factions in hopes of stopping the fighting, though with little success.[6]

The second point at which early action could have changed the course of events was in mid-1991. At that time, a smaller-scale relief effort, coupled with a UN or American force to contain and disarm the rival factions, could have prevented the massive refugee exodus and civil violence for a fraction of the eventual cost. Supported by a resumption of some economic and development aid, these actions would have saved hundreds of thousands of lives, prevented a mass flow of refugees into neighboring countries, and saved most of the money that was later spent. A small force of 5,000–7,000 troops, similar to the early UN presence, and refashioned economic development aid could have achieved these goals. A three-year deployment of 5,000–7,000 troops and $50–$100 million per year in development aid would have cost less than $1 billion and saved many thousands of lives, as well as $3 billion.

Given the feasibility of intervention, policymakers' awareness of the situation, and the costs involved, this case study supports the hypothesis that early intervention is cost-effective. The case study also refutes the null hypothesis that early intervention would have had no impact on the costs borne by the international community, since significant savings would have been realized in both early intervention scenarios.

Origins of the Conflict

The two primary factors causing internal conflict in Somalia were the termination of all Western economic and military aid and the decline in world prices of Somalia's main export, livestock.[7] The loss of foreign aid coupled with the decline in export earnings led to the collapse of the Somali economy and then to the fall of the Somali government. Once the global military rivalry between the United States and the Soviet Union receded, there was no geostrategic reason for either nation to supply aid to countries in the horn of Africa.

Somali dependence on foreign aid began in 1969 after a military coup overthrew the postcolonial democracy. Somalia soon became a Soviet client, and from 1971 to 1973 received $87 million in economic aid from the Soviet Union.[8] From 1974 to 1977, the Soviet Union sent $435 million in military support to Somalia. The death of pro-American Emperor Haile Selassie in Ethiopia and the rise of Mengistu Haile Mariam dictated a new pattern of alliances. The Soviet Union had always coveted Ethiopia as the most important potential client in East Africa, and soon abandoned Somalia. In response, Cold War rivalry led the United States to recruit Somalia as a replacement for Ethiopia and to maintain the regional balance of power. Somalia became a firm U.S. ally in 1977 when the Soviets began to support Ethiopia and Mengistu in territorial disputes against Somalia. Gradually, American involvement in Somalia increased and came to include substantial cash payments, food and agricultural programs, health services, and economic advice. Unfortunately, little of the aid went to sustainable economic development projects.[9] The people remained dependent on American economic assistance, and the government needed American military aid. Yet with all the assistance, only 11 percent of the population had access to treated drinking water in 1987.[10]

From 1985 to 1989, the United States provided $300 million in economic aid, and from 1980 to 1989, $33.5 million in military aid. During this period, the American-Somali relationship was quite strong and the Barre regime cooperated with American military units in the area. The U.S. Air Force had landing rights at Somali airports, one of which maintained the longest runway in Africa (built by the Soviet Union), and the U.S. Navy had port-of-call privileges.

In the late 1980s both superpowers reduced overseas commitments, since there seemed to be less need to pay for military allies and greater reasons to address economic problems at home. Somalia, which was in the worst economic position in East Africa and suffered from an absence of effective government, was hard hit by their decisions. The Somali regime, like some other Cold War allies, was also undemocratic and had a poor human rights record. As the threat to the United States from the Soviet Union receded and Soviet support for its allies diminished, human rights issues came to dwarf the remaining strategic value of Somalia. In response to congressional pressure and in the absence of compelling strategic need, the United States cut off all military aid to Somalia in mid-1988 and diverted $21 million in economic aid to other African nations. In 1988 Somalia's GDP was only $1.7 billion and declining, inflation was rising, and the annual trade deficit approached $400 million.[11] Later congressional action, in October 1989, closed the door on Somalia.[12] The sudden removal of Western aid, about 25 percent of GDP,[13] combined with drought and low export prices for livestock, led to internal economic collapse.[14] The civil war that followed was particularly bloody since Somalia was well endowed with Western weapons, mostly arms made in the United States.

The Somali political structure had been directly supported by American military aid and arms transfers. Barre's forces were the best armed in the country and could effectively control rival factions. These factors allowed him to keep rival clans at bay and keep a grip on political power. Barre had used the economic aid to maintain at least a subsistence level of nutrition for most of the populace. He also instituted programs to reach rural Somalis and increase their dependence on his regime, seeking to eliminate potentially competing social and political organizations. Therefore, when his government fell, there were no institutions that could take over the critical functions of providing public order, administering food aid, and enforcing laws and contracts throughout the country. The United Nations, recognizing this problem, made the establishment of replacement institutions a primary goal of its mission in Somalia.[15] In summary, the total and sudden absence of economic aid led to economic collapse. Economic collapse in turn produced internal conflict. Political ineffectiveness, drought, and other environmental factors hastened and worsened the regional crisis. The national government's inability to provide food, coupled with the absence of a viable private economy, resulted in mass migration, a devolution of power to the clans, and starvation. The civil war that followed further weakened the economy. Since no faction had the strength to hold an economically viable area, continued conflict was inevitable unless an external force intervened. In retrospect, it would have been cheaper to continue the $20–$100 million per year in American aid.[16] This was enough for the country to function and would have averted the crisis and the costly intervention that ensued. By 1989, total Western expenditures in Somalia were $360 million, though this was largely famine relief.[17] Continued American aid, coupled with investments from other Western nations, the World Bank, and other NGOs, would have mitigated the cost of famine relief and kept the country together.

Overview of the Conflict

The path to the crisis in Somalia began in 1988 when a faction opposed to the Barre regime, known as the Somali National Movement (SNM), took over the capital of the northwestern province of Glabeed and transformed what had been a guerrilla resistance movement into a civil war. Fighting in the region in late 1988 cost 50,000 lives, made 500,000 people homeless, and destroyed the provincial capital.

By the end of 1989 and the beginning of 1990, widespread fighting had broken out, and the Barre regime was rapidly losing control of the country. Two additional factions, the United Somali Congress (USC) and the Somali Patriotic Movement (SPM), based on clans that were in opposition to Barre, joined together to fight the government in the Somali capital of Mogadishu. In response to this new threat, Barre declared a national state of emergency and concentrated all his energies on staying in power. He was, however, quickly defeated and on January 5, 1991, the American Embassy was evacuated as the capital fell to rebel forces. Barre, also defeated in Northern Somalia, fled to the southern part of the country.

Throughout 1991 civil war spread. Rival factions fought over territory and loot, and putative allies turned on one another. In May 1991 one faction, the SNM, declared that the northwest region of Somalia had seceded to become the independent republic of Somaliland. These events led to the first of many international efforts to negotiate peace between the rival factions in June and July 1991. These conferences, organized by Egypt, Italy, and Djibouti, failed to achieve any substantial result. As the conflict continued, fighting between the forces led by Barre and Aideed became the focus of an increasingly brutal civil war. Both sides destroyed wells and canals, burned fields and homes, and plundered grain supplies. This forced people to move, and those farmers who remained were unable to plant grain for the next harvest.

In November of 1991 full-scale war over Mogadishu began in earnest and lasted for four months. There were more than 25,000 civilian casualties, 600,000 cross-border refugees, and several hundred thousand internal refugees. Areas south of Somalia also became battlegrounds as fighting continued throughout the country. In May 1992 Barre was finally defeated by a coalition of rival factions led by Aideed. He then fled to Kenya and later to Nigeria.

After the fall of the Somali government, local, regional, and clan rulers took over areas of the country. There was no central government to administer food aid, distribute medical supplies, or maintain infrastructure (power, roads, and port facilities). Lack of electricity, fuel, and sanitation in turn idled plants. Fields lay fallow in the countryside. Plant equipment, wiring, and other portable items were looted by contending clans and militia, thus destroying the little industry and infrastructure that had existed before the civil war began.

The United Nations resumed activity in Somalia in response to the heightened humanitarian crisis. UN officials, who had left Mogadishu in January 1991, returned in August 1991 and attempted to get relief supplies to the Somali people. Throughout the rest of 1991 and early 1992, Aideed and rival factions fought in the capital and in other cities, continuing to prey upon aid workers. In response to the deepening crisis, the United Nations passed Security Council Resolution 733, which urged the parties to cease fighting, reconcile their differences, and allow humanitarian aid to flow into the country. The Security Council followed this resolution with a global arms embargo on Somalia.

During March and April, 1992, the United Nations attempted to negotiate a lasting cease-fire between the rival factions, with little success. Finally, on April 24, 1992, UN Security Council Resolution 751 established the United Nations Operation in Somalia (UNOSOM I). A UN force of 500 light infantrymen was approved, and its mission was to protect aid workers and supplies, and escort aid convoys into the countryside. An additional fifty cease-fire observers were asked to report on violations of the cease-fire. Unfortunately, the United Nations required an agreement with the clans fighting over Mogadishu before these troops could be deployed. Reaching an agreement took several months, and the cease-fire observers were not sent until July 23, 1992. The lightly armed infantry was not deployed until September 14, 1992.

Sadly, as early as July 1992, drought and disease had pushed nearly two-thirds of the Somali population to the brink of starvation. The United Nations and other relief agencies continued to feed 4.5 million people every day in increasingly dangerous conditions. Since no political solution had been reached, fighting continued in Mogadishu and in the surrounding regions. From January until May 1992, no seaborne relief supplies had been unloaded as rival factions shelled ships in the port of Mogadishu.

Through July and August the situation deteriorated further and the international community began to take notice. Prompted by the United Nations, relief supplies and logistical support were provided by member countries, and in August 1992 Operation Provide Relief was authorized by U.S. President George Bush. Initially this American operation gave relief supplies to southern Somalia and to refugee camps in Kenya, though no American ground forces were committed. However, the lack of both a central authority and agreement between the rival factions made delivery of humanitarian relief difficult. On August 16, 1992, one Somali faction stole the first relief supplies in the southern town of Kismayo where many thousands were on the brink of starvation. Raids on relief supplies continued throughout Somalia.

On August 28, 1992, the United Nations proposed that UNOSOM be augmented by 3,000 additional troops; however, these troops were never actually deployed, as Somali faction leaders would not give their assent. The Somali factions became increasingly resistant to UN requests for security forces to protect humanitarian supplies and workers. By the end of October 1992, General Aideed, now the most powerful man in Mogadishu, objected to the deployment of the first UNOSOM troops, demanded they be removed, and expelled a UN official. By the end of November, when the flow of relief supplies to the starving was further slowed by factional fighting, the United Nations began to consider changing its mission objectives.

During Operations Provide Relief and UNOSOM I, which lasted from August 15 through December 1992, there was a growing consensus that a more forceful intervention would be necessary to stop the famine from claiming further lives. After losing the presidential election in November, President Bush considered a full-scale intervention and informed the United Nations that American troops were available for a large-scale deployment in Somalia.

On December 3, 1992, the United Nations passed Security Council

Resolution 794, which approved a military intervention in Somalia and authorized member states to use "all necessary force." The U.S. intervention plan was named Operation Restore Hope, and the UN mission was dubbed Unified Task Force (UNITAF). These missions lasted from December 9, 1992, through May 4, 1993. The United States assumed operational command of UNITAF and provided the largest contingent of troops. By the end of December, American troops had occupied key points in Somalia. At its peak, UNITAF deployed 37,000 troops, including 8,000 troops on U.S. Navy ships offshore. Of these troops, 28,000 were provided by the United States. By early March 1993, however, the UNITAF force had been reduced to 28,000 troops.

During the UNITAF operation, humanitarian efforts achieved their maximum effect. The famine was finally contained to a few small areas, and most Somalis were receiving food aid. Medical care was increasingly available, and supplies entered various Somali ports without resistance. In addition, the United Nations began programs to restore agricultural and livestock production and made various attempts at state building, realizing that only a stable, central government could avert a replay of the recent crisis.

In January 1993 and again in March, Somali faction leaders met with UN officials and delegates from African nations in an attempt at national reconciliation. While agreements were reached for a cease-fire and the disarming of faction troops, the peace did not last. By late March the fighting had resumed. It was soon evident that a strong international presence in Somalia would have to continue.

On March 26, 1993, UNOSOM II was approved for comprehensive peacekeeping and had the additional mission of disarming faction troops and local militia. Compared to UNITAF, UNOSOM II had an expanded mission and fewer troops. The United Nations assumed command of UNOSOM II, and American forces, deployed as an offshore Quick Reaction Force, operated with their own commanders in support of UN operations. Some additional American forces were deployed to Mogadishu, though they were small, special operations units. Though these forces imposed a continued peace, humanitarian efforts were still necessary to cope with the large refugee population. On March 27, 1993, the United Nations allocated $142 million for relief and rehabilitation efforts in addition to peacekeeping expenses.

These steps, however, did not resolve the crisis. Previous cease-fire agreements were ignored, and UN forces and relief workers were threatened. On June 5, 1993, a Pakistani force of UN peacekeepers was ambushed by Aideed loyalists. Twenty-four Pakistani troops were killed. UN efforts to punish those responsible were unsuccessful. Operationally, UNOSOM II was experiencing severe problems in achieving its mission.

There were constant coordination problems between contingents from different nations, and the definition of mission goals remained unclear. The United Nations admitted it had no operational blueprint, and that without better planning and information, mission success was in danger. Coupled with an expanded set of goals and fewer resources, these problems made success unlikely.

The failure of UN efforts led to increased American actions to disarm the factions. During one of these missions on October 3, 1993, an American Ranger unit suffered eighteen dead and seventy-five wounded in a raid on a weapons storage site. Frustrated by UN failures and under increasing domestic political pressure, American President Bill Clinton announced on October 7, 1993, that all American combat forces and most logistics units would leave Somalia by the end of March 1994.[18] Other nations followed suit, and by March 1994 two-thirds of UNOSOM II troops had been withdrawn. The remaining UN troops turned to keeping the peace in smaller areas of Somalia, though factional fighting continued.

Over the next twelve months, UN troops and humanitarian aid workers continued in decreasing numbers to keep the peace and feed the hungry in Somalia. Mass starvation had been averted, but no new national government was installed, and factional violence continued. The UN mission officially ended in March 1995, having achieved some measure of humanitarian success but failing in its mission to settle an ongoing internal conflict.

Costs of the Conflict to International Actors

The following sections provide estimates for the costs to international actors and the United Nations for operations conducted in Somalia from 1990 to 1995. The bulk of documented expenditures are direct costs of intervention and include the cost of military operations, famine relief, and actual grants for economic recovery. Military costs are presented first, followed by humanitarian costs, other direct economic costs, and indirect (opportunity) costs.

Military Costs

The final total of American intervention costs in Somalia is about $2 billion.[19] This includes the cost of American intervention through the UN operations UNOSOM I and II and UNITAF, as well as the U.S. Forces in Somalia (USFORSOM). This figure is adjusted for American contributions to the United Nations for peacekeeping, which are counted in the UN estimates in table 4.1. UNOSOM II, the UN operation that replaced American troops, cost over $1 billion per year and lasted over two years.

TABLE 4.1
Somalia: Military Costs ($U.S. Billions)

U.S. costs for all military operations	2.0
UN costs: UNOSOM I	0.4
UN costs: UNOSOM II	1.6
Additional direct costs, U.S. and UN combined	0.4
TOTAL	**4.4**

Sources: "The Final Cost of a Mission of Hope," *Newsweek* (April 4, 1994), 44. Tom Pfeiffer, "US Hands Over Somali Mission to New UN Peacekeeping Force," *Arms Control Today* 23 (June 1993): 28. UNDPI, *The United Nations and Somalia, 1992–1995,* Document 110, 482–83. Michael Maren, "Spoiled," *The New Republic* (December 12, 1994): 13.

The prospect of a continuing civil war and the failure to build a state where one no longer existed eventually forced the United Nations out of Somalia.[20]

Cost of equipment left behind and donated to local communities was valued by the United Nations at $235.7 million.[21] In addition to equipment, the United Nations abandoned the American Embassy that it used as a headquarters.[22] The costs involved are all in addition to the figures cited above.

The UN cost for UNOSOM I was $351.5 million.[23] It involved the maintenance of a small military force as well as sustained and widespread relief efforts. A summary of military costs is presented in table 4.1.

Humanitarian Costs

Major American costs were incurred before the intervention, including nearly $600 million for the three months immediately preceding deployment.[24] These were spent for humanitarian relief and continued to accumulate as the crisis continued. Total American relief aid, not including military costs counted above, was about $800 million over the entire crisis.

Food aid costs continued after the intervention, largely donated by international organizations, though at a reduced annual amount. For example, the World Food Programme (WFP) spent $50 million in 1994, after the crisis was over, and planned to continue that level of spending. The Oxford Committee for Famine Relief (OXFAM) spent over $500,000 received from the British government to feed returnees in 1994.[25] The United Nations spent nearly $500 million in famine and other relief operations during various phases of operation in Somalia, including $142 million through March 1993, which accumulated to $160 million by the end of 1993. Similar amounts were disbursed in 1994.[26] (See table 4.2.)

TABLE 4.2
Somalia: Total International Costs of Conflict ($U.S. Billions)

U.S. costs: Intervention	2.0
U.S. costs: Humanitarian, rebuilding, refugees, and other nonintervention costs	0.8
UN costs: Intervention	1.9
UN and other humanitarian aid costs	0.5
Costs of debt write-off to the international community	2.1
TOTAL	**7.3**

Sources: E. Palmer, "Putting a Price on Global Aid," *Congressional Quarterly Weekly* 51 (January 23, 1993): 186. *Somalia News Update* 3 (January 7, 1994); UNDPI, The United Nations and Somalia, 1992–1995 (New York: United Nations, 1995). Central Intelligence Agency, *World Factbook,* assorted years (Washington, D.C.: CIA). Tom Pfeiffer, "US Hands Over Somali Mission to New UN Peacekeeping Force," *Arms Control Today* 23 (June 1993): 28.

Other Direct Economic Costs

After the conflict was settled, the United Nations estimated that creating and maintaining a judicial system and police force to guarantee internal order would cost the United Nations and donor nations $45 million for the first year and an additional $10 million per year for several years.[27] Actual costs incurred by member states for UNOSOM police development efforts included $20.6 million in cash payments and $43 million in in-kind contributions that consisted largely of equipment and facilities.[28]

Somalia also had in excess of $2 billion in external debt at the beginning of the crisis. This equals roughly 120 percent of precrisis export earnings.[29] Current export earnings are a small fraction of precrisis amounts, and there is little reason to believe that any increased export earnings will be used to pay back this debt, especially since there is no Somali government willing to assume these liabilities. This combination of circumstances suggests that the entire portfolio of Somali debt, already in technical default, will be written off. This is a further expense to international actors like the World Bank and decreases the capital available for development projects worldwide. The capital to rebuild Somalia must come from external sources. Prior to the conflict, net capital expenditures were $111 million per year, and some amount must be spent to replace destroyed infrastructure and encourage development.[30]

Indirect and Opportunity Costs

According to UN estimates, at least 1.8 million refugees needed to be resettled. Ethiopia had 300,000 Somali refugees and Kenya had 500,000. Somalis fleeing within their own country and to Djibouti made up the remainder.[31] Precise estimates of these costs to neighboring states are unavailable, but they are substantial. Refugees received food and shelter while in other countries, though some of this aid was paid for by NGOs. The refugee crisis disrupted trade, including nonmonetized trade, which is important in subsistence areas and inherently difficult to estimate. Areas closest to the fighting experienced a sharp decline in economic activity.

Somalia exports livestock and bananas, and imports mostly petroleum products and foodstuffs. Its trade proportion of GDP prior to the crisis was 9.3 percent (1.8 percent for imports and 7.5 percent for exports). The small absolute value of this level of trade coupled with the wide distribution of trading partners indicates that there was little external monetary loss due to trade disruption.

Significant costs were nonetheless incurred by regional actors in terms of nonmonetary trade in livestock. Animal husbandry, which accounts for 40 percent of GDP and 60 percent of export earnings, was severely disrupted. Groups in neighboring states that relied on livestock trade with Somalia were severely affected and the famine in Somalia, which resulted in the slaughter of livestock, spread to other nations in the region.

In Kenya one consequence of the influx of Somali refugees was increased inflation. Since August 1991, prices for basic staples such as sugar and rice have doubled throughout the economy and apartment rents have tripled.[32] Refugees also smuggled goods across borders and evaded customs taxes. Camps were turned into bazaars where all sorts of goods were sold without payment of sales tax, costing the local governments uncounted millions.

In aggregate, regional opportunity costs were quite high. The regional GDP in 1989 was $25.4 billion, whereas the 1994 figure was only $18.6 billion, a 27 percent decline. Some of this was due to the effects of the civil war in Somalia. States have lost the potential benefit from economic activity that could not occur.

Total Costs

A summary of the international costs of the internal conflict in Somalia is presented in table 4.2. Opportunity losses to economies in the region are not included, as it is difficult to measure to what extent the regional decline in GDP was due to the conflict in Somalia or the drought. East African states had to spend more on their militaries to protect themselves during the war, impinging on economic development. While these costs are difficult to estimate, they are real and substantial.

For several reasons the direct costs presented in table 4.2 almost certainly underestimate the actual direct cost of the internal conflict in Somalia to the international community. First, these figures do not include a full accounting of costs incurred by other nations involved in UN operations that were borne directly by these nations and not spent through the United Nations. For example, the costs over and above UN assessments paid by France and Italy are not included as they were not readily available. Second, private organizations undertook large-scale humanitarian efforts in Somalia, and only a fraction of their costs is known and included above. Red Cross, Cooperative for Assistance and Relief Everywhere (CARE), and other organizations were in Somalia throughout the crisis and incurred considerable costs in food and medical supplies that are not publicly reported. These costs are not reported because they are difficult to quantify and are not as clearly a direct cost of conflict as those costs recounted earlier.

Estimated Costs of Preventive Action

There were at least two points in time when early intervention in Somalia would have saved lives and billions of dollars. Early intervention was feasible in both cases. In the first scenario, intervention would not have required the large-scale troop deployments that are regarded as a great political risk by most Western leaders.

The first intervention point when the conflict in Somalia might have been deferred or prevented had to do with economic choices in 1989. If American foreign aid had been continued, the crisis might never have occurred. This aid was sufficient to maintain internal stability prior to the crisis and would likely have prevented the civil war as well as mitigated the cost of famine relief. Continued Western economic aid of $40–$60 million per year would have maintained the status quo. During the drought period, this aid might have been doubled to cover the costs of feeding those who relied on livestock in the affected rural areas. At most, the incremental cost for this "crisis" period would have amounted to $30 million per year for four years. This stream of aid need not have been continued forever. If the character of the aid had been altered according to World Bank strategies, it is possible that a stable and self-sufficient economy could have developed. Instead of food shipments and arms, capital to develop raw materials extraction capabilities and expand banana production could have boosted export earnings. Modern farming and irrigation, programs to vaccinate livestock and increase herds, together with a stimulus to some industrial sectors, would have allowed Somalia to become self-sufficient, reducing the likelihood of later famine. These measures would have stimulated trade and private capital inflows, creating the basis for a more stable economy.[33] Even vastly increasing the previous aid, creating new conditions and purposes for the grants, and continuing it for a decade would have cost the international community less than $1 billion, or less than 25 percent of the direct military costs of intervention.

A second opportunity to preempt the eventual crisis occurred in mid-1991.[34] After the Barre regime ultimately fell, in January 1991, no military force capable of opposing American troops existed in Somalia. The absence of any potential opposition to a U.S. Marine landing was a necessary precondition to intervention. Opposition by heavily armed, though poorly trained, soldiers would have made the costs of intervention prohibitive in economic and political terms. By mid-1991, however, there was no faction able to oppose intervention. There was also some support for external help, especially among the displaced population.

By this time, the central government had fallen and rival clans seized what assets they could to survive. Interclan warfare was beginning to spread and this generated large refugee populations. The situation was rapidly deteriorating, and the humanitarian and regional costs were rising. At this time, a small, well-armed, mobile force could have secured the important ports and city areas and separated warring factions. This would have also facilitated the distribution of food aid, slowing and eventually reversing the refugee flow into neighboring countries.

A preemption mission in mid-1991 would have consisted of 5,000–7,000 troops broken down into three elements. The first element would have combined U.S. Marines, mechanized equipment, and organic air support with the primary mission of separating groups in conflict and making peace in the countryside. These units would have also secured the airports.[35] The second element of light infantry or additional U.S. Marines would have swept and held the cities and ports and responded when fighting broke out.[36] These combat elements would have deployed sufficient heavy weapons support, and their superior tactical ability would have enabled them to accomplish their primary mission of pacifying the cities. Removing heavy weapons and reducing the amount of small arms available would also have been an early goal of the first two elements.[37] The third element would have consisted of military police and civil affairs personnel who would have kept order in the cities after the other elements had removed the threat of armed clan units. The third element would have also facilitated the distribution of food and medical aid throughout the country, and begun the process of reconstituting the state apparatus while fostering an interclan bargain that might have ended the fighting.

As early as mid-1991, no remaining clan or faction would have been able to oppose an American landing force or mount an effective, long-term resistance to American forces. Recognition of the actual tactical situation would have allowed a deployment far smaller than the 29,000 specified in the American operational plan and in the actual operation. Even early deployment plans under consideration in late 1991 envisaged only 12,000–

15,000 troops.[38] An earlier preemption force would have faced a less threatening environment and could have been small compared to the actual forces deployed.[39] This smaller contingent would have been large enough to remove heavy weapons from the clans and enforce peace.

The original proposal for a rapid reaction force during the Carter administration, which led to the development of the Central Command (CENTCOM) with pre-positioned stores at Diego Garcia and Oman, could have formed the nucleus for the proposed preemption force.[40] Additional units from NATO deployments and from the continental United States would have rounded out the force. To succeed, however, new political institutions would have had to be crafted to facilitate internal peace and economic development.

Using the costs of USFORSOM as a baseline for estimation, this smaller intervention force would have cost $500 million over a four-year period.[41] The cost of an expanded economic assistance program, similar to that proposed in the first preemption scenario, would have represented no more than $1 billion over a ten-year period. This brings the total cost for this proposal to $1.5 billion.

Conclusions

The Somalia case demonstrates the high cost of waiting too long. Even in the more expensive of the two proposed early action scenarios, the international community would have saved billions. The international community was certainly aware of the growing crisis and the need for outside intervention.

By mid-1990 the United States was making contingency plans for an intervention in Somalia, and the West knew well in advance that a costly internal conflict and humanitarian crisis were imminent. Despite forewarnings, the international efforts undertaken were insufficient to stop the crisis before it became acute. As the crisis worsened, the economic costs of intervention mounted as did the humanitarian costs. The lateness of international intervention is most often blamed on domestic political concerns. Few elected governments commit troops to an area where no compelling vital interest is at stake. However, governments need to recognize that risking a small yet decisive military intervention early in a crisis could produce domestic political success.

Since it was clear to the West early in the crisis that some deployment would eventually be necessary, waiting only increased the costs that would eventually be incurred. The case clearly supports the hypothesis that early intervention is cost-effective and refutes the null hypothesis that early intervention would lead to no savings.

The cost analysis of this case provides a clear economic rationale for early intervention. Continued economic aid, proposed in the first alternative scenario, would have saved nearly $6.5 billion. The second proposal, a small, early preemption operation launched in mid-1991, would have saved nearly $6 billion.

The cost savings generated by early intervention are even greater if indirect and economic opportunity costs are counted. For example, if only 10 percent of the decline in regional GDP is attributed to the Somali conflict, the total cost savings generated by early intervention would increase by $680 million. Additional costs would have been saved by preventing refugee movements, increased inflation, and opportunity costs. These costs are also large, though difficult to estimate precisely. The cost savings that would be generated by early intervention indicate that there is a purely economic rationale for the proposed policy.

The peace provided by an early, preemptive strategy would have allowed for increased foreign assistance and capital investment. Of course, ultimately, only the development of stable economic and political institutions in Somalia would prevent a recurrence of the crisis. Early intervention would have made this much more likely.

5
Haiti

Mike Blakley

Case Preview

THE AMERICAN AND UN OPERATIONS in Haiti represent another instance of belated intervention in an internal conflict. While Haiti is a poor country possessing only local strategic significance, U.S. policymakers perceived that the crisis in Haiti was directly relevant to American interests. Like Rwanda and Somalia, Haiti's unfortunate plight raised American concerns—economic, political, and humanitarian. The tide of Haitian refugees to the United States increased economic and political costs and became a factor in Florida's local politics. Consequently, the United Nations played a less important role in this case than in Rwanda, Somalia, and Cambodia. The following case history thus centers on American policy and to a lesser extent on the role of other international actors. Haiti is the only case where refugees came to the United States directly from the site of the conflict. In addition, Haiti was not so much a case of civil war as of national collapse in the wake of a military coup, an embargo, and a predatory ruling elite that used political and economic means to strip the nation of its assets.

As with the other cases in this study, the central research question is whether early intervention in Haiti would have cost the international community less in purely economic terms than the actual operation. Therefore, this chapter centers on the costs to external actors stemming from Haiti's internal conflict. These costs included humanitarian assistance, the direct expenses of intervention, and the costs of rebuilding the country. These are then compared to the costs involved in a projected counterfactual intervention scenario that could have been launched at two different points in the historical development of the crisis.

Haiti is an important case in this study for many reasons. First, it is the only instance of an internal conflict on the sea approaching the U.S. border. As a result, policymakers could cite a direct threat to American security as a reason for intervention.[1] Thousands of refugees from the conflict headed for America. Most of them were intercepted by the U.S. Coast Guard and interned at the U.S. naval base at Guantanamo Bay, Cuba. However, the possible resettlement of Haitian refugees in the United States had important domestic political implications.

Second, unlike Somalia and Bosnia, the Haiti issue did not arise because of foreign policy shifts in the aftermath of the Cold War. Haitian internal conflicts were domestic in character and grew out of a long history of repressive dictatorship that systematically eliminated all competing political and economic centers of power. Though there was international interest in and some assistance given to Haiti, it was a low-priority issue to Western nations until the conflict escalated.

Third, the Clinton administration used cost savings as an explicit rationale for intervention. This represents a new approach to what are traditionally called "humanitarian efforts" and marks the beginning of an emergent foreign policy doctrine: early intervention saves money. In this case the savings would have been over $2.7 billion. One indication of this new approach came during Deputy Secretary of State Strobe Talbott's testimony before the Senate Foreign Relations Committee on March 9, 1995. When asked about the cost of American operations in Haiti, Talbott argued that intervention in Haiti was justified on purely economic grounds and that the United States could either continue to bear the costs of internal conflict in Haiti indefinitely or mount an intervention to halt it that would be less expensive in the long run.[2] He also alluded to the tremendous opportunity costs of conflict, noting that a peaceful Haiti would be valuable as a trading partner.

Fourth, this conflict demonstrates the enormous cost to the international community of belated intervention in internal conflict. The United States and other nations took action in Haiti at a cost of $5 billion. The situation was addressed only after early opportunities for cost-effective action had passed. Of this amount, the international community spent over $2 billion on operations to relieve hunger, support and interdict refugees, assist subsequent economic development, and restore and maintain democracy in Haiti.[3] Most of this came from the United States, while Canada and France contributed smaller, though still significant, amounts. The

United States directly spent another $2 billion for intervention in Haiti. American assessments for UN operations are included in the international community costs.

There were at least two periods prior to the actual intervention in Haiti when international action would have been at least as effective and far less expensive. The first of these occurred in the months immediately following the election of Jean-Bertrand Aristide; the second took place after the Washington Accord was signed in February 1992. Given the feasibility of intervention and the costs involved, we can conclude that this case supports the hypothesis that early intervention is cost-effective. Since significant savings would have been realized in both early intervention scenarios, the Haiti case also supports rejecting the null hypothesis that early intervention would have had no impact on the costs borne by the international community.

Origins of the Conflict

Problems in Haiti arose from the disjunction between political leadership and civil society that characterized the Duvalier period, from 1957 to 1986.[4] The Haitian government apparatus was predatory, appropriating wealth from its people while offering few welfare benefits, public goods, or sustainable economic policies. Eventually, such a state needs external support since it cannot continue indefinitely to squeeze resources from its people, who will ultimately either avoid paying the state or cease all economic activity.

The Haitian government was supported by some foreign aid. But the lack of conditions governing aid and little outside pressure offered the regime few incentives to change domestic policy so long as Haiti supported the U.S. policy against Cuba. What financial resources existed in Haiti were confined to a small number of elites who maintained that wealth by force. Yet donors continued to send money to Haiti despite the obvious social and economic problems.[5]

In addition to this fundamental disequilibrium and the regime's need for external support, population pressure compounded the instability brought on by decades of repressive economic policy and a failure to invest in productive capacity.[6] This repressive policy and the lack of arable land had led to migration from rural to urban areas. The urban population grew so rapidly that there was no way for Haiti to produce enough food domestically. The rising specter of hunger and large-scale internal migration caused severe problems for the government, and the situation steadily worsened. Large-scale emigration was difficult because no other nation was willing to accept a large number of economic refugees. Continued economic problems caused Haitians to flee the island any way they could.

When Haitian democracy first emerged, it was thus a very fragile creation, resting on poor economic foundations and vulnerable to elements of the previous autocratic regime, which eventually staged a coup. The economic basis for the failure of Haitian democracy has many similarities with the problems of democratic consolidation in other parts of Latin America and Eastern Europe in the late 1980s.[7]

As the Aristide government began its tenure in Haiti on February 7, 1991, the army and the militia groups, as well as the people, saw little hope for economic improvement. Few effective economic reforms were initiated, and in rural areas supporters of the previous autocracy still held sway. There was little incentive for foreign investment to enter; as a result, scarcely any new jobs were created. The United Nations and the community of established democracies continued to provide food aid, but the international community saw little reason to believe that there was a permanent solution to Haiti's inability to feed its population. Domestic economic policy reform was also slowed by political instability.

Aristide was unable to discipline the military for its repressive role during the Duvalier years, nor was he effective in breaking the power of paramilitary supporters of the old regime. Caught in a trap of increased expectations and limited resources, and unable to please the military, the fragile democracy was easily overthrown on September 29 and 30, 1991. An embargo, in response to the coup that overthrew Aristide, was imposed by the Organization of American States (OAS) and later supported by the United Nations. It was the final factor leading to the collapse of the Haitian state.

The worsening of internal conflict, together with a greater refugee and humanitarian crisis, ultimately generated an international response. The international community, led by the United States, intervened to restore democracy and order.

Overview of the Conflict

Haiti has never had a stable, democratic government, and peaceful power transitions are rare in Haitian history. There have been forty-one rulers since Haiti gained independence from France in 1804. Of these, seventeen fled the country, six were overthrown, three died of illnesses, three resigned, two were assassinated, one committed suicide, one was executed, one died of natural causes, one was killed by a bomb explosion, one was murdered in jail, one was killed by mayhem, and one was removed by the United States. The disposition of the remaining three leaders is unknown.[8]

Haiti's economy has been even less successful than its political system, and Haiti has been a long-term recipient of Western aid. From 1973 through 1981, Haiti received $477 million in foreign aid.[9] Foreign assistance accounted for approximately 25 percent of GDP prior to the coup.[10] The termination of this aid and the imposition of the embargo shattered the economy.

The First Election

On December 16, 1990, Haitian voters elected Aristide after an often bloody campaign waged in the streets by both reformist and conservative sides. This first free and fair election in Haitian history was supposed to relieve the repression of the Duvalier years, create a stable democracy, and produce prosperity. However, the plan did not include continued benefits for the military elite and gangs of their paramilitary allies loyal to the previous regime, and these groups soon began to oppose the new democracy.

In addition to a president, a parliament was elected that included many representatives of the previous leadership. Parliament often opposed the new president, and this conflict was mirrored by conflict in the streets. By August 1991 there had been little progress toward reform and almost no structural change in local government or economic policy. Dissatisfaction with the government mounted, and parliamentary leadership changed, becoming even more stridently anti-Aristide.

By late September the remaining middle-class and wealthy Haitians, as well as the military, were completely dissatisfied with the new democratic regime. Speculation grew that a coup was imminent. Aristide addressed the United Nations on September 27 and called for his people and the international community to join him in the struggle against corruption and to maintain the rule of law.

The Coup and the Crisis

The crisis was precipitated by the coup that overthrew Aristide on September 29 and 30, 1991. Lieutenant General Raoul Cedras, who had been recently promoted to army chief of staff by Aristide, took over the government with the support of the military, and Aristide escaped to Venezuela. Immediately after the coup, the OAS denounced the coup and its leader and demanded the restoration of President Aristide. The United Nations later followed suit. Aristide addressed the UN Security Council on October 3 in an attempt to rally international support for his return. On October 8 the OAS urged member states to freeze Haitian assets abroad and impose a trade embargo on Haiti. This was followed by UN General Assembly Resolution 46/7, which demanded the legal government be restored to power in Haiti and that human rights not be violated.[11] The Security Council also expressed support for the OAS recommendation for a freeze of Haitian assets and a trade embargo.

In the weeks following the coup, thousands of Haitians were gunned down in the streets by the police, the military, and armed factions loyal to the previous regime. The army arrested Aristide supporters, looted homes, kidnapped opponents, and waged a comprehensive campaign against prodemocracy groups. Army units loyal to Cedras seized radio and television stations and controlled or shut down the press. The army continued to weed out Aristide supporters, and 200,000 residents fled the capital for the relative safety of the countryside. About 25,000 went to the Dominican Republic, which had recently expelled earlier refugees. On October 7 an OAS mission visited Haiti, condemned the coup, and noted the large-scale human rights violations. The United Nations issued a similar statement on October 11.

Taking note of the failure of diplomatic efforts and responding to the brutality of the military regime, American President George Bush imposed a commercial embargo on Haiti, exempting only humanitarian food and medical supplies. Mass demonstrations, broken up by military units, led to more civilian casualties. The military began arresting students and foreign journalists and continued to suppress pro-democracy demonstrations. The number of internal and external refugees rose.

As the crisis intensified, American refugee policy changed. On November 15, 1991, reversing previous policy, the U.S. Coast Guard repatriated 535 refugees. Eventually, over 30,000 were repatriated to Haiti over the course of the crisis. On December 5 the first formal declaration that international action would be necessary to restore peace in Haiti was issued by the OAS. This declaration called for the coup leaders to step down, requested that Aristide appoint a new prime minister, and called for an international force from neighboring countries to make peace. This proposal was largely ignored by both the international community and the Haitian regime.

Large-scale riots and street fighting broke out on the anniversary of Aristide's election. Many of his remaining supporters in parliament fled the capital or were murdered by the police or the army. During this period, several ships defied the embargo and contraband shipments of diesel and petroleum allowed the coup leaders to maintain power. Humanitarian aid continued, though the refugee crisis intensified. There was a growing realization that the embargo hurt the people of Haiti far more than the coup leaders. During the first three months of 1992, American policy remained essentially unchanged; though the embargo against intermediate goods assembled in Haitian factories for export was lifted, the rest of the embargo remained in place. This step was supposed to allow poor, unemployed Haitians to return to work and earn enough money to buy food.

In February the parties to the dispute, including Cedras and Aristide, were invited to Washington, D.C., for talks that explored ways to resolve the crisis, though Cedras did not attend the meetings himself. On February 21 the Washington Accord was announced. It called for a return of Aristide and a general, military amnesty, though Aristide later excluded Cedras from the amnesty provision. While there was some hope that the Washington Accord might be implemented, there were few clear indications from the coup leaders that they intended to abide by the agreement. On April 9 Cedras rejected the Washington Accord and expressed his intention to remain in power. The economic situation continued to deteriorate.

Frustrated by Cedras's intransigence and the growing refugee problem, President Bush ordered all seaborne refugees interdicted and repatriated to Haiti without hearing on May 24, 1992. He hoped that this policy would halt the refugee flow into the United States and encourage the populace to overthrow Cedras, though how these returnees would overthrow the military government was unclear. This policy did raise the level of desperation in Haiti. People could no longer flee from violence. But there was also a growing perception in Haiti that the international community was flagging in its resolve to overthrow Cedras. In addition, the repatriations further strained the already limited supply of food. Democratic presidential candidate Bill Clinton promised to revoke Bush's order and grant asylum to Haitian refugees until "we restore the elected government of Haiti."[12] During the months of June and July, the Haitian military shot refugees attempting to leave the island, and international pressure to stop human rights abuses grew. In September an OAS human rights mission was held under house arrest. Street violence continued.

In late September Canadian Prime Minister Brian Mulroney called for a complete blockade to pressure the de facto Haitian government into resigning. After his election Bill Clinton announced, on January 14, 1993, that he would continue Bush's refugee policy and ordered the Coast Guard to increase its interdiction efforts. During January and February, Aristide supporters were pursued and beaten by the military. A joint UN/OAS mission was deployed throughout the country to monitor human rights abuses on March 7, 1993. Rumors that the military regime engaged in drug smuggling surfaced and added to the international pressure to overthrow the Cedras regime. Continued and stricter economic sanctions further depressed the Haitian economy. Food supplies decreased.

The United Nations imposed a global fuel and arms embargo on Haiti on June 13, 1993, and internal violence increased. Riots and human rights abuses continued. On June 26 Cedras and a delegation went to New York for another attempt to negotiate an end to the crisis. Under intense pressure from the United States, Aristide and Cedras signed the Governor's Island Accord on July 3, 1993. The accord called for parliamentary, police, and military reforms under UN oversight, a total amnesty, the quiet retirement of Cedras, and the restoration of Aristide. Later in July Aristide asked for 600 UN troops to keep peace in Haiti.

Despite the Governor's Island Accord, by August 1993 peace seemed as distant as ever. International observers in Haiti reported a dramatic rise in murders and kidnapping of pro-democracy citizens. Despite this, the United Nations suspended the embargo on August 27, 1993, when a compromise prime minister, Robert Malval, was confirmed by parliament. Violence continued, however, and on September 6 Cedras condemned the Malval government. Public executions continued, and by mid-September Aristide called once again for a new government and Cedras's resignation.

Throughout September and October it became clear that the Governor's Island Accord had dissolved. The parties were still far from resolving the conflict, and no further meetings were planned. In these circumstances, the USS *Harlan County,* which contained a contingent of U.S. military advisers and trainers, as well as some seabees, docked in Port-au-Prince on October 11, 1993, only to decide that it was too dangerous to disembark. Members of the anti-Aristide faction demonstrated at the docks, and the entire ship's complement was forced to remain on board. The United States quickly ordered the ship back to Guantanamo. The next day, President Clinton declared that Aristide had complied with the terms of the Governor's Island Accord and called for the removal of Cedras. The UN Security Council voted to reimpose the embargo on October 13, 1993, unless Cedras resigned. He refused, and the embargo was resumed on schedule.

Through the rest of October and November the killing continued and additional refugees fled into the hills. In a section of the capital where Aristide had support, over 1,000 homes were burned on December 27. During March and April Aristide and the Clinton administration attempted a third time to negotiate a compromise agreement to restore democracy. These negotiations failed even to produce a draft agreement. In April Clinton appointed a new special adviser on Haiti, former Congressman William Gray, who advised a tougher American policy toward the coup leaders.

On May 6 the United Nations called for the resignation of the coup perpetrators and threatened an even tighter embargo.[13] President Clinton demanded the immediate removal of Cedras. New enforcement mechanisms to police the embargo took effect on May 19. The United States deployed additional ships to enforce the blockade. Despite this, the policy of automatic repatriation of Haitian refugees by the U.S. Coast Guard was halted in late May, and there was a growing realization that current American policy had become ineffective. In response to the tightened blockade, Cedras ordered UN personnel out of Haiti on July 11, 1994. Within forty-eight hours the United Nations had complied. On July 31 the Security Council approved Resolution 940, authorizing member states to use "all necessary means" to restore the legally elected Haitian government of President Aristide. This resolution was the prelude to intervention.

Intervention

Diplomatic efforts continued as the United States and the international community hesitated to act. However, on September 15 President Clinton stated that twenty countries had offered to participate in an American-led intervention to topple the de facto Haitian government and restore democracy. The U.S. Defense Department made final preparations for plans to invade Haiti.

A last-ditch mission to negotiate the return of democracy and the departure of the coup leaders, led by former President Jimmy Carter, arrived in Port-au-Prince on September 17. This final effort was successful, as Carter persuaded Cedras that the allied invasion was imminent and that there was no way for the coup leaders to remain in power. On September 19, lead elements of the American-led Multinational Force (MNF) landed unopposed.

During the next few weeks, the MNF established peace in the cities and rural areas and searched for weapons caches. Cooperative relationships were established between the MNF, the Haitian people, and some elements of the local police, though human rights abuses continued, especially in rural areas still under the control of Cedras's sympathizers. The MNF soon took a more aggressive stance and disarmed the Haitian military and confined many Haitian troops to their barracks.

It was soon apparent that the 21,000-member force initially deployed was far more than necessary to accomplish mission goals, and some combat units were replaced by military police and civilian affairs personnel.[14] By the end of September, the United Nations began planning for the reintroduction of the International Civilian Mission in Haiti (MICIVIH) and United Nations Mission in Haiti (UNMIH) to replace the MNF. Though still outside Haiti, President Aristide convened an extraordinary session of parliament on September 29, 1994, which passed legislation allowing the coup leaders to leave Haiti. By October 10 Cedras and other coup leaders had left Haiti for exile. This left the anti-democracy faction headless, and resistance within the army to the MNF ceased.

On October 15 Aristide returned to Haiti, and the United Nations lifted the economic sanctions and embargo the next day. Aristide reduced the power of the military over the next few months and introduced a series of reforms aimed at retraining military and police personnel for civilian jobs. By early 1996 over 5,000 former soldiers had become involved in American-sponsored jobs programs, and it was envisioned that such programs would be expanded.

American Troops in Haiti

Order was soon restored in Haiti, though economic prosperity did not immediately follow. American troops easily broke up the remaining opposition elements, confiscated their weapons, and acted to create an independent police force. American and UN troops also began to repair the devastated infrastructure. The United Nations and other NGOs continued to feed thousands of Haitians, and there was no return to the violence of the past months. There seemed little more for the large MNF contingent to accomplish in Haiti, and as the gradual draw-down continued, the United Nations began to assume greater operational control. The focus of the mission shifted from peacemaking to peacekeeping. Plans for a smaller force were outlined. This force would ensure that elections, in July 1995, would take place in a peaceful manner.

UN Takeover

On November 29, 1994, the UN Security Council approved Resolution 964 authorizing the deployment of advance elements of UNMIH to take over peacekeeping from the MNF. MICIVIH, the UN civilian mission, had already been on the ground for several weeks and was asked to monitor human rights issues. UNMIH had an authorized troop strength of 6,000 and an additional 600 police and military trainers. Even at this late date, the United Nations continued to feed nearly 1 million Haitians. This UN operation lasted until May 31, 1996, and was replaced by UNSMIH (United Nations Support Mission in Haiti), which still continues.

After most American troops left Haiti, it remained clear that some external help was still needed to prop up Haiti's new and fragile institutions. Approximately 1,300 UN troops from the UNSMIH remained, along with 300 foreign policemen who assisted the 5,200 newly trained Haitian police.[15] An international presence was necessary to keep the peace and pave the way for elections and continued international development assistance. In January 1995 a new package of development aid was pledged by fourteen governments and nineteen NGOs. This aid was used to support imports of vital reconstruction material to Haiti, restore destroyed infrastructure, and support continued food aid.

The Canadian and UN presence continued into 1996 and ensured the peaceful transition from President Aristide to his elected successor, René

Preval, who was sworn in on February 7, 1996. The economic problems continued, however, and Haiti remained the poorest country in the Americas, though the continued American distribution of food aid lessened the flow of refugees. Steps to improve the economy included reduced tariffs and privatization, but these did not fully solve the problem. International economic assistance continued to support Haiti, yet despite the presence of peacekeeping forces and the restoration of democracy, economic conditions have not greatly improved.

In summary, the international intervention in Haiti has been a qualified success. While the democratically elected government was restored, and new elections were held, only a further improvement in the Haitian economy will be likely to keep the peace over the long run. The international donor community continues to support Haiti, and such aid will remain the mainstay of the economy for many years to come. The military operation was successful. The military presence, however, was unnecessarily large and expensive, and was deployed later than it might have been. The actual cost of the internal conflict in Haiti to the international community is discussed below.

Costs of the Conflict to International Actors

Economic costs of the Haitian conflict borne by international actors include direct military costs, humanitarian costs, other direct costs, and opportunity costs. The cost estimates presented represent largely American and UN expenditures.

Military Costs

Domestic politics complicate the assessment of American costs in Haiti. Hearings held before the Senate Armed Services Committee, the Senate Subcommittee on Western Hemisphere and Peace Corps Affairs of the Committee on Foreign Relations, and the House Subcommittee on the Western Hemisphere of the Committee on International Relations addressed the cost issue. Caught in a dilemma of conflicting policy priorities, the Clinton administration at times attempted to downplay intervention costs in an attempt to show that the operation to restore democracy in Haiti was a cost-effective success. Conversely, the Defense Department has frequently tried to show far greater intervention costs in order to secure additional budget allocations.

The final, official U.S. government estimate evolved over several months. Testimony given before the Senate Armed Services Committee on September 28, 1994, put the cost at $200 million for migration operations and sanctions enforcement, $500–$600 million for peacekeeping operations, and $295 million for reconstruction assistance, totaling $995–$1,095 million for fiscal years 1994/95 and 1995/96.[16] By March of 1995 that figure had grown to "at least $1.3 billion" for 1994 and 1995.[17] Also, during congressional hearings the administration continued to make the point that intervention saved money, stating that nonintervention involved an expense of $300 million per year and could continue indefinitely.[18] This was compared to an intervention that was projected to cost only $700 million. Later on in the same hearing, however, the actual cost of intervention was admitted to have been $1.351 billion when expenditures from all federal agencies were included. Actual costs before the intervention were subsequently acknowledged to be in the range of $200 million per year.

During later hearings before the House Committee on International Relations on February 28, 1996, the cost estimates for operations in Haiti increased further. The estimate for the American intervention in Haiti was now $2 billion, and questions were focused on whether this was money well spent. Having presented a cost-benefit rationale, the Clinton administration needed to demonstrate the soundness of the investment.

This American expenditure was in addition to UN peacekeeping assessments the United States owed, and did not include the $56 million spent in six months of postintervention peacekeeping, of which the United States would pay 25 percent. In the later hearings on February 28, 1996, it was admitted that the total American cost of operations in Haiti from early 1993 to February 1996 was at least $3 billion and probably more.[19] Testimony from various experts lends credibility to these later figures. In this hearing Dr. Ernest H. Preeg, a noted expert on Haiti, put the intervention costs at $2 billion from 1994 to 1996 and economic aid costs at $235 million for 1995 alone. Other economic aid, loan guarantees, and program support easily brings the total American cost to over $3 billion dollars.

Budget figures from the United Nations Security Council show that in addition to the cost borne directly by the United States and other nations, the United Nations spent nearly $6.5 million on UNMIH, the UN mission in Haiti. Prior to the intervention, the United Nations spent $24 million on MICIVIH, the civilian mission to Haiti. The United Nations also estimated that the continuation and expansion of the UN presence after American troop withdrawal involved the disbursement of $215 million for the first six months.[20] While these figures may seem small, most of the external costs of this conflict were paid directly by the United States, Canada, and other nations. The United Nations was less involved, for example, than it had been in Somalia.

Final estimates on the complete UNMIH mission report the cost as $315.8 million from September 1993 through June 1996. The follow-on mission, the UN Support Mission in Haiti, from July 1996 through July

1997 cost $71.1 million, the UN Transition Mission in Haiti (UNTMIH) from August 1997 until November 1997 cost $20.6 million, and the UN Civil Police Mission in Haiti, which began in December 1997, costs $14 million every six months.[21] Thus the total cost of UN operations in Haiti from September 1993 through May 1998 was $421.5 million.

Humanitarian Costs

The United States was already spending a substantial sum on humanitarian relief efforts and refugee operations in Haiti before the military intervention. In the months immediately preceding the September 1994 deployment of American troops in Operation Uphold Democracy, the United States spent $200 million in operations to rescue and divert Haitian seaborne refugees, $100 million to expand existing facilities and to build new facilities for refugees at Guantanamo Bay, Cuba, and allocated $20 million per month to provide food, water, and medical services for these refugees.[22] These figures include the costs of increased Coast Guard efforts to interdict refugees and either return them to Haiti or to the U.S. naval base at Guantanamo. The United Nations estimated that its cost for humanitarian and refugee assistance was approximately $63 million immediately prior to the intervention.[23]

These costs do not include the expense to private charitable organizations and other NGOs. No firm and reliable cost estimates are currently available for the latter. These figures also leave out the direct cost of refugees to the Dominican Republic or other nations in the Caribbean. Despite these omissions, the cost of humanitarian aid prior to the intervention and the costs of interdicting, housing, and repatriating refugees involved the international community in expenditures of over $500 million.

Other Direct Economic Costs

International donors have pledged and already paid over $1.2 billion for postintervention reconstruction costs, economic aid, and fiscal relief for the indebted Haitian government.[24] Later pledges have increased the total foreign aid pledged to $1.8 billion.[25] Non-American donors accounted for 75 percent of that total.

American strategy also included support for private investment in Haiti. To that end, American agencies have created a program of loan guarantees for American businesses that invested in Haiti. The total amount of loans guaranteed was $100 million, and these guarantees were quickly used by American firms eager to do business in Haiti.[26] The actual cost of these guarantees will not be known for some time and depends on whether the projects guaranteed succeed. To a great extent, the program of loan guarantees and further foreign investment depends on improvements in the Haitian political situation, since a period of renewed disorder could waste the expensive efforts of the international donor community.

After the restoration of Aristide, the international costs of the conflict continued to mount. There were many parts of the Haitian economy in need of repair after the military phase of intervention and also a continued need to dampen internal conflict. Costs for these activities included $2.5 million to equip and train a new Haitian police force and $68 million per year for continued international police enforcement.[27] Through 1996, peacekeeping troops remained in Haiti at a cost of $25 million for Canada and $22 million for the United States.[28] These costs are in addition to the UN figures noted above.

Economic Opportunity Costs

Haiti shares the island of Hispaniola with the Dominican Republic, and the two nations have many similarities. The internal conflict in Haiti not only deepened domestic economic problems but also spilled over into Haiti's only land neighbor. Table 5.1 compares the Dominican GDP and military spending before and after the crisis.

The Dominican economy's performance had been relatively strong prior to the Haiti crisis. After an increase of nearly 8 percent in 1992, GDP growth fell to 3 percent in 1993 and declined in 1994. Gross domestic product for 1994 was $8 billion, however.[29] Haiti-related events on Hispaniola had a negative effect on the Dominican Republic. These figures above suggest that the Dominican Republic lost approximately $1 billion in GDP from 1993 to 1995. In defense terms, the increased military cost during the crisis totaled approximately $57 million from the baseline of the 1992 defense budget.

While the GDP losses may not be fully attributable to the Haitian crisis, some portion is a direct consequence since the two countries were impor-

TABLE 5.1
Gross Domestic Product and Defense Expenditures by the Dominican Republic before and after the Crisis in Haiti

Year	GDP ($U.S. Billions)	Defense Expenditures ($U.S. Millions)
1993	9.1	108
1994	8.0	113
1995	8.3	112

Sources: International Institute for Strategic Studies, *The Military Balance 1994–95* and *1995–96* (London: Oxford University Press).

tant trading partners and some of the decline in regional economic activity is attributable to the Haitian crisis. At least some portion of the increased defense budget was a direct response to the internal conflict in Haiti and is included. Therefore, the final cost to the Dominican Republic for the crisis in Haiti is conservatively estimated at $50 million.

Total Costs

The total international costs of the internal conflict in Haiti are presented in table 5.2. Total costs of American intervention in Haiti are conservatively estimated at $3 billion. UN costs were approximately $0.6 billion, and international donor aid in the aftermath of the crisis reached $1.35 billion.

The opportunity costs of this conflict are not counted. The income losses due to this conflict and their cumulative effects are difficult to estimate, though these costs are probably quite high. Future work needs to address this issue and present ways to estimate the international impact of internal crises.

The direct costs presented in the table probably underestimate the true costs for several reasons. First, efforts are continuing in Haiti. There is no reason to believe that they will end in the near future. Peacekeeping costs approximately $110 million per year. Second, the economy is not recovering in any meaningful way, and the amount of foreign aid Haiti receives will remain at $300–$400 million per year for several more years.[30] Third, given the Clinton administration's attempts to portray Haiti as a cost-ef-

TABLE 5.2
Haiti: Total International Costs of Conflict ($U.S. Billions)

U.S. costs: Intervention	2.00
U.S. costs: Humanitarian, rebuilding, refugees, and other nonintervention costs	1.00
UN costs: Missions in Haiti, including UNMIH, MICIVIH, UNSMIH	0.60
International donor aid for rebuilding and humanitarian relief (net of U.S. share)	1.35
Direct costs to Dominican Republic	0.05
TOTAL	**5.00**

Sources: The United States and the Situation in Haiti, UN Reference Paper (March 1995), 2. *Implementation and Costs of U.S. Policy in Haiti,* Senate Foreign Relations Committee, 104th Congress, 1st session, 1995, S. Hrg 104–52. UN Internet site available at UNMIH.-HTM. Eric Schmitt, "Pentagon Estimates It Will Cost $427 Million to Invade Haiti," *New York Times* (September 2, 1994), A7. Donald Schulz, "Whither Haiti," *SSI US Army College* (April 1, 1996): 15. "US Releases Some Aid to Haitian Police," *Facts on File* 56 (February 1, 1996): 46.

fective operation, there are compelling reasons to underestimate the actual costs in order to depict a foreign policy success. This would seem to suggest that the actual cost of all American operations in Haiti may be greater than reported to date. Finally, the estimation method used here is highly conservative and only counts the known direct costs.

Estimated Costs of Preventive Action

The next step is to determine the estimated cost of earlier intervention to see if there was a time when intervention would have been successful in achieving its goals at a lower cost. There were at least two periods prior to the actual intervention in Haiti when international action would have been at least as effective and far less expensive. The first of these occurred in the months immediately following the election of Aristide; the second took place after the Washington Accord was signed in February 1992.

At both of these points it is assumed that an American, or a combined U.S. and UN force would have landed unopposed, with the support of Aristide and at least the tacit assent of Cedras and other military leaders. There were overriding incentives for both Aristide and Cedras to order their forces to permit unopposed landings. Aristide would have returned to power in Haiti as he wished, and Cedras would have been offered the same terms of exile that he later accepted from the Carter mission. If the U.S. government had played a more active role and promised to make peace, break the power of the military, and uphold the democratic process, Aristide would certainly have complied with early American action. By allowing Cedras and his faction leaders free passage out of Haiti, together with some financial incentives, the United States eventually did cause them to leave. The United States had the power, the resources, and sufficient international support, and could have easily mobilized an effective military force that provided an additional incentive to encourage cooperation.

An early intervention force, deployed after the election of Aristide or after the Washington Accord was signed, would have resembled the force that eventually took over from the United States and MNF in 1995. This force consisted of 6,000 troops at its peak, along with police and military training units, and was able to keep the peace and permit free and fair elections in 1995. This force would have been heavily armed in the beginning in order to deter remaining military opposition. After the peace was made, the power of the military broken, and their arms confiscated, the mission personnel would have been reoriented to provide infrastructure and continued humanitarian relief.

In the actual intervention, the initial force of U.S. Marines and elements of the 82nd Airborne Division had more than enough firepower and tactical advantage to suppress any armed resistance the Haitian military could have mounted, and were able to confiscate the weapons held by various factions. A smaller force could have accomplished the mission's peacemaking and peacekeeping goals, especially after the coup leaders had conceded.

A force of 5,000–6,000 troops, as projected in this scenario, actually cost the United Nations about $315 million per year for operations in Haiti. Using this as a baseline, we can conclude that an early U.S. or UN intervention force, composed of well-trained and heavily armed personnel, would have been able to quickly defeat remnant armed resistance and would have cost $400–$500 million per year. This estimate is comparable to a U.S. Defense Department estimate for an early intervention force that was considered during the first few months of the crisis, though their plans called for more troops than those suggested here.[31] Even allowing for significant cost overruns and a longer mission, the cost of early intervention would have been only $600 million. The United States would also have saved $200–$500 million in refugee costs that were spent between the proposed intervention points and the time of the actual intervention. Even assuming that the costs of reconstruction aid and other economic assistance pledged to Haiti would have remained constant (at $1.8 billion), the total expenditure would have been greatly reduced if earlier intervention had taken place. The total cost for early intervention would have ranged from $2.1 to $2.3 billion.

Conclusions

The Haitian case suggests that an early intervention in the internal conflict would have saved the international community nearly $3 billion in direct costs, using conservative estimation guidelines. When the final and additional costs are finally counted and the expenditures from all American, UN, and other international actors is tallied, the savings from an early intervention would undoubtedly have been even higher.

An international mission at the early intervention points described above is consistent with planning documents prepared by the U.S. Defense Department and the actual costs of UN operations in Haiti. The assumption that Aristide and Cedras would have allowed an unopposed international force is necessary to allow for the lower costs projected, but it is quite reasonable. While it is impossible to state with perfect accuracy what might have happened, it is reasonable to accept the following conclusions. First, an earlier intervention would have been cheaper no matter how the costs were measured. The direct military costs would have been far less, the humanitarian costs would have been less, the cost of refugee interdiction and repatriation would have shrunk, and the indirect costs, while difficult to measure, would have also decreased.

Second, an early intervention was therefore justified on purely economic grounds. While there was considerable pressure on the international community to respond to the suffering in Haiti, such pressure was insufficient to spur an early intervention. Since this is often the case, the Haitian study supports the conclusion that intervention in internal conflicts may be justified on economic grounds. This case study supports the hypothesis that early intervention is cost-effective. The case study also contradicts the null hypothesis that early intervention would have had no impact on the costs borne by the international community since significant savings would have been realized in both early intervention scenarios.

Finally, the crisis in Haiti has important implications for American and international foreign policy. This research suggests an evolution in American foreign policy on internal conflict. The Clinton administration, in dealing with Congress, used the argument that intervention was economically justified in the Haitian crisis. This adds an additional motivation for intervention and supports the argument that early intervention may be warranted. If so, an ounce of early international prevention is easily worth a pound of subsequent military cure.

6

The Persian Gulf

Mike Blakley

Case Preview

THE GULF WAR IS OFTEN CITED as the post–Cold War model of multilateral response to military adventurism. Larger than the Vietnam War, such a conventional military operation had not been seen since the Korean War, when American and UN forces also beat back an invasion and restored the status quo ante. The massive efforts to expel Iraqi forces from Kuwait in the winter of 1991 by American-led coalition forces also confirmed the value of a multilateral approach and the importance of modern weapons, tactics, and communications technology.

The Gulf War was also an instance of costly and belated Western intervention in a local or regional conflict. What distinguished this event from interventions in Somalia and Haiti, however, were the high political and economic stakes for the West and the large scale of military operations.

The Gulf War case is different from other cases in this study because it involves a cross-border or interstate conflict. While less frequent than internal conflicts in the post–World War II era, cross-border conflicts remain an important threat to world stability and can be the most costly type of encounter in human and economic terms.

As with the other cases in this volume, the central research question is whether early intervention in the Iraq-Kuwait crisis would have cost the international community less in purely economic terms than the actual operations of Desert Shield and Desert Storm. Therefore, this chapter focuses on the economic costs and losses from this conflict to external actors.[1] These costs included direct costs of intervention, trade disruption, debt write-offs, decreased tourism, and higher oil prices. These costs are then compared to the costs of two projected counterfactual intervention and deterrent scenarios. This case study supports the hypothesis that early intervention is cost-effective. Since significant savings would have been realized in both early intervention scenarios, this case study also refutes the null hypothesis that early intervention would have no impact on the costs borne by the international community.

The Gulf War is an important case in this study for many reasons. First, the Iraqi invasion of Kuwait was the first post–Cold War conflict that directly involved Western economic and political interests. The case therefore set a precedent for foreign policy and is likely to influence future decision makers. Second, the Gulf War was the first war that took place in "real time," that is, while people were watching it. During the Vietnam War, the West saw daily pictures from the battlefield, usually on the evening news. During the Gulf War, there was twenty-four hour coverage of events as they happened. This created new political challenges for the West in justifying war aims and battlefield conduct. Third, the Gulf War demonstrated the increasing military power gap between advanced and less developed nations. The Soviet-oriented Iraqi military was no match for the West's sophisticated weapons. This weapons quality gap also kept the West's human cost surprisingly low, though the economic cost was enormous. Last, this case demonstrates the enormous cost of regional interstate conflict to the international community: the total external cost of this conflict exceeded $100 billion.

There were early indications that this conflict was likely to occur and at least two opportunities to preempt the Iraqi invasion of Kuwait. There were four clear signals that Iraq intended to solve its economic and financial problems by invading Kuwait, and there were two time periods when early, cost-effective action could have averted the crisis and reduced the cost of intervention.[2] The first signal that Iraq was moving toward a military solution came in February 1990 at an Arab Cooperation Council meeting in Jordan. Saddam Hussein placed his Arab neighbors on notice that a redistribution of oil wealth was necessary and that the United States must have no influence in the region. In response to this aggressive stance, Egyptian President Hosni Mubarak called for an early end to the meeting, clearly disturbed by this new, aggressive Iraqi position.

The second signal of growing Iraqi aggressiveness came on April 2, 1990, when Saddam announced that Iraq had developed chemical weapons and would use them against Israel. While this drew some response from Washington, there was no clear change in American policy. Israel responded by stating that any chemical attack would provoke a serious response, and they attempted to convince the United States that Iraq was preparing for military action.

The third signal came during the Arab League summit in May 1990. Here, Saddam added his fellow Arabs, especially Kuwait, to the list of Iraqi enemies, for waging economic warfare against Iraq. By the middle of 1990 Saddam Hussein had called for the removal of all American forces from the Middle East, had threatened Israel with chemical attack, and had demanded a forcible redistribution of Arab oil wealth. Together these actions clearly indicated that military action by Iraq was at least possible and would likely be directed against the only two targets within reach: Kuwait and Israel.

The final signal came on July 17, 1990. Saddam delivered a speech combining previous themes and proposed himself as the defender of the Arab people. He praised his armed forces, noting their reach and power. He also sent to Kuwait a formal list of Iraqi grievances, demanded that these be addressed, and accused Kuwait of conspiring with the United States and Israel against Iraq.

By May, or at least by the middle of July, 1990, the West had clear indications that Iraq was preparing for military action and that the likely target was Kuwait; yet the United States did nothing to deter Iraq. Israel was out of the reach of Iraqi conventional forces and could threaten to use nuclear weapons if Iraq dared to employ chemical weapons. Iraq's strength lay in its tank divisions, and these could only be used against Kuwait. During July the United States had detected the movement of Iraqi ground forces toward the Kuwaiti border at the same time Saddam had scheduled his attack on Kuwait.[3]

The West could have taken early, preventive measures to forestall the invasion. Even though the United States was engaged in an ongoing attempt to co-opt Iraq, the U.S. leaders knew that the Iraqi military was preparing for action and might be deterred. However, the United States failed to act. It is reasonable to believe that the West knew of the danger and could have acted to preempt this conflict in May or June, after the third signal that Iraq was becoming more dangerous. At this time Western action could have preempted this conflict and saved hundreds of thousands of Iraqi lives as well as billions of dollars. Action in late July would have proved to Saddam that the gamble of invading Kuwait would not pay off, saving the West some $100 billion. If this had failed and Iraq had attempted some cross-border action, the presence of militarily superior American troops would have quickly demonstrated the futility of an invasion. Even if Western policymakers thought an invasion of Kuwait was unlikely despite the warning signs (as probably was the case), the dangers of such an invasion made preventive action reasonable.

Origins of the Conflict

Iraq was in desperate shape on the eve of the Gulf War. Exhausted by the war with Iran, troubled by Kurdish and Shi'ite separatist movements, and faced with a low price for crude oil and declining government revenues, Iraq could not easily solve its economic problems. Saddam, while exercising considerable control of the country, was faced with difficult trade-offs and financial constraints. Iraq's economic infrastructure had been severely damaged during the war with Iran, the economy had become almost entirely dependent on oil revenues, and the capital needed to diversify was unavailable. The military was consuming the lion's share of revenue and Saddam decided to keep the army in uniform rather than turn them out into the streets.[4] Iraq also owed at least $30 billion to the West, as well as another $30 billion to Middle Eastern states, and debt service was increasingly expensive. In addition, no further loans were forthcoming and Western sources of advanced technology were shut down during the late 1980s.[5]

In addition to the West, Saddam had several reasons to blame Kuwait for his troubles. Long-standing claims Iraq held against Kuwait included: a territorial claim based on the fact that Kuwait had been governed from Basra during the Ottoman Empire; Kuwait's refusal to allow Iraq the use of two small coastal islands for shipping purposes; Iraq's belief that Kuwait was stealing oil from the Rumaila oil field shared by both countries; Kuwaiti overproduction of oil that kept prices low;[6] and the large debt that Iraq owed Kuwait.[7] This amounted to "economic warfare" against Iraq and underscores the large and growing losses incurred by Iraq, and the increasingly desperate situation that Saddam faced.

Various accounts of the origin of the Gulf War rely on miscalculation by Saddam of American willingness to fight, his ability to threaten Israel and therefore restrain the United States, and Saudi unwillingness to host Western troops.[8] Accounts in the popular press blame the war on Saddam—his aggressiveness or foolishness—and go no further. Others blame the United States for giving permission for an Iraqi attack or at least for sending mixed signals about the American reaction,[9] or cite a bid for hegemony or Iraqi domestic unrest as motivating the invasion.[10] However, none of this explains what happened to change Saddam's mind from pressuring Kuwait to invading Kuwait. The permission argument seems quite unconvincing after examining the transcript of the meeting between American Ambassador to Iraq April Glaspie and Saddam. The other explanations are also incomplete or unconvincing.

The questions, simply put, are what happened in 1990 to change Saddam's actions from threat to attack, and why did he choose occupation of the entire country instead of only the disputed oil field and off-shore islands? The tensions between Iraq and Kuwait were substantial as early as 1988, when many of the issues were first raised, and some analysts felt even then that it was only a matter of time until Iraq would attack.[11] There were few feasible policy options available to Saddam, and Iraq had reached a point where only a high-risk/high-return strategy would reverse the declining economic situation. Given the set of options, the choice narrows to an invasion of Kuwait.

In the decision process prior to the Gulf War, Saddam was like the gambler who had been losing steadily for quite some time and was nearly out of chips. His losses mounted and his endowments shrank, and the only remaining asset he had was an army. This biased all his policy choices toward high-risk/high-return options using his remaining asset. Saddam came to view his position as increasingly desperate and eventually made a very risky choice. The gamble Saddam chose, while risky, had to provide a large enough reward, and only complete occupation of Kuwait and access to the entire Kuwaiti endowment would have been sufficient. In one stroke Saddam could literally have gone from rags to riches.[12] Thus the invasion of Kuwait was a classic example of a high-risk/high-reward choice made after accumulating huge losses.

It was quite clear from the beginning that Saddam's war aim was to loot Kuwait. Once the Iraqi army controlled the territory of Kuwait, Saddam installed a client regime and attempted to access Kuwait's substantial international investments. However, the gamble did not pay off. The world financial community denied Iraq access to the accounts. So Saddam announced the annexation of Kuwait and turned to a longer-term strategy of gaining revenue from control of the oil export market.[13]

Once Saddam had Kuwait, the fact that he stopped there and did not move against Saudi Arabia needs additional explanation. Once he had Kuwait, a valuable gain that included a large debt write-off as well as proven oil reserves, Saddam adopted a less risky policy. The prospect of American action if he invaded Saudi Arabia seemed certain, and having already won a prize, Saddam chose a less dangerous strategy. Taking into account the chain of reasoning and risk-acceptant nature of the Iraqi regime, analysts can construct a plausible explanation for Saddam's choices.[14]

Feasible Options

The feasible set of policy options may be broken down along two axes, and some options are presented in table 6.1. Saddam selects a policy or set of policies that meet his needs. The policies in the upper-left quadrant are the most risky and yet are the most rewarding if the policy goals are met. The upper-right and lower-left quadrants are less risky, while the lower-right quadrant has the lowest risk/return.

TABLE 6.1
The Persian Gulf: Feasible Set of Policy Options for Saddam Hussein

	International	Domestic
Aggressive	Invade and annex Kuwait	Use army versus Kurds/ Shi'ites
	Increase pressure on Kuwait/ Israel	Declare martial law
	Occupy off-shore islands/oil field	Nationalize remaining assets
	Increase terrorism	
Conciliatory	Demobilize and ask for debt relief	Privatize businesses
	Sell assets overseas	Encourage capital to stay
	Take Kuwait to an international organization arbitrator	Use army for public goods creation
	Stop arms purchases	Allow regional autonomy

We can clarify his options by examining the state of the Iraqi economy and the available policy implementation tools remaining to Saddam. It is immediately apparent that none of the domestic options would have been likely to generate the payoffs necessary for the regime to stay afloat and that they also might endanger Saddam's domestic power base.

Of the international options, some of the more conciliatory choices had already been used to little effect or closed out. Iraqi arms purchases ceased, but only because Iraq had defaulted on many previous promises to pay. Iraq had only one asset that was salable overseas, and that was oil. Oil prices, however, were low, and the Iraqi oil production infrastructure was in poor and declining condition. It was unlikely that Iraq could increase oil production, and Saddam's grip on power made foreign investors unwilling to risk large investments that could be expropriated.

The aggressive international options were all that remained. Only one option contained a payoff high enough to merit its high risk, and Iraq still possessed the capabilities to make the policy feasible. This option was to invade and hold Kuwait. The end of Kuwait as a state would immediately cancel billions in Iraqi debt, and the overseas holdings of the Kuwaiti state exceeded $100 billion at the time of the invasion. In addition, Iraq would control a far larger fraction of proven world oil reserves and would have more bargaining power in the Organization of Petroleum Exporting Countries (OPEC) to keep prices high. So this policy option contained a short-term fix for Iraq's financial crisis and the long-term potential for substantial returns.

Of course, Saddam ran a significant risk. The West might respond and defend Kuwait or even evict Iraqi troops from Kuwait. Presumably, Saddam believed that there was some chance that the West would not intervene. Preemptive action by the West assuring that a response was certain would have closed out the invasion option. Other policy options chosen to support the invasion choice included threatening Israel, which cost Iraq little and had at least a small chance of increasing the odds of holding on to Kuwait.

Additionally, the choice of an invasion was also conditioned by the fact that by the end of 1990, the military was the only functional part of the Iraqi government apparatus. There was no private sector to plunder, and the army could do little domestically to rescue Iraq from financial ruin. If Saddam had demobilized the army he would have reduced his political support, since these troops would be unemployed and likely to incite public unrest. The combination of increasing losses led Saddam to adopt a high-risk strategy—the only option that could recoup his losses and had a chance of success—occupation and annexation of Kuwait.

This raises the question of whether any deterrent action would have been successful. Saddam was sometimes portrayed as unstable or irrational, and therefore might not be deterrable. This, however, seems extreme. Iraqi policy appears rational given the circumstances and set of options available. If there had been incontrovertible proof that an invasion of Kuwait would not be allowed to stand, no full-scale invasion would have taken place. An American blocking force might have been probed by Iraqi units and some cross-border incidents would almost certainly have occurred; however, the invasion would have been prevented.

Overview of the Conflict

The U.S.-Iraq relationship may be divided into four periods: Reagan's policy during the Iran-Iraq War, the period after the gas attacks on Iraqi Kurds, the Bush strategy of accommodation, and Bush foreign policy through the invasion of Kuwait.[15]

For this study, the first period, covering American foreign policy during the Iran-Iraq War, does not impact the research question. The second period, however, begins the story when support for Iraq began to contravene American interests as well as treaties the United States had signed. The United States had supported Iraq in the war with Iran and viewed Iraqi power as a counterbalance to radical Iranian policy. However, support for Iraq was subordinated to the overall goals of American Middle East policy: regional stability and free-flowing oil. At times, however, American support for Iraq continued in the face of growing evidence that Iraq was becoming an obstacle to attaining these goals.

The controversy surrounding Iraqi involvement in the BNL loan scandal did not change the Bush administration's support for Iraq. In fact, after Congress placed Iraq on the list of countries that supported terrorism, President Bush granted Iraq a waiver "in the interests of national security" to receive loan guarantees as well as support from the Export-Import Bank. The administration could easily have signaled Iraq that its support was not unqualified at this point and blamed Congress. A shift toward containment and support for the moderate Arab states, including Kuwait, might have signaled a shift in American policy toward maintaining the regional status quo. The United States continued a policy of engagement with Iraq instead of taking a more aggressive and proactive stand that might have demonstrated that the United States would preserve the status quo.

Events Preceding the Invasion

The initial phase of the Gulf War began on June 26, 1990.[16] On that date Saddam sent a personal message to the emir of Kuwait demanding that Kuwait reduce its oil production since overproduction had lowered oil prices substantially. This meant lower revenue for Iraq, which was already laden with debt from the war with Iran. The message also criticized the United Arab Emirates and OPEC, and stated that $25 per barrel was a reasonable price for oil. By July 10, 1990, the Gulf States agreed to a Saudi proposal to reduce oil production and set a target price of $18 per barrel. World market oil prices were $14 per barrel at this time.

Unsatisfied with this proposal, Iraq wrote a letter to the Arab League accusing Kuwait of stealing oil from the contested Rumaila oil field. The letter also accused Kuwait of building military installations on Iraqi territory. In a speech the next day, Saddam threatened to use force against Arab states that were overproducing oil. On July 21 two Iraqi armored divisions were moved toward the Kuwaiti border.

As tensions mounted during July, the United States issued a statement in support of the Gulf States and placed American military forces in the region on alert, but made no move to station troops in the region. On July 23 Egyptian President Hosni Mubarak hosted a meeting with Jordan's King Hussein and Iraqi Foreign Minister Tariq Aziz in an attempt to start a negotiation process to resolve the situation. Later in the month Mubarak traveled to Kuwait, Iraq, and Saudi Arabia hoping to diffuse the crisis; however, the Iraqi position remained unchanged.

Next, the infamous meeting between Ambassador Glaspie, Foreign Minister Aziz, and Saddam took place in Baghdad. The Iraqis expressed their position that Kuwait was stealing Iraqi oil and waging economic warfare on Iraq, keeping oil prices low by overproduction. Saddam also expressed concern over deployments of U.S. Navy ships to the region. The ambassador's response that the United States had "no opinion on the Arab-Arab conflicts, like your border disagreement with Kuwait" was seen by some as permission to invade Kuwait.[17] However, the ongoing American military response and statements by American President Bush clearly indicated that the United States had some interest in maintaining peace in the region. At the very least, Saddam could be sure that there was some chance that the West would not intervene if Iraq invaded Kuwait.

By the end of July, over 100,000 Iraqi troops were massed along the Kuwait border. There were no further official contacts between the United States and Iraq, though Iraq and Kuwait continued talks concerning the status of Iraqi debts to Kuwait. No agreement was reached, and on the evening of August 1, 1,800 Iraqi tanks and 140,000 Iraqi troops crossed the border.[18] By nightfall on August 2, Kuwait was occupied by Iraqi troops.

Desert Shield

The United States immediately condemned the invasion, ordered an embargo on all Iraqi commerce, and froze both Kuwaiti and Iraqi assets in the United States. Most Western European countries immediately followed suit and the Soviet Union halted all arms transfers, effectively isolating Saddam. Iran also demanded the immediate withdrawal of Iraqi troops from Kuwait, and Israel announced that any movement by Iraqi troops into Jordan would be met with an immediate military response. Within twenty-four hours of occupying Kuwait, Iraq stood alone.

Apparently unaffected by these reactions, Saddam moved 60,000 troops further south toward the Saudi Arabian border on August 3. This move drew increased threats from the West, and President Bush warned Iraq that protecting the territorial integrity of Saudi Arabia was vital to American interests. The Arab League issued a statement on the same day demanding that Iraq withdraw from Kuwait.

Over the next few days, Saudi Arabia mobilized its military and China and Japan joined the arms and economic embargoes against Iraq. On August 6 the UN Security Council passed Resolution 660, which imposed a global trade embargo on Iraq. That same day Saddam met with the senior American diplomat in Baghdad and stated that Iraqi forces would remain in Kuwait. On August 7 the first American troops left for Saudi Arabia. The next day Saddam announced that Iraq had annexed Kuwait. On August 8 the United Nations declared this annexation null and void, and most nations continued to recognize the Kuwaiti government in exile.

Over the next few weeks, a coalition to protect Saudi Arabia and threaten Iraq was built under American leadership. Egypt played a critical role in rallying Arab support, and on August 11 the first Egyptian troops arrived in Saudi Arabia. These troops were soon followed by contingents from Syria and Pakistan. On August 22 Bush recalled thousands of reservists to active duty in connection with Operation Desert Shield. European Union members began plans to support the American operations in the Gulf, and on August 21 dispatched a group of naval vessels to enforce the embargo against Iraq.

During this period Saddam made no offers to get out of Kuwait. The Iraqi military presence in Kuwait was increased and these troops prepared to defend Kuwait from an attack. On August 26 Saudi Arabia announced plans to increase oil production, making up for the shortfall left by the embargo on Iraqi oil exports. OPEC, in a meeting later in August, raised production quotas, effectively reallocating the Iraqi quota to other OPEC members. World oil prices continued to rise and reached $40 a barrel by early October.

American efforts to forge a coalition to contribute troops and funds to remove Iraqi troops from Kuwait continued throughout September. Financial contributions from Kuwait and Saudi Arabia totaling several billion dollars were soon made, and troop commitments were sought from the United Kingdom and France. Japan offered $4 billion in military and economic aid to the coalition.

In response to the growing coalition arrayed against him, Saddam, on September 23, threatened to destroy well heads and oil fields in Kuwait and Saudi Arabia and attack Israel if the embargo against Iraq was not lifted. The United Nations responded by extending the embargo against Iraq with Security Council Resolution 670, and Syria and Iran issued statements in support of American operations in the Gulf against Iraq.

The U.S. Congress voted to support President Bush's Gulf policy in early October. During the rest of the month, increased arms shipments were made to the Gulf States and political support mounted for military operations to remove Iraqi troops from Kuwait. Iraqi troops in Kuwait remained on alert in expectation of a U.S.-led invasion, and on November 3 Saddam issued a statement that any resolution of the Gulf crisis that returned Kuwait to its former rulers would not be acceptable.

Additional coalition troops were deployed to Saudi Arabia by November, including 15,000 troops from Syria and 200,000 additional American troops. This deployment brought the total number of American troops in the area to 430,000. American and Saudi troops performed joint exercises, and statements issued in various coalition capitals indicated an increased willingness to use force to resolve the crisis. Iraq deployed an additional 250,000 troops to counter the building strength of coalition forces during the month. On November 29 the UN Security Council passed Resolution 678, which called on member states to "use all necessary means" to resolve the situation unless Iraq withdrew from Kuwait by January 15, 1991. This set the stage for Operation Desert Storm. Iraq rejected this resolution on November 30.

During December the crisis continued to simmer. Saudi Arabia canceled $4 billion in Egyptian debts in response to Egypt's strong support against Iraq. Overtures to Iraq for a meeting between Saddam and American Secretary of State James Baker III were rejected. By December 13 the last American "detainees" in Iraq were released, and the use of hostages as human shields ceased. Iraq recalled its personnel from most Western countries, and on December 22 designated Tel Aviv the next target for the Iraqi military. On December 24 Israel promised massive retaliation in response to Iraqi threats.

The coalition's military buildup continued through January, and on January 8 Bush requested congressional permission to use force in the Gulf against Iraq. On January 12 the U.S. Congress authorized the president to use the military in the Gulf pursuant to the War Powers Act and in accordance with UN Resolution 678. The UN deadline for Iraq to withdraw from Kuwait passed quietly on January 15. Massive coalition bombing of Iraqi military targets began on January 17, and the stated aim of coalition policy was the liberation of Kuwait and the removal of Iraqi weapons of mass destruction. Iraq responded by launching Scud surface-to-surface missiles against Israel and Saudi Arabia in late January. On January 22 Iraqi troops set fire to Kuwaiti oil refineries and oil fields and released crude oil into the Gulf. Over 9,000 air sorties were flown by coalition planes by January 21, causing heavy damage to Iraqi forces in and around Kuwait. Most of Iraq's air force fled to Iran.

Border clashes between Iraqi and coalition forces occurred during early February, and the damage to Iraqi forces caused by coalition air power continued to mount. Iraqi casualties were estimated at 20,000 dead and 60,000 wounded while coalition losses were minimal. President Bush delivered an ultimatum to Iraq on February 22 that demanded the immediate withdrawal from Kuwait of all Iraqi forces. The Iraqi response was to ignite more oil well fires. At 8:00 P.M. February 23, Bush ordered the U.S.-led forces in the Gulf—now numbering over 270,000 combat troops—to begin operations to liberate Kuwait.

The Ground War

During the next four days the "one hundred hour war" was fought. Iraqi troops offered sporadic and uncoordinated resistance and proved no match for the modern tanks, air power, and accurate intelligence of the coalition forces. Iraq did continue to fire Scud missiles at targets in Saudi Arabia, killing twenty-eight American troops in a barracks in Dhahran on February 25.

On February 27 President Bush announced that Kuwait had been liberated. Coalition forces continued to destroy Iraqi military targets and accept surrenders from Iraqi soldiers. On March 3 Iraq accepted UN terms for a cease-fire and asked that the trade embargo be lifted. Also on that day Iraq canceled its annexation of Kuwait and released all remaining coalition prisoners of war. Domestic unrest in Iraq began to spread during March. Coalition forces eventually protected rebel Kurds in northern Iraq and Shi'ites in southern Iraq from air attack.

On March 14 the emir of Kuwait, Jabir al-Ahmad al-Sabah, returned to Kuwait. By this time most captured Kuwaiti citizens had been returned home, and the process of rebuilding Kuwait, dousing oil fires, and assessing the impact of the war on the economy and the environment had begun. While internal conflict continued in Iraq during this period, American forces did little to aid rebel factions, though American policy was to encourage the Iraqi people to overthrow Saddam.

The UN Security Council passed Resolution 687 on April 3, 1991, which dictated final surrender terms requiring Iraq to recognize the previous border, destroy its weapons of mass destruction, and pay reparations. Three days later Iraq accepted these terms and effectively ended the Gulf War. By the end of June 1991, the last coalition ground forces had withdrawn from Kuwait and Saudi Arabia. No-fly zones enforced by coalition air power remained in effect in northern Iraq to protect the Kurds and in southern Iraq to protect the Shi'ites.

Aftermath

A review of American foreign policy immediately prior to the invasion shows no signal to Iraq that the United States would definitely intervene to defend Kuwait. Laying the blame on Ambassador Glaspie ignores the fact that the United States had given no indication that policy had changed, and Glaspie's actions were simply in line with the extant, stated American position. At any of several points a strong American statement of intentions in the region or even of American goals or preferences might have deterred the invasion of Kuwait. When it seemed that such an invasion was imminent, a trip wire force of American troops would also have prevented an invasion. This trip wire strategy is one of many actions that would have sent a clear signal to Iraq that maintenance of the borders as they existed was the goal of American policy.

Costs of the Conflict to International Actors

Military Costs

The cost of removing Iraq from Kuwait totaled $61.1 billion. Of this total, $53.8 billion was paid by American allies, including $16 billion each from Saudi Arabia and Kuwait, $6.5 billion from Germany, $4 billion from the United Arab Emirates, and $10 billion from Japan.[19] The United States paid $7.3 billion, and the rest came from other Arab and Western nations.[20] Subtracting the Kuwaiti contribution makes the total external military cost of this conflict $45.1 billion.

Other Direct Economic Costs

A study commissioned after the Gulf War by the Arab Monetary Fund estimated that the regional cost of the conflict, including assets destruction, trade losses, increased defense expenditures, and so on, was $676 billion.[21] Others have estimated the economic impact at $438 billion.[22] These sums do not include costs borne by nations outside the Middle East. Costs were partially offset by increased OPEC revenue due to higher oil prices. This is estimated at $54.3 billion for Middle East states.[23] This makes total regional economic losses approximately $384 billion. From this amount, the losses from the two combatants—Iraq and Kuwait—are subtracted, leaving an external, regional cost of $24 billion. The estimates presented below, country by country, generate a more comprehensive, yet conservative, estimate. Also included are economic losses to states outside the region.

The United States

The United States absorbed costs other than military expenditures due to the Gulf War. Oil prices increased dramatically during the crisis period. Since oil is a vital part of the American economy, an increase in its price tends to slow economic growth and increase inflation. Oil price increases due to the crisis are estimated to have cost the U.S. economy $29–$30 billion for 1990–91.[24]

Egypt

Egypt, a critical American ally in the Gulf War, received some benefits as well as incurring costs. The most important benefit to Egypt was the cancellation of external debt. This included $6.7 billion in debts owed to the United States for military equipment. Other nations who canceled Egyptian debts include Germany ($2.5 billion), France ($2.8 billion), the Gulf States ($6.6 billion), and Finland ($78 million). Altogether, the West forgave nearly $25 billion that Egypt owed. While this was good for Egypt, this was a cost to the West and counts as a necessary price incurred to create and maintain the coalition that drove Iraqi forces out of Kuwait.

Egypt also received additional economic and development aid, including $1.5 billion from Saudi Arabia. France and Germany added over $1 billion in new aid tied to the Gulf War. There is no reason to believe that any of this money would have been granted to Egypt without the need for Egyptian support against Iraq. So while Egypt gained, the West paid over $27 billion to get and keep Egypt in the coalition.[25]

Losses Egypt incurred include the lost remittances from Egyptian workers in the Gulf States as well as the cost of sending troops to the theater. This total was approximately $1 billion.[26] In addition, Egypt lost $0.5 billion in revenue from the Suez Canal, since ship traffic decreased during the war, and $1.25 billion in tourism revenue.[27] Even considering debt cancellation and economic aid as internal transfers between coalition partners and therefore not as net costs, Egypt still sustained at least $3.75 billion in economic losses from the Gulf War.

Jordan

The Jordanian economy was severely damaged by the war. Over 500,000 Palestinians, most of whom held Jordanian passports and remitted money to family members in Jordan, were made homeless and unemployed by the war. These guest workers also lost their assets in Kuwait and are unlikely to ever recover them. This, as well as the embargo against Iraq, which was Jordan's primary supplier of petroleum products, nearly crippled the Jordanian economy.[28]

Jordan was also forced to write off loans to Iraq that totaled nearly $1 billion.[29] In addition to this debt write-off, Jordan estimated that the Gulf War cost $3 billion, largely through disruption of trade and tourism.[30] Total Jordanian losses totaled $4 billion net of assistance from other nations.

Turkey

No Iraqi neighbor escaped incurring large costs associated with the Gulf War. Turkey, an American NATO ally, did not send troops to the Gulf, although the Turkish army deployed more than 100,000 troops and several Turkish air force squadrons to the Iraqi border. Iraq left nine divisions of their troops on the border to counter any possible Turkish move. This meant that fewer Iraqi divisions were available to resist coalition forces. The cost to Turkey for this deployment, other actions taken to support the coalition, reduced exports, and the costs incurred by the government due to higher oil prices were estimated by the Turkish government to be $10 billion. Turkey also absorbed over 200,000 refugees from Iraq, largely as a result of fighting between Kurdish separatists and Iraqi troops.[31] Even counting American support for Turkey during this period, as well as using a more conservative estimation technique, still leaves Turkey with a $4 billion bill for the conflict.[32] In addition to this bill, Iraq also seized $1.5 billion in Turkish assets in Iraq[33] and defaulted on $1 billion in loans owed to Turkey.[34] This brings Turkey's cost for the Gulf War to $6.5 billion.

Japan

Japan paid over $9 billion for Gulf War operations that is counted in the military costs noted above.[35] However, in addition to that amount, Japan also made an additional $2 billion in "soft" loans to Turkey, Jordan, and Egypt. These loans were not expected to be nor ever were repaid.

Saudi Arabia

Saudi Arabian estimates of the Gulf War cost reached $64 billion in military costs, asset destruction, in-kind payments of fuel, lost trade, and other costs. That figure does not include the cost of additional arms purchases—approximately $20 billion—but does include the billions paid to the United States and counted in the military cost above.[36] Therefore the Saudi Arabian cost for this conflict can conservatively be estimated at $64 billion, less the $16 billion contributed to the United States and counted above, for a total of $48 billion.

Iraqi Debt

The West was forced to write off Iraqi debt of between $30 and $40 billion. Arab states wrote off an additional $30–$40 billion over and above the amounts given above.[37] At a minimum, this is an additional $60 billion cost from the Gulf War.[38]

Other States

The Gulf states employed a large number of Pakistani workers prior to the Gulf War. Most of these workers were concentrated in Iraq and Kuwait and were unable to work during and after the crisis. The loss of these remittances is estimated to have cost the Pakistani economy in excess of

$500 million. Also, oil price increases due to the conflict cost Pakistan an additional $600 million. This brings the Pakistani Gulf War cost to $1.1 billion. Costs to India from the Gulf War were similar.[39] Estimated Gulf War economic losses for other nations not mentioned above are reported in table 6.2.

Spillover Effects and Asset Losses

The Gulf War also caused severe environmental damage in the region. Oil spills polluted the Gulf waters, and oil fires set by retreating Iraqi troops poisoned the air. Damage from these events spread from Eastern Europe to India, where acid rain from the oil fires damaged crops. The cost of cleaning up the oil spills was over $2.5 billion.[40] Estimates of additional damage are not available.

Total Costs

Table 6.3 summarizes the cost of the Gulf War to external actors. The most conservative estimates are presented and the actual costs were almost certainly far greater. Internal transfers between coalition partners are not included. Direct economic costs are net of military costs and include offsets for increased oil revenue where applicable. Table 6.4 summarizes the cost to the West only and includes costs of debt write-offs for non–Western coalition partners.

Estimated Costs of Preventive Action

The West had a clear signal that Iraq was preparing a military strike in May 1990. An early intervention in the Gulf at this point would have looked much like the British intervention in Iraq-Kuwait relations in 1961, and

TABLE 6.2
Estimated Gulf War Losses ($U.S. Billions)

United Arab Emirates	4.0
Yemen	1.5
Morocco	1.0
Other Arab nations	2.0
TOTAL	**8.5**

Source: Ibrahim M. Oweiss, "The Economic Impact of the War," in *The Gulf Crisis: Background and Consequences,* ed. Ibrahim M. Oweiss (Washington, D.C.: Center for Contemporary Arab Studies, 1991), 296.

TABLE 6.3
Costs of the Gulf War to the International Community ($U.S. Billions)

Type	Amount
Military costs	45.10
Direct economic losses:	
United States	29.00
Egypt	3.75
Jordan	4.00
Turkey	6.50
Saudi Arabia	48.00
Iraqi debt write-offs:	
Middle Eastern states	30.00
Western nations	30.00
Losses to other non–Western states	10.70
Cost of environmental damage	2.50
TOTAL	**209.55**

Sources: Lawrence Freedman and Efraim Karsh, *The Gulf Conflict: 1990–1991* (Princeton: Princeton University Press, 1993). Youssef M. Ibrahim, "Gulf War Is Said to Have Cost the Region $676 Billion in 1990–91," *New York Times* (April 25, 1993), 7. K. S. Ramachandran, *Gulf War and Environmental Problems* (New Delhi: Ashish Publishing, 1991), 30. David R. Henderson, "The Myth of Saddam's Oil Stranglehold," in *American Entangled,* ed. T. G. Carpenter (Washington, D.C.: Cato Institute, 1992). Yoram Meital, "Egypt in the Gulf Crisis," in *Iraq's Road to War,* ed. Amatzia Baram and Barry Rubin (New York: St. Martin's Press, 1993), 191–99. Ibrahim M. Oweiss, "The Economic Impact of the War," in *The Gulf Crisis: Background and Consequences,* ed. Ibrahim M. Oweiss (Washington, D.C.: Center for Contemporary Arab Studies, 1991), 296. Hisham H. Ahmed, "The Impact of the Gulf Crisis on Jordan's Economic Infrastructure," *Arab Studies Quarterly* 15 (Fall 1993): 33. Joseph Nevo, "Jordan's Relations with Iraq: Ally or Victim?" in *Iraq's Road to War,* ed. Baram and Rubin. Mustafa B. Hamarneh, "Jordan Responds to the Gulf Crisis," in *Beyond the Storm,* ed. Phyllis Bennis and Michel Moushabeck (New York: Olive Branch Press, 1991), 228–29. David Kushner, "Turkey: Iraq's European Neighbor," in *Iraq's Road to War,* ed. Baram and Rubin (New York: St. Martin's Press, 1993), 213–17.

would have been far less costly than the actual operation to evict Iraq from Kuwait. After the British protectorate of Kuwait ended in 1961, the Iraqi dictator, ʻAbd al-Karim Qasim, quickly prepared an invasion force to occupy Kuwait. The United Kingdom dispatched a small force to guard the border, and this deterred the Iraqi invasion. This force was soon withdrawn after having made the point that the United Kingdom was prepared to defend the border.[41]

A force deployed in May 1990 would have unequivocally signaled the West's intention to maintain the status quo in the region and cost far less than the actual operations. Using the intervention in Somalia as a tem-

TABLE 6.4
Costs of the Gulf War to the West ($U.S. Billions)

Type	Amount
Military costs	25
Direct economic losses:	
United States	29
Western debt relief to Egypt	25
Support for Turkey	3
Japanese loans to coalition states	2
Iraqi debt write-offs	30
Total cost to the West	**114**

Sources: Ibrahim M. Oweiss, "The Economic Impact of the War," in *The Gulf Crisis: Background and Consequences,* ed. Ibrahim M. Oweiss (Washington, D.C.: Center for Contemporary Arab Studies, 1991). Amatzia Baram and Barry Rubin, eds., *Iraq's Road to War* (New York: St. Martin's Press, 1993). Micah L. Sifry and Christopher Cerf, eds., *The Gulf War Reader* (New York: Times Books, 1991). Les Aspin, *The Aspin Papers: Sanctions, Diplomacy, and the War in the Persian Gulf* (Washington, D.C.: Center for Strategic and International Studies, 1991).

plate, a blocking force of 20,000–30,000 troops would have cost approximately $4 billion for a deployment lasting 18–24 months. This ground force would need to be augmented by either ground- or naval-based air forces, which would have cost an additional $500 million to $1 billion for the mission duration.

Compared with the actual cost of allowing Iraq to occupy Kuwait, the cost for this type of force seems easily justified. It is also possible that a smaller force could have been used and that Kuwait might have paid at least part of this cost.

The second intervention point came in July 1990. While this would have left little time for an American or coalition response, a trip wire force could have been landed and would also have deterred Saddam. A rapid reaction force of approximately 5,000 men could have been quickly deployed and supported with pre-positioned equipment in the area and from Diego Garcia. This force would have been supported by naval aircraft already in the region and by land-based bombers from Europe and Guam.[42]

This type of deployment, while rushed and less well equipped than the eventual forces used in Desert Storm, would still have served as a clear signal that Iraq would not be allowed to take Kuwait. Iraq might have probed these defenses and some skirmishes would likely have occurred, thus increasing the cost, but also increasing the clarity of the signal that this border was sacrosanct. The cost of such an initial deployment, its augmentation by both air and ground units, and its extended presence in the region might have cost $10 billion. Even if this force was tripled by bringing in troops from Europe, and supported by a large-scale naval and marine presence, the cost would not have exceeded $30 billion, even in an extended deployment.

Either early intervention scenario contains significant cost savings for the West as well as the Middle East region. While it might have been difficult to implement a preemption strategy in this case, even assembling the force and having it ready at a moment's notice for deployment on the eve of the invasion would likely have generated significant cost savings. Intervention in May or July and a continued Western presence would have been the most cost-effective option, saving the West nearly $100 billion.

Conclusions

Intervention in the Persian Gulf cost the West a staggering sum. In an area of such vital economic and political interest, it seems to have been money well spent. However, equal or superior results could have been achieved by a strategy of conflict preemption.

The West knew well in advance that a conflict was likely to start, and even given the powerful forces urging Saddam to strike, there would have been no possible payoff to Iraq for an invasion if the West's response had been assured. While this raises the problem of how best to clearly signal potential opponents in the noisy environment of international relations, some tactics work better than others. When nations station troops on a border, including nations under a nuclear "umbrella," and when they sign formal alliance treaties, they signal their readiness to enter a conflict. A demonstrated commitment to intervention and preemption in regional conflict is another way to make sure signals are clear.

A deployment of Western troops with firm backing from the United States would have sent an unequivocal signal. Saddam based his gamble on the chance that the West would not respond with a policy of restoring the status quo. Ensuring the clarity of Western intentions in the area might have been expensive, but far less costly than the Gulf War. This case supports the hypothesis that early preventive efforts are cost-effective and negates the null hypothesis that early action does not generate savings.

This case also provides important foreign policy lessons that may be applied to other situations. The small force on the Macedonia-Yugoslavia border has kept the Balkan conflict from spreading by providing a clear signal that the West will fight to maintain that border. Small contingents of UN troops have also kept the peace in Cyprus, and the American commitment to South Korea has kept the peace for forty-five years.

In conclusion, while clear signaling may be difficult and expensive, the expense of misunderstood intentions is far more costly. The $10 billion or even $30 billion cost of signaling Iraq that an invasion of Kuwait would not be allowed to stand seems paltry compared with the actual cost of the Gulf War.

Part Two

Initial Prevention

7

Macedonia

Bradley Thayer

Case Preview

SINCE MACEDONIA DECLARED its independence from Yugoslavia in 1991, the potential for war has existed between the new state and Serbia, Albania, and Greece.[1] U.S. decision makers and international observers feared that war might occur with one or more of the neighboring states: Serbia would strike to incorporate it into a Greater Serbia; Albania might attack to protect the ethnic Albanian minority; or Greece might invade, which in turn might compel Turkish involvement, causing a wider Balkan war and straining the North Atlantic Treaty Organization (NATO) alliance. These fears, particularly the threat from Serbia, prompted the dispatch of the first ever UN preventive peacekeeping operation to Macedonia, the UN Preventive Deployment Force (UNPREDEP).[2]

The intention of this case study is first to present the history of UNPREDEP, focusing particularly on the threats from Serbia, Greece, and Albania; second, to determine the costs of the preventive action taken by the United Nations; and third, to estimate the costs of a conflict to regional and international actors if one had occurred. The conclusion of this study is that the cost of the peacekeeping operation is modest in comparison to the cost of a conflict in Macedonia, thus supporting the contention that intervention is cost-effective. Further, the Macedonian case provides evidence to reject the null hypothesis that the costs of preventive action outweigh the costs of inaction.

Origins and Overview of the Conflict

The threats to Macedonia from Greece, Albania, and Serbia are important to understand because UNPREDEP was deployed to mitigate them.[3] Macedonians are a distinct ethnic group who possess their own culture, language, and history that dates back to antiquity—Philip of Macedon and Alexander the Great were perhaps the most famous Macedonians.[4] Despite its ancient identity, Macedonia did not become an independent state until 1991, when it, unlike Bosnia, Croatia, and Slovenia, emerged peacefully from the collapse of the former Yugoslavia.[5] In a referendum held on September 8, 1991, Macedonians voted overwhelmingly in favor of establishing an independent state. Support for independence was widespread throughout all ethnic groups in Macedonia, including the large minority of ethnic Albanians.[6]

In December 1991 Macedonia applied for recognition by the European Community (EC, now the European Union, EU) along with Bosnia-Herzegovina, Croatia, and Slovenia.[7] These applications were considered by a five-member Arbitration Commission, under the leadership of Judge Robert Badinter of France. In January 1992 the Badinter Commission submitted its report that only Slovenia and Macedonia be recognized. However, on January 15 the EC recognized Slovenia and Croatia, but not Macedonia. Greece vetoed the recognition of Macedonia by the EC.

The Threat from Greece

From the date of its independence, tension has existed between Greece and Macedonia. Greece refused to recognize Macedonia's independence for two reasons. First, Athens argued that the use of the name "Macedonia" implied a territorial ambition toward northern Greece, and an attempt to establish a state from Skopje, the capital, to Thessaloniki, the Greek port on the Aegean Sea. In support of its claim, the Greek government cited several passages in the 1992 Macedonian constitution that offer support to Macedonians living in other countries. Macedonia "cares for the status and the rights" of Macedonians in neighboring countries and "assists them in their cultural development and promotes ties to them."[8] Greeks objected because they interpreted these passages "as legitmating efforts to 'liberate enslaved Macedonians' living in Greece. More generally, however, Greece objects to all references to a Macedonian minority in Greece since the Greek government denies the existence of any such minority."[9]

The second reason concerns national symbols and culture. The use on commemorative currency of the image of the White Tower, the traditional symbol of the city of Thessaloniki, enraged many Greeks. But perhaps most offensive was the Macedonian parliament's adoption, in August 1992, of the sixteen-ray star or sun of Vergina as a state symbol. This symbol is widely recognized as the emblem of the ancient Macedonian royal family. The adoption of it was perceived by the Greeks as another indication of Macedonia's expansionist design on Greek territory and as theft of Greek culture.[10]

Despite Greece's objections, Macedonia was admitted to the United Nations in April 1993, under the provisional name Former Yugoslav Republic of Macedonia (FYROM) because of the unsettled dipute with Greece over its name.[11] In 1993 special UN envoy Cyrus Vance was assigned to mediate the dispute between Macedonia and Greece. This effort was unsuccessful, and relations worsened when the government of Andreas Papandreou introduced an economic blockade, except for food and medicine, in February 1994 that denied a landlocked Macedonia access to the Aegean Sea.[12]

The Greek blockade had a devastating effect on the Macedonian economy, which was already weakened by the UN embargo imposed on Serbia, Macedonia's largest trading partner, in May 1992.[13] By denying it access to Thessaloniki, the Greek blockade hindered its export earnings and the import of vital supplies such as oil. Greece insisted that Macedonia be barred from international organizations, and having failed in that goal only reluctantly accepted it as the Former Yugoslav Republic of Macedonia. The cause of Greek obstreperousness may be that it fears regional isolation. Athens sees Albania, Bulgaria, and Turkey as potential foes, and Macedonia independence, especially a Macedonia that is allied with Turkey, isolates Greece from its traditional ally, Serbia.[14]

In addition, statements by Turkish and Macedonian politicians have not helped to resolve the dispute. The president of Turkey, Turgut Ozal, explicitly referred to Turkey as "the guardian of Macedonia and Bosnia-Herzegovina."[15] These statements are perceived to be threatening by Greece, given its history of conflict with Turkey, which threatens to erupt once again over Cyprus or the demarcation of sovereignty over islands in the Aegean.[16] The deputy speaker of the parliament in Skopje asserted that Greece "has no legitimate right over Aegean Macedonia."[17] This caused great alarm in Athens because "Aegean Macedonia" is Greek Macedonia. Moreover, the major opposition party in Macedonia, the Internal Macedonian Revolutionary Organization–Democratic Party for Macedonian National Unity (VMRO-DPMNE), a powerful nationalistic party, has adopted an irredentist platform that calls for the creation of a "United Macedonia."[18] In support of this goal they have published maps that show "Greater Macedonia" consisting of the present state of Macedonia, as well as large portions of Greek territory and part of western Bulgaria.[19]

However, since 1995 relations have improved. An Interim Accord was signed on September 13, 1995, between Greece and Macedonia. Greece ended its blockade, which had cost Macedonia about $40 million in lost trade and revenue each month.[20] Macedonia has dropped the Vergina symbol from its flag and amended its constitution to remove the passages that had been interpreted by Greece as irredentist. While the states have achieved a modus vivendi in their relations, the dispute over the territory of Macedonia and its symbols may always resume.

The Threat from Albania and the Albanian Minority within Macedonia

While the threat from Greece appears to be diminishing as the countries resolve their disputes, there are significant tensions between Albania and Macedonia, as well as between the ethnic Albanian minority and the Slavic Macedonian majority within Macedonia. Macedonian forces reportedly have fired at Albanian armed forces on patrol along the border, causing dozens of casualties.[21] This fighting continues on a small scale and thus presents the possibility of escalation. But the greater danger is internal. As one official was quoted as saying in 1994, "We have problems on our borders, but our biggest problem is the Albanians living here."[22] Macedonia has a large Albanian minority, 21 to 23 percent of the population, and there is significant support in it for a separate state or confederation with Albania.[23] Tahir Xhema, a prominent Albanian nationalist, depicts the sentiment of the Albanian minority: "the feeling is that this is our land, the land we lived on, and soon it will be our republic."[24]

Albanian leaders believe that the actual number of Albanians in Macedonia is greater than Skopje admits. Albania's President Sali Berisha stated that Albanians make up almost 40 percent of the population in Macedonia, and this opinion is echoed by the Party for Democratic Prosperity (PPD), which is the principal representative of Macedonia's Albanian population in parliament. While Berisha advocates a diplomatic solution to the problem of greater Albanian rights in Macedonia, he has stated that if war occurs, Albania will come to the assistance of the Albanian minority.[25]

There are indications that elements within the Albanian minority are acting upon their irredentist beliefs. Macedonian authorities have discovered a secret paramilitary organization, called the All-Albanian Army, which existed within the Army of the Republic of Macedonia and was allegedly in contact with Albanian officials.[26] In early November 1993, police arrested a small group of Albanians, among them a deputy minister of defense in the FYROM government, who they said were trying to establish an "autonomous province of Ilirida" in western Macedonia, adjacent to Albania.[27] Presumably, the goal of the group would have been to separate "Ilirida" by force and unify with Albania, and possibly Kosovo as well. Moreover, the Albanians have formed their own paramilitary units, which the government considers illegal but tolerates.[28]

The political leaders of the ethnic Albanians demand that the Albanians be recognized by the government as a constituent people, and receive representation in all governmental and educational structures in proportion to their percentage of the population.[29] Arben Xhaferi, the leader of a branch of the PPD, warned of violence if these conditions are not met, while another leader, Menduh Thaci, demands "space" within Macedonia for Albanians.[30]

Some of the worst interethnic violence occurred in February 1995. On February 9 all eighteen ethnic Albanian parliamentarians walked out of parliament to protest a draft law banning the use of the Albanian language on Macedonian identity cards and passports.[31] A week later, on February 17, violence erupted when Albanians attempted to establish a private Albanian-language university near Tetovo in the heart of Albanian Macedonia.[32] University education had been only available in Macedonian because of concern that education in Albanian would contribute to greater ethnic fragmentation, and thus Skopje forbade it to open. The leader of the Albanian protesters, Fadilj Sulejmani, won praise from many Macedonian Albanians and from Berisha for leading this effort. Sulejmani warned the government that "200,000 Albanians will rise to our defense, and they will have guns and grenades," and asked that the police avoid a confrontation that "would take us directly to war."[33] The university opened and this prompted a police crackdown that left one ethnic Albanian dead and about sixty wounded.[34]

After these events the government undertook several reforms intended to increase the numbers of Albanians in the state university, but it refuses to permit education in the Albanian language. This in turn reinforces suspicions among ethnic Albanians that the government wants them to remain undereducated and thus unqualified to participate in politics.[35]

Skopje is worried that unrest among the Albanians will lead to unification of western Macedonia with Albania and the largely Albanian population, 90 percent, of Kosovo in Serbia, and so is reluctant to accede to the demands of the Albanian population for greater autonomy.[36] There is also a strong sentiment against the Albanian minority by the Macedonian majority.[37] An anti-Albanian riot at an open market in Skopje in November 1992 resulted in the deaths of three Albanian men and a Macedonian woman.[38]

More recently, one well-known Macedonian commentator, Slavko Milosavlevski, expressed the fears of many Macedonians by observing a "clear tendency . . . among the ethnic Albanian population, which is totally possessed by the idea of a 'Greater Albania' and which is consistently directed toward preparing conditions for the separation of a part . . . of the Republic of Macedonia . . . to realize that idea."[39] Many Macedonians believe that steps to placate the ethnic Albanians in education, government, and other institutions is the beginning of the end of Macedonia.

While the irredentism found in the Albanian minority is the principal danger they pose to Macedonia, Albanians also have other disputes with Skopje. They object to the mention of the Macedonian Orthodox Church in the constitution, as well as the depiction of Orthodox church buildings on new currency, and decry the lack of professional opportunities available to them.[40] Thus, the threats from Albania and the ethnic Albanians within Macedonia are significant and present the possibility of either a civil or Balkan war arising from ethnic conflict.

The Threat from Serbia

Macedonia faces a threat from Serbia as well. Although a significant one, this threat is not as great as those from Albania or from the Albanian minority, for three reasons. First, Serbs do not perceive Macedonia to be traditional Serbian territory. The Serbian-dominated Yugoslav People's Army occupied Macedonia until April 1992, when it left peacefully. It is unlikely that the Serbian leadership would have given up a favorable position only to return later by force, particularly after the international monitors from the Conference on Security and Cooperation in Europe (CSCE, now OSCE, the Organization for Security and Cooperation in Europe) and UNPREDEP had been deployed.[41] This would risk a war with NATO. Second, unlike Bosnia and Croatia, Macedonia has no significant Serb minority. Serbs in Macedonia are about 2.2 percent of the population, or 40,000 people, who are geographically dispersed throughout Macedonia.[42] Thus there is little prospect of having an effective fifth column that is capable of playing a role analogous to the Bosnian and Croatian Serbs. Third, since most of the population of Macedonia is anti-Serbian, there is little possibility of the Serbs being invited into the country—a Macedonian-Serbian *anschluss.* According to Stefan Troebst, "the Macedonian nationalists are fiercely anti-Yugoslav and thus primarily anti-Serbian, as their antipathy against the Albanian and other Muslim minorities is not sufficient to form a strong, pan-Slavic bond" with the Serbs.[43] Similarly, the Albanian minority "due to the Kosovo problem, are among the staunchest anti-Serbs in the country."[44]

Nonetheless, there are disputes that could trigger a Serbian invasion. A dispute exists between the Serbian Orthodox Church and the Macedonian Orthodox Church, which was established in 1967 with the approval of the

Yugoslav government as a way to increase Macedonian nationalism, to combat Albanian nationalism, and to arrest the spread of Islam in western Macedonia.[45] The Macedonian Church has never been recognized as autocephalous by the Serbian Orthodox Church. Politicians within Macedonia, especially the VMRO-DPMNE, generally support the Macedonian Church and promote it as part of building Macedonian nationalism.[46] Despite the vitriol expressed by partisans in this dispute, it is unlikely that it could cause a war between Macedonia and Serbia.

More disturbing, however, is the possibility that an aggressive Serbia will seek to reclaim as much of the former Yugoslavia as possible. Greece might agree to a Balkan Molotov-Ribbentrop pact, to join this attack and divide Macedonia between them. This also introduces the possibility that the war might widen to involve neighboring countries—Bulgaria and Turkey—and result in a general Balkan war. Such a war would directly affect U.S. and Western European interests—the strain on the NATO alliance would be great since Greece and Turkey are members of the alliance.

A third and perhaps the greatest danger is a Macedonian-Serbian conflict over Kosovo.[47] This is the greatest danger Macedonia faces due to the increasing violence in Kosovo. The emergence in late 1997 of an ethnic Albanian terrorist group, the Kosovo Liberation Army (KLA), and its battles with Serbian special police units beginning in late February 1998, which at the time of this writing, in May 1998, have left over 100 people killed, demonstrate that large-scale violence in Kosovo is a genuine danger.[48] This violence may result in a wave of ethnic Albanian refugees from Kosovo to Macedonia, thus destabilizing the tenuous ethnic balance of the country.[49] Conflict might also arise as the result of an Albanian attack on Kosovo initiated either by the Albanian army, the KLA, paramilitary formations of Macedonian Albanians, or by all three groups, to protect the Kosovo Albanians from increased Serbian oppression or from ethnic cleansing there.[50] Either would greatly threaten Macedonia and increase the chances that war would escalate to include it. These dangers were recognized by the international community, who deployed UNPREDEP largely to avoid them.

In 1996 the sanctions against Serbia were lifted by the United Nations, and Macedonia normalized its links with Greece and Serbia. For the first time since Macedonia's independence, Skopje has open borders in all directions, and the possibility exists for improved diplomatic and economic relations with Serbia, as well as a lessening of tension along the border. As this brief analysis of Macedonia's disputes with Greece, Albania, and Serbia shows, there are significant external and internal threats to Macedonia.

The Deployment of UNPREDEP

By mid-1992 many international observers were apprehensive that threats from Serbia, Greece, and Albania would result in war.[51] Macedonia is unable to defend itself against these threats because its army is poorly trained and equipped, and lacks armor, heavy artillery, and an air force.[52] Moreover, Macedonia has no allies to aid it in the event of an attack. To address these threats, and at the request of Macedonia's President Kiro Gligorov, the UN Security Council authorized the deployment of a peacekeeping force in December 1992.

UNPREDEP was given the mission of deterring any threats against Macedonia and reporting any developments in border areas that could undermine confidence and stability in Macedonia or threaten its territory. One hundred forty-seven Canadian troops were dispatched immediately in January 1993; these were later replaced by about 500 Nordic troops.[53] About 300 U.S. troops joined the force in July 1993, and this force was later augmented to 350.[54] The U.S. force monitors the eastern half of the border while the Nordic force patrols the western half of Macedonia's border with Serbia and Albania.[55] UNPREDEP is a trip wire that serves to reassure Macedonia and to deter its neighbors from intervening.[56]

By 1996 UNPREDEP consisted of 1,050 soldiers: a Nordic composite battalion and a U.S. Army task force supported by a heavy engineering platoon from Indonesia.[57] This force operated twenty-four permanent observation posts in Macedonia along 420 kilometers of its borders with Serbia and Albania. It also operates thirty-three temporary observation posts on the border. From these posts about forty border and community patrols are conducted daily.[58]

Thus far, UNPREDEP has accomplished its mission without major incidents. Both it and Macedonia have survived despite the turmoil that has occurred within Macedonia, such as the October 1995 assassination attempt on Macedonia's president in Skopje.[59]

Costs of Conflict Prevention to International Actors

The costs of the conflict prevention effort to date have largely been those of the UNPREDEP peacekeeping operation because there has not been actual combat in Macedonia. Therefore, many of the costs—economic, humanitarian, and military—that were significant in other cases are less so here.

The Costs of UNPREDEP

The cost of UNPREDEP was $204 million through the end of 1996. When UNPREDEP was a part of UNPROFOR it cost about $25 million every six months, or $50 million per year.[60] Once it became an independent mission on February 1, 1996, its costs rose slightly to an estimated

$29 million for six months, or about $60 million a year.[61] As the mission continues, costs should be calculated on the basis of $29 million every six months, so that by the end of June 1997, UNPREDEP cost $234 million.

Economic Costs

The direct economic costs incurred by the international community are very modest. Macedonia itself has shouldered most of the direct economic costs of conflict prevention efforts, largely as a result of the UN sanctions against Serbia, which closed Macedonia's northern border.[62] About 70 percent of Macedonia's trade at the time of independence had been with Yugoslavia, so the sanctions against Serbia closed off Macedonia's northern border and hit its economy hard, halting production entirely in some sectors of industry.[63] By demonstrating such resolve, especially given great economic incentives to break the embargo, Macedonia may have helped to deter Serbian aggression against Macedonia.

The direct economic cost to the international community is largely the cumulative foreign direct investment in Macedonia, which totaled $21 million as of the end of 1995.[64] Table 7.1 summarizes the costs of the conflict prevention effort to the international community.

While the $255 million conflict prevention cost to the international community was modest and borne by many states, the economic cost to Macedonia as a result of complying with UN sanctions against Serbia and of the Greek embargo was borne by a small economy and has helped to create a desperate economic situation within Macedonia.[65]

Estimated Costs of Conflict

The intention here is to estimate the costs of a war to regional and international powers had one occurred in Macedonia. While it is not possible to compare the costs of an actual event, the conflict prevention effort of UN-

TABLE 7.1
Macedonia: Estimated Conflict Prevention Costs to the International Community ($U.S. Millions)

Cost of UNPREDEP to July 1997	234
Direct economic cost to international community	21
TOTAL	**255**

Sources: Economic Commission for Europe, *Economic Survey of Europe in 1995–1996* (New York: United Nations, 1996), 150. UNDPI, *Information Notes, United Nations Peace-keeping* (New York: United Nations, 1994).

PREDEP, with something that did not happen, a war in Macedonia, it is possible to generate a cost estimate based on the costs of comparable operations launched elsewhere in the world.

Had war occurred, it probably would have been on the scale of the conflict in Bosnia—if not worse. This is because the danger of escalation to a wider Balkan war would have been significant due to the dangers from Greece, Albania, and Serbia described above. Put into the context of this study, it would require tens of thousands of troops, such as the United Nations and NATO's Implementation Force (IFOR) operation, for an intermediate conflict if not hundreds of thousands of troops, such as Desert Storm (a large conflict), to end a war once it started.

The Costs of an Intermediate Conflict

The estimate for an intermediate conflict is calculated using the Bosnian case as a yardstick, and is bounded by two conditions. First, it would have involved only two belligerents—Macedonia and Albania, for example. Second, the conflict would not have lasted as long as Bosnia due to the difference in relative power (in population, military effectiveness, and geography, among other factors) between these states. Given these parameters, the costs of an intermediate conflict would be comparable to the $44 billion total cost of the Bosnian war.[66]

Macedonia is weaker than all of the neighboring states, and thus would have been unable to stop any attack by its neighbors. Nonetheless, the potential for a conventional and guerrilla war would be present, given the large number of men who received military training in the Yugoslav army, and the relative simplicity of tactics and equipment involved in guerrilla warfare.[67] While it is impossible to determine with certainty, it is likely that an invasion of Macedonia would take perhaps a month to complete; but a much longer time would be required to pacify the countryside—perhaps two years, in a guerrilla war. Using two years as a time frame, and the costs of similar operations in Bosnia to provide a metric for cost estimation, the total cost to international powers would be $15 billion. These costs are summarized in table 7.2.

Military costs would be similar to the costs of the joint UN-NATO operation IFOR, now SFOR (Stabilization Force), which are approximately $2 billion per year. Macedonia has about half the territory and the population of Bosnia, thus the cost of an IFOR/SFOR operation should be lower—about $1 billion per year for two years, or $2 billion.[68]

Similarly, the humanitarian costs would be about half what they were per annum in Bosnia. UN agencies, including the UN High Commissioner for Refugees, the World Health Organization, World Food Programme, and the United Nations Children's Fund spent about $3.7 billion

TABLE 7.2
Macedonia: Estimated Costs to Outside Powers of an Intermediate Conflict Lasting Two years ($U.S. Billions)

Military	2.0
Humanitarian	4.1
Economic: Direct	6.0
Economic: Opportunity	2.6
Individual nations	0.3
TOTAL	**15.0**

through 1996 in Bosnia to assist over 2 million citizens. The costs of similar operations in Macedonia would be about $1 billion per year, or $2 billion for two years.

The refugee costs would be significant. Macedonia has relatively long open borders with four states, so it should be easy for refugees to flee. For the Bosnian conflict, costs to national hosts, principally Germany, were about $2.5 billion a year. In addition, private and nongovernmental organizations provided $200 million through 1995. An intermediate conflict would produce fewer refugees due to the smaller population and estimated shorter time of the conflict, so we may estimate that the costs to a national host would be about $1 billion per year, with about $50 million spent per annum by private and nongovernmental agencies, for a total of $2.1 billion for two years.

Direct economic costs to Bosnia were $60 billion. In the case of Macedonia these costs would be a fraction of that amount because its economy is smaller than Bosnia's, and we are postulating that the war would not last as long. The direct economic costs to Macedonia would be at least one-tenth of Bosnia's cost, or $6 billion. Of Bosnia's $60 billion direct economic cost, the World Bank, the European Bank for Reconstruction and Development, and the EU have given or pledged $6.3 billion to aid the reconstruction of its economy. Aid to assist Macedonia would probably be as modest, a 10:1 cost to aid ratio, so that about $600 million would be given in aid.

The economic opportunity costs of any conflict would also be significant. Macedonian exports and imports would be severely disrupted by a conflict. In 1995 the country exported about $1.2 billion in goods and services and imported about $1.4 billion.[69] The GNP was estimated to be $1.6 billion, indicating that the economy is highly dependent upon trade, which would be severely disrupted in a conflict, especially because Macedonia is dependent upon roads to Serbia and to Greece that would be disrupted in a war. Thus, the economic opportunity costs of a conflict to regional and international actors should be at least half of Macedonia's total of yearly exports/imports—about $1.3 billion per year or $2.6 billion for a two-year conflict.

In the case of Bosnia, the cost to individual nations was approximately $3 billion. This amount was bilateral aid donated principally by the United States, the United Kingdom, and Japan. These countries, as well as others, such as Germany, may be expected to provide a proportional degree of aid in the event of a war between Macedonia and a neighboring state. Given that Macedonia has only half the population of Bosnia, and the conflict is postulated to last only half the time as the Bosnian war, a good estimate is that one-tenth of the total amount would be donated to Macedonia, or $300 million in bilateral donations by major countries. This figure is an estimate and probably understates the true cost of a conflict if there were one. The human costs of such a war, of course, cannot be as easily quantified, but would be great.

The Costs of a Large Conflict

If the conflict were large, the costs could be estimated at approximately $144 billion. The metric against which to measure the costs of such a war would be the Gulf War. A large Balkan war would be of that scale because it would probably involve Macedonia, Albania, Serbia, Greece, Turkey, and the United States. Such a large number of states might quietly become involved in conflict due to their competing security interests. If Greece or Serbia were to engage in conflict with Macedonia, then Turkey and possibly Albania might come to its assistance in order to prevent Greek or Serbian domination of the Balkans. If Albania were to attack, then Greece or Serbia, or both, might be compelled to come to Macedonia's assistance. If the conflict were to involve Greece or Turkey, then the United States would be compelled to intervene to save NATO from destruction. The potential for rapid escalation of a conflict is genuine, and fear of a larger Balkan war driven by Serb expansion largely explains why the international community was motivated to send a preventive deployment force to Macedonia. U.S. involvement in a larger war would probably shorten the timescale of the conflict to about a year, principally due to the military power of the United States. The costs of a large conflict to the international community are summarized in table 7.3.

The military costs of intervention to international actors would be as large as the $45.1 billion total incurred by them during the Gulf War.[70] U.S. involvement would be at about the same scale, 500,000 troops, but would take longer. Moreover, the operation would require that the logistical infrastructure—ports, roads, airports—of the area be developed so U.S. forces could be supported. The hostile forces the United States would be

TABLE 7.3
Macedonia: Estimated Costs to Outside Powers of a Large Conflict Lasting One Year ($U.S. Billions)

Military	45.10
Humanitarian	30.00
Economic: Direct	28.00
Economic: Opportunity	23.60
Individual nations	17.24
TOTAL	**143.94**

likely to face would be much smaller than Iraq's, which in 1990 were the fourth largest in the world, but a similar number of U.S. forces would be needed due to the mountainous terrain of the southern Balkans.

Unlike the Gulf War, for which it paid only $7.3 billion of the total cost to international actors, the United States would pay a greater amount of the military costs due to the absence of wealthy allies like Saudi Arabia and the United Arab Emirates. In addition, Japan would probably contribute less than the $10 billion it did during the Gulf War, because it has no direct interests in the Balkans.

The humanitarian costs incurred by a large conflict may be determined by using the figures from the Bosnia case study. The Bosnia figures provide a good baseline because population rates, weather, infrastructure, and terrain are similar in the southern Balkans. The humanitarian costs to international actors in Bosnia from 1992 through 1996 were about $12 billion. This amount is approximately $3 billion per year for Bosnia's two million people. The population of the southern Balkans may be conservatively estimated to be 10 million—3.5 million in Albania, 2 million in Macedonia, 2 million in Kosovo, and 2.5 million in the Macedonian provinces of Greece.[71] The humanitarian costs to the international community of a one-year, large-scale conflict would be at least $30 billion. This number was calculated on the basis of intensity of the conflict, which would be at least twice that of the war in Bosnia, or $3 billion per year for each million in population. The actual humanitarian cost would no doubt be greater.

The direct economic costs would be much lower than the $91.25 billion estimate of the direct economic losses suffered by the United States and the major regional actors—Egypt, Jordan, Saudi Arabia, and Turkey. In contrast to the Persian Gulf states, the Balkan states lack valuable natural resources, have modest economies, and do relatively little trading with the United States, the rest of Europe, or with Japan. These states, in turn, have few investments in the Balkans. The value of imports to the Balkan states, all of which are dependent on trade, permits an estimate of direct economic costs to the international community due to the loss of direct trade. A one-year, large-scale war would cost the international community about half of the total volume of imports to these states, or about $28 billion.

The economic opportunity costs to the international community may be calculated from the value of Balkan exports. To avoid overestimating the opportunity costs to the international community, this analysis will not count the value of imports to these states since this figure was included in the direct economic costs. The economic opportunity costs will be calculated using the value of exports from these countries. In the event of a large war, exports from these states to the international economy would be significantly reduced, by at least one-half, although substitute suppliers would be found at a marginally higher cost. Thus the economic opportunity costs to the international community would be slightly greater than $23.6 billion.

Although it is difficult to predict what the costs to individual nations of a Balkan war would be, an estimate may best be calculated using the numbers from the Bosnian war because, unlike the Gulf, no international actors have vital interests in the southern Balkans and they would therefore be less likely to be as generous. Total costs to individual nations in Bosnia were about $3 billion: the United States provided about $2.8 billion, the United Kingdom $200 million, and Japan $24 million. In a large conflict these states, and other European states, such as Germany, would donate perhaps an order of magnitude greater. Therefore, the United States would provide about $13 billion, the United Kingdom and Germany $2 billion each, and Japan $240 million, for a total cost of $17.24 billion. As with the estimate of the intermediate conflict, this probably underestimates the costs, and makes no effort to estimate the human cost, which would certainly be great.

Conclusions

The cost to the international community of conflict prevention measures in Macedonia was about $60 million a year, or $234 million to July 1997, for UNPREDEP, plus an additional $21 million in direct economic costs, calculated through 1995, for a total of $255 million. The cost of a conflict to outside powers would be $15 billion or $144 billion for a medium-size or large conflict, respectively. The total savings to the international community yielded by preventive action, then, range from $14.7 to $143.6 billion; this clearly supports the contention that intervention is cost-effective. While it is impossible to prove that the presence of UNPREDEP in Macedonia prevented aggression, either from Serbia or Albania, the significant threats to Macedonia and the modest cost of the conflict prevention effort makes it an excellent investment—especially when this cost is compared to the much greater costs of war.

8

Slovakia

Renée de Nevers

Case Preview

THIS CHAPTER EXAMINES THE POTENTIAL for conflict in Slovakia, and Western efforts since 1989 to keep conflict from erupting. There are two related possibilities. First, internal conflict, stimulated by tensions between ethnic Slovaks and ethnic Hungarians in the southern and southeastern parts of the state could erupt in violence. Second, external conflict with neighboring Hungary could break out. The former is more likely than the latter; indeed, only if conflict breaks out within Slovakia is a clash with Hungary at all probable.[1]

Slovak-Hungarian tensions were of historic origins and reemerged after the collapse of the Soviet-dominated Warsaw Pact in 1991, followed by the dissolution of Czechoslovakia at the end of 1992.[2] Vladimir Meciar, Slovakia's prime minister within the federated state, exploited latent nationalist tensions in Slovakia to demand more power for the Slovak government within Czechoslovakia. Disagreements between Czech and Slovak leaders over an acceptable constitutional structure for the state, and over the pace of economic reforms, led by mid-1992 to the conclusion that a unified state could not be sustained; subsequently, the Czech and Slovak republics became independent states on January 1, 1993.

Tensions between Slovaks and the sizable ethnic Hungarian minority inhabiting much of the land along Slovakia's border with Hungary emerged prior to the breakup of Czechoslovakia, fueled by nationalist sentiment in Slovakia. Relations within Slovakia and with neighboring Hungary were further complicated by the stress Hungary's first non-Communist government placed on protecting the rights of "all" Hungarians in the early 1990s. While the Hungarian government has adopted a more conciliatory attitude that gives priority to relations with neighboring governments over its ethnic diaspora, strains between Hungarians and Slovaks remain.

The dominant concern of both Hungary and Slovakia since 1989 has been to integrate with the West by joining Western institutions. While this has mitigated significantly the likelihood of conflict between Slovakia and Hungary, Slovakia's treatment of its ethnic Hungarian minority continues to aggravate relations between these two states. Several Western institutions, notably the Council of Europe and the High Commissioner on National Minorities appointed by the Organization for Security and Cooperation in Europe (OSCE), have worked to ease tensions by advocating a European standard for treatment of minorities, while at the same time making clear that border revisions are unacceptable to the international community. Moreover, specific efforts have been made by external bodies to ease ethnic relations both within Slovakia and between Slovakia and Hungary. These have included mediating particular disputes between ethnic Hungarians and the Slovak government regarding legal rights of minorities, working to resolve the dispute between Slovakia and Hungary over the Gabcikovo-Nagymoros dam project on their common border, and improving political relations between the two states.

Mediation efforts have been proceeding since 1993. The total cost of mediation between 1993 and 1997 was roughly $1.8 million. Since 1990 the international community spent roughly $890 million to assist Slovakia's transition to a market economy and a more democratic political system. This adds up to less than $1 billion over a seven-year period, during which violent conflict did not emerge despite fluctuating tensions between Slovakia and Hungary, and within Slovakia itself. The low costs of these exertions, in comparison with the higher price of halting conflicts later, makes their emulation worthwhile.

This chapter will analyze the tensions within Slovakia and between it and Hungary. It will then assess the steps that have been taken to lessen tensions both within Slovakia and between Slovakia and Hungary. Finally, it will evaluate the costs of these efforts and compare them to estimated costs of either a full-blown prevention effort or actual intervention to stop fighting.

Origins and Overview of the Conflict

Czechoslovakia had a short history as a unified independent state. Prior to World War I, most of this territory was part of the Austro-Hungarian Empire, while parts of Slovakia were directly under Hungarian jurisdiction within the empire. The state created at the end of World War I had a variety of structures over the ensuing seventy years.[3] Between 1939 and 1945 Czechoslovakia disappeared; the Czech lands were absorbed by Hitler's empire, while the remaining territory of Slovakia was established as an independent state, but one ruled by a fascist government in alliance with Nazi Germany. In 1945 a new state was again created from Czech and Slovak lands, granting Slovaks increased autonomy; this structure was then superseded by a more centralized structure when the Communists took control after a coup in February 1948. Finally, some steps back toward federalism were enacted during the Prague Spring in 1968; these were not completely abandoned after the crackdown in August of that year, and remained in place until the "Velvet Revolution" of November 1989.[4]

This history gave both the Czechs and the Slovaks some cause for grievance against the other. Czechs resented the Slovaks for their abandonment of the Czech lands in favor of an independent, fascist state in 1939; Slovak nationalism played a role in the decapitation of Czechoslovakia by Hitler in 1939. The increased political visibility of Slovaks after 1968, due to federal reforms that gave them greater voting weight in the national assembly, also fostered resentment. The Slovaks in turn resented the lack of autonomy granted to Slovakia during the interwar period, and remained discontented with their unequal representation in the federal government under the Communists, as well as the uneven economic development of the two states, with Slovakia lagging behind the Czech lands.[5] Slovakia's previous domination by the Magyars under the Austro-Hungarian Empire also created simmering resentments against Hungarians.[6]

Czech-Slovak Tensions Since 1989

During the revolution of 1989, Czechs and Slovaks were united in their opposition to the Communist regime. Civic Forum (CF), which was formed in the Czech Republic, worked closely with its Slovak counterpart, the Public against Violence (PAV), in the overthrow of the Communist regime; and indeed, though the first elected president of the federal state, Vaclav Havel, is Czech, Alexander Dubcek, the former proponent of the Prague Spring who was made head of the Federal Assembly in December 1989, was a Slovak. In the run-up to the first free elections held in 1990, CF and the PAV continued to work together, and they clearly shared their opposition to the Communist Party, as did most of the newly emerging political parties in both parts of Czechoslovakia. However, some nationalist-oriented parties emerged in Slovakia almost immediately after the collapse of the old regime, as well as some with a distinct ethnic base.

The new non-Communist government instituted some measures to decentralize the federal government and to shift more power to the republics early in 1990. Signs of friction between the two republics emerged shortly after the change in power. The very name of the country became an issue in March 1990, when Havel proposed dropping the word "Socialist" from its title. Slovak activists balked at his suggestion of the "Czechoslovak Republic" as the country's new name. Several versions were debated before the "Czech and Slovak Federated Republic" was finally accepted on April 20, 1990. Before agreement was reached, however, several thousand Slovaks demonstrated for the outright separation of the Czech lands and Slovakia.[7]

Partly as a result of the strains that emerged over this issue, Czechoslovakia's three governments—the federal, Czech, and Slovak—held discussions during the summer of 1990 that culminated in the Trencianske Teplice agreement on August 8 and 9, 1990. This set out guidelines for the drafting of new constitutions at both the federal and republican levels. However, several Slovak political parties vetoed this agreement, and called instead for a sovereign and independent Slovak republic.[8] Several of the parties that objected to the Trencianske Teplice agreement argued that a new Slovak constitution ought to be designed to make federal laws superfluous, and also proposed that Slovak immediately be declared the official and state language in Slovakia.[9]

Signs of antagonism toward Czechs within Slovakia accompanied the debate over the relative rights of the federal and state governments during the summer of 1990.[10] The success of the Slovak National Party, which won 14 percent of the vote in the Slovak parliamentary elections held in June 1990, reinforced the appeal of nationalism as a rallying cry.[11] This led some of the other parties in Slovakia, notably the Christian Democratic Party, led by Jan Carnogursky, to adopt more nationalist positions.[12]

Negotiations over a power-sharing agreement between the federal and republican governments were further exacerbated by the adoption of a language law by the federal government in the fall of 1990. Slovak nationalist groups protested a provision granting the right to schooling and legal representation in a minority mother tongue in places where 20 percent of the population belonged to a given group. The main effect of this federal law, however, was to induce Slovak nationalists to demand more actively that Slovak laws be given precedence over federal ones. As the debate over state's rights in Slovakia became increasingly radicalized, Slovak nationalists, angered by the prospective accord, held a march in Bratislava on November 17, 1990, demanding independence.[13]

Sovereignty became an increasingly potent tool in the struggle for popular support in Slovakia in 1991. Prime Minister Meciar, in an unsuccessful bid to take control of the PAV in February 1991, began to question the organization's aims, and to argue that nationalist concerns ought to be given a higher priority than simply as one of five equal pillars in the PAV's political platform, as had been agreed in the fall of 1992.[14] Meciar and his supporters took an increasingly populist stand, decrying the pace of the national economic reforms that had been introduced early in 1991 as "unsuitable for Slovakia," and proposing that a referendum be held on the future of the federal state.[15] Indeed, following his unsuccessful bid to gain control of the PAV, Meciar and his followers established a new group, called the Public Against Violence—for a Democratic Slovakia (MDS).[16] There were further demonstrations in Slovakia in mid-March advocating the primacy of Slovak laws over federal ones, as well as demands for a separate Slovak economic system and armed forces, and independence.[17]

This discord culminated on April 23, 1991, in the recall of Meciar and seven of his ministers by the Presidium of the Slovak National Council, and the appointment of Carnogursky as new prime minister. Meciar's critics accused him of subverting the democratic system in Slovakia by acting without consulting the Slovak government.[18] Yet Meciar's populist stand had made him, by the spring of 1991, the most popular politician in Slovakia. His recall provoked a demonstration of 50,000 people in Bratislava supporting him, which again underlined the utility of nationalism as a political tool in Slovakia.[19]

In 1991 the general response of the federal—predominantly Czech—leadership to this resurgence of Slovak nationalism was restrained. Rather than denouncing these proposals, government figures confirmed several times that if the Slovaks wanted independence, they had the right to choose this option. Both the president and his spokesmen noted that two independent states would be better than a dysfunctional federation. Yet they were careful to note that there were a variety of options in considering changes to either sovereignty or the internal makeup of a federated state, and Havel stressed the importance of ensuring that any moves toward independence follow constitutional guidelines.[20]

As the impasse over constitutional issues continued, however, federal officials started proposing that a referendum on the federated state's future be held to resolve this question.[21] This idea was rejected by several leading Slovak politicians. In good part, this was based on the knowledge that in opinion polls held in Slovakia, the majority of the population had repeatedly favored the unified state, which meant that those leaders basing their popularity on nationalist rhetoric stood to lose if an open vote on the federation were held.[22]

The prolonged stalemate over this issue left the federal government of Czechoslovakia paralyzed. Growing Czech frustration with Slovak recalcitrance led to counter moves by the Czech parliament; by late summer 1991, both republican parliaments were developing contingency plans to be utilized in the event of an actual split. In the fall of 1991, the Czech parliament stated its claim to be the legal successor to the existing federal state should a breakup occur.[23] This latter move came in response to a narrowly averted attempt by Slovak nationalist groups in September 1991 to compel the Slovak National Council to hold a vote on a declaration of Slovak sovereignty; a similar demand was again barely avoided in November. By that time, Havel had requested changes in the newly established referendum law to give not only the Federal Assembly but also the president power to call a referendum, since the federal parliament had been deadlocked on this issue due to Slovak resistance and disagreements over wording of any referendum questions. Havel failed to gain approval for such a move, and by early 1992 even he was noting that the breakup of the state seemed increasingly likely, given the inability of the two groups to find any acceptable compromise.[24]

The irony of these calls for Slovak independence was that virtually no one in either republic disputed the fact that Slovakia would suffer from such a step far more than would the Czech lands. Though it would obviously be hurt as well, the Czech economy was far more advanced, and more likely to be able to expand its ties with the West through trade and foreign investment. Slovakia, in contrast, was far less technologically developed, and was saddled with most of the federated state's outdated heavy industry and munitions plants that had been built to meet Soviet goals in the aftermath of World War II.[25]

Growing nationalist sentiment in Slovakia had led by early 1992 to a situation in which at least a minority in the republic was pushing for the right to form an independent state, while at the same time rejecting the rights of minorities in Slovakia.[26] The paralysis caused by the political stalemate hindered the federal government's efforts to address the state's urgent economic problems.

The spring 1992 elections, therefore, took on additional significance for the future of the republic. The two issues that appear to have been critical to the course of this election were nationalism and economic policies. In the Czech lands, Vaclav Klaus's Civic Democratic Party focused its campaign on continuing the economic reforms at all costs; the strong support Klaus received suggested that a significant part of the population favored economic reform even if it complicated relations between the Czech lands and Slovakia.

The election results in Slovakia confirmed Meciar's strength, reinforcing his popularity, the increasing pull of nationalism, and differing attitudes toward economic reforms. The contrast with the Czech lands was pointed, since Meciar advocated slowing the reform process to make it less painful for Slovakia, and insisted that he would not halt arms production, in deference to the importance of the arms industry in Slovakia. Meciar's success was also based on the anti-Hungarian sentiment expressed in his campaign.

The June elections for the federal state thus doomed Czechoslovakia. The economic aims of the governments in Slovakia and the Czech lands were seriously at odds, as were their views on possible solutions to the federal crisis. While Meciar continued to advocate the maintenance of a loose confederation, rather than a complete break, the Czech leadership rejected this option, stating that if the states could not agree to remain in a workable federation, then they should make a clean break, so both could move forward.

The June elections led to Klaus's appointment as prime minister in the Czech lands. When negotiations between Klaus and Meciar in late June ended in stalemate, an agreement was reached to create a weak and clearly temporary federal government until the country's future could be settled. An integrated solution was clearly no longer an option, however. Klaus's determination to proceed with market economic reforms (and his irritation with Meciar's obstructionism) led him to favor the dissolution of Czechoslovakia, and by the end of July 1992, Klaus and Meciar had agreed on the division of the country.[27] Ironically, once it became apparent that the Czech lands were prepared to go their own way, Meciar tried to sustain at least a confederation;[28] nonetheless, the dissolution of the federal state took place at the end of 1992, leading to the establishment of the Czech Republic and Slovakia as independent countries on January 1, 1993.

Ethnic Hungarians in Slovakia

Slovak nationalism was clearly central to the breakup of Czechoslovakia. The achievement of an independent state did not ease the Slovak need for recognition and "justice," however; instead it fueled tensions between ethnic Slovaks and minorities in the new state, especially the Hungarian minority.[29]

A sizable Hungarian minority lives in Slovakia along the southern border with Hungary, some of the most fertile land in Slovakia. The post-Communist Hungarian government affirmed its recognition of its existing borders, but some Hungarian politicians have also vehemently insisted that the government must defend the interests of all Hungarians regardless of their state of residence, which created tensions with most of Hungary's neighbors.[30] While the actual threat of border encroachments by Hungary is virtually nonexistent, this tension fed Slovak nationalist sentiment against minority rights in Slovakia.

The Hungarian minority makes up 11 percent of Slovakia's population. During the revolution in November 1989, some ethnic Hungarians joined the PAV, the Slovak counterpart of the Czech Civic Forum, in the struggle to overthrow the existing government. A variety of Hungarian cultural and pseudo–trade union organizations were set up shortly after the government shake-up began in November 1989.[31] But the most important organizations to emerge were two major Hungarian political parties in Slovakia: the Coexistence Movement and the Hungarian Christian Democratic Movement (HCDM).[32]

In contrast to Romania, there have been marked differences of opinion between the new Hungarian political movements in Slovakia since the introduction of pluralism in 1990. The main split to emerge was between those who cooperated with the PAV (the Independent Hungarian Initiative, FMK), and the alliance formed by the Coexistence Movement and the Christian Democratic Movement, which was backed by Csemadok, which had been the only officially recognized Hungarian organization in Czechoslovakia prior to November 1989.[33] The main disagreement between these groups was based on the priority they placed on the collective and individual rights of minorities.[34] The political differences between these organizations led to mutual recriminations, including attacks by the FMK on Csemadok's "Stalinist" past.

The split within the PAV in 1990 over the issue of Slovak nationalism, fomented by Meciar, had a definite impact on the FMK's attitude toward both the PAV and the other Hungarian political organizations in Slovakia. Over the course of the summer of 1990, Meciar adopted a more confrontational stance with regard to Hungary and the rights of the Hungarian minority in Slovakia, declaring after talks with the Hungarian president that Slovakia would not be willing to cooperate with Hungary on questions regarding the problems of minorities until Hungary took similar actions with regard to minorities in Hungary, especially the Slovak minority there. In spite of objections by the FMK, ostensibly one of its members, the PAV also began to attack groups such as the Coexistence Movement, charging that it, along with groups like the Slovak Nationalist Party, was spreading disinformation and deliberately radicalizing the domestic situation in Slovakia. The PAV also protested that the Hungarian Republic was interfering in Czechoslovak internal affairs.[35]

As Slovak nationalist sentiment gradually built during the summer of 1990, greater animosity toward the Hungarian minority began to emerge.[36] One consequence of this was that three of the main Hungarian parties in Slovakia—The Coexistence Movement, the Hungarian Christian Democratic Movement, and the Hungarian People's Party (HPP)—formed a coalition in April 1992 in order to improve their chances of representation in the upcoming elections.[37] This coalition succeeded in winning 7.4 percent of the vote, thus gaining fourteen seats in the Slovak National Council, as well as representation in the Federal Assembly.[38] The results of the June elections in Slovakia made clear that a majority of ethnic Hungarians placed higher priority on minority rights than on other issues facing the state, and that they favored a position independent of Meciar's PAV—even in alliance with organizations that had a questionable past.

The ethnic Hungarian minority in Slovakia, like that elsewhere in East-Central Europe, insisted that minorities have the right to separate schools with instruction only in the Hungarian language, from elementary school to the university level, as well as the right to use their native language at all levels of public administration in districts where they make up a significant portion of the population, and to have their own churches.[39] The issue of restorating Hungarian-language schools met with serious resistance from Slovak officials and the Slovak population in 1990, as some groups argued that Hungarian schools in Slovakia would be sources of nationalism and potential irredentism.[40] Slovak concerns about Hungarian intentions were undoubtedly exacerbated by Hungarian Prime Minister Jozef Antall's claims in the spring of 1990 that he represented all Hungarians, including those outside Hungary.[41]

Both ethnic Hungarian groups and nationalist-minded Slovak groups tended, over the next year, to exaggerate the strains between these different groups in Slovakia, and the role played by the Hungarian government in fomenting problems in the country. Leading Csemadok officials, for example, complained of an anti-Hungarian campaign in the media, citing charges that Hungarians in southern Slovakia were demanding border revisions and were insulting Slovaks.[42] Other mutual accusations included claims that a high-ranking official of the PAV had said that Hungarian-language schools had been closed in Slovakia because of economic difficulties—and a lack of interest; while a leading Czech newspaper reported that units of the Hungarian army were being deployed along the border with Slovakia, and that Hungarian reconnaissance officers were operating in parts of Slovakia inhabited by ethnic Hungarians.[43]

The stimulus of the most heated objection by the Hungarian minority, however, was the adoption of a new language law in Slovakia. Debate over a new language law began in the spring of 1990. Three different versions were proposed by the Slovak Heritage Foundation, the PAV and the Christian Democratic Movement together, and the Coexistence Movement. The last of these was not considered by the parliament in its deliberations. These proposals clearly reflected the political leanings of each group; the Slovak Heritage Foundation, for example, called for recognizing Slovak as the only official language in the republic. In October 1990, the Slovak parliament adopted a law on languages that granted minorities the right to use their language for official dealings in those cities and communities in which they made up at least 20 percent of the population. The Hungarian community considered this a serious setback. The fact that employees of state institutions were not required to speak or use minority languages, and that public documents, official correspondence, and geographic names would remain only in the state's "official" language, also angered the Hungarian minority. Even this law, however, triggered protests from Slovak nationalists.[44]

The federal reaction to this debate was muted. Though the federal government did not specifically object to the debate in Slovakia on a new language bill, Havel cautioned the Slovak parliament prior to the vote, noting that Czechoslovakia's return to Europe might be complicated if it ignored the norms of European organizations on this subject.[45] On the federal level, the adoption of a Bill of Fundamental Rights and Liberties on January 9, 1991, was probably a more important indication of the federal government's hopes to resolve this question; this guaranteed minorities the right to develop their own culture and language without discrimination.[46] Hungarian representatives in the parliament were unhappy with this as well, calling the provision on language rights too vague to be useful. Thus, though far less problematic than the rift between Czechs and Slovaks, the Hungarian issue continued to be a nagging concern in Czechoslovakia throughout 1991.[47]

Sources of Tension in Slovakia: External and Internal

Since Slovakia announced its independence on January 1, 1993, three issues have strained Slovak-Hungarian relations: the controversy over the Gabcikovo-Nagymoros dam project; concerns about the Hungarian-Slovak border; and Slovakia's treatment of its ethnic Hungarian minority.

The Gabcikovo-Nagymoros project grew out of a Soviet proposal initially made in the 1950s, which resulted in a treaty between Hungary and Czechoslovakia, signed in 1977, agreeing jointly to build a hydroelectric project on the Danube River. In 1989, following several years of environmental protests and growing government concerns, and despite the project's near completion, the Hungarian government decided to withdraw from the project, citing financial, economic, and domestic political reasons.[48] Czechoslovakia continued construction on its part of the project at Gabcikovo, though this required changes in the plans for damming the Danube. Hungary and the ethnic Hungarian minority in Slovakia opposed this construction, the latter primarily on ecological grounds.[49]

In spite of strong lobbying from Hungary in 1992, Slovak Prime Minister Meciar began the diversion of the Danube into the new channel, which would fill the dam and start the hydroelectric plant, on October 24, 1992. This led to increased protests from both Hungary and the international community. On October 28, Hungary and Czechoslovakia agreed to submit their dispute over Gabcikovo-Nagymoros to the International Court of Justice (ICJ), and Czechoslovakia agreed to allow 95 percent of the Danube's flow to return to its original channel. This would preclude the ecological changes that Hungary feared until a decision was reached.[50] Slovakia, however, did not honor this agreement, returning only 20 percent of the Danube's flow to its previous channel.[51] While Slovakia and Hungary agreed on April 7, 1993, to accede to the ICJ's judgment, this did not provide an immediate solution, since a ruling could not be expected for several years.

Hungary further exacerbated the situation in October 1993 by declaring that it would begin dismantling the construction that had been completed earlier on its part of the original project. Slovakia objected to this, arguing that Hungary must await the ICJ's ruling on the entire dispute. Slovakia also announced its intention to complete the diversion of the river, and to put its power plant at Gabcikovo into full operation.

The judgment on this dispute by the International Court of Justice left the resolution of the Gabcikovo-Nagymoros project in doubt. In September 1997 the court ruled that both Hungary and (Czecho-)Slovakia violated certain provisions of the 1977 treaty. It called on Slovakia and Hungary to negotiate in good faith to find a means to achieve the objectives of the treaty, while taking into account environmental and other concerns, and it called on each side to compensate the other for the consequences of their treaty violations.[52] How the two states would respond to the ICJ's ruling in the long run remains uncertain.

Second, resolving historical questions about the Hungarian-Slovak border proved to be an obstacle to smooth relations between these states. Despite their limited initial interest in cooperation with each other following the collapse of the Warsaw Pact, the new governments of East-Central Europe realized that cooperation with each other was a necessary prerequisite to the coveted membership in Western institutions. This led, in February 1991, to the establishment of the Visegrad Triangle as a loose consulting group including Poland, Hungary, and Czechoslovakia.[53] Additionally, the East European states continued the Soviet practice of signing bilateral treaties as the basis for friendly relations.

The new Hungarian government, however, was slow to sign treaties with several of its neighbors. There were two complicating factors: Hungary's desire to include regard for minority rights in these treaties, meaning the ethnic Hungarian minority outside its borders, and its neighbors' insistence that Hungary renounce any territorial claims. Hungary had previously signed a bilateral treaty with Ukraine that included both of these provisions. Yet the Hungarian government demurred from offering a formal guarantee of the present borders to other states, absent the minority clauses it favored. Slovakia and Romania, the two states with substantial Hungarian minorities, rejected the codification of minority rights in such a treaty. Slovakia's Prime Minister Meciar argued that individual rights were sufficient and group rights immaterial under European law.[54]

This stalemate lasted until March 1995, when a bilateral Hungarian-Slovak treaty on Good Neighborly Relations and Friendly Cooperation was finally signed. Slovakia did not formally ratify the treaty until March 1996, and it only did so after adding a unilateral declaration that this treaty did not provide for "collective" autonomy for Slovakia's ethnic Hungarians, since the formal treaty language had stipulated that the Hungarian minority as a "community" be protected.[55] Budapest has continued to support the autonomy of minority communities outside its borders "in accordance with European practice," though it has not pressed either Slovakia or other neighboring states to grant autonomy.

Critical to even the partial resolution of the minority issue between Hungary and Slovakia was the change in government in Hungary in the summer of 1994, which led to a shift in policy priorities. Under Prime Minister Gyula Horn, Hungary gave good relations with its neighbors greater precedence than protection of the Hungarian minority abroad. This was a marked shift from the preceding Antall government's position.[56]

Clearly, the border issue was entangled with the third source of friction between Hungary and Slovakia: the Slovak government's treatment of its ethnic Hungarian minority. Several factors have exacerbated tensions over the Hungarian minority, including historical resentment and anxiety, Hungarian government statements, the rise of nationalism in Slovakia, and the Slovak leadership's willingness to both fuel and exploit this nationalism for its own purposes.

Historical resentment and anxieties exist on both sides. Slovaks resent the history of Hungarian rule, which they considered (with some justification) repressive and assimilationist.[57] More recently, Slovakia has feared the loss of the territory it gained at Hungary's expense in the Peace Treaty of Trianon in 1920. These fears were exacerbated by the statement of Hungary's first democratically elected prime minister, Jozef Antall, that he was "in spirit" the prime minister of 15 million Hungarians. The population of Hungary is only 10.5 million, and since the remaining 4.5 million Hungarians reside mostly in neighboring states, these states viewed this statement as an indication of revisionist aims.[58]

Hungary's efforts to codify minority rights in its bilateral treaties with neighboring states and its advocacy of autonomy for these communities while Antall was prime minister aggravated fears that it endorsed autonomy as a first step toward secession.[59] The Slovak leadership, in turn, heightened the concerns of both Hungary and its own Hungarian minority by passing laws establishing Slovak as the official state language. Though the first language law in the post-Communist state allowed for the use of minority languages in areas where a minority made up 20 percent or more of the population, this led to heated objections from the radical nationalist Slovak parties. Subsequent laws to "protect" Slovak language and culture led to insistence on the Slovakization of foreign names and the rejection of bilingual street signs even in minority-dominated communities.[60]

The dispute between Hungary and Slovakia over Slovakia's treatment of its minority eased once Horn's government came to power in Hungary, due to Hungary's larger interest in European integration. The removal of Prime Minister Meciar from power in Slovakia in the spring of 1994 aided the improvement of relations with Hungary; the new government under Jozef Moravcik reiterated its interest in Western integration and, as a result, continued its consultations both with Hungary over bilateral relations and with European organizations over broader questions of the treatment of minorities.[61]

Treatment of the Hungarian minority remained doubtful, however. Meciar was reelected in October 1994, which both slowed Slovakia's economic reforms and kept nationalist sentiment as a central part of the political debate.[62] Indeed, a new Slovak language law, passed in November 1995, restricted the use of any language other than Slovak, in contradiction to both the Slovak constitution and to the 1990 language law that guaranteed minority language rights.[63] An additional source of tension was Meciar's proposal to redraw administrative units in Slovakia. The ethnic Hungarian minority viewed this as a clear attempt to weaken its political representation and voice, since the territory where most ethnic Hungarians reside would be parceled into several administrative districts, rather than one.[64]

Hungarian concerns were further exacerbated by Meciar's suggestion to Hungarian President Horn in September 1997 that the two countries initiate "voluntary" repatriation of their ethnic minorities. This suggestion raised particular concern because it appeared to be an effort to exploit nationalist sentiment as Slovakia began to prepare for elections in 1998.[65]

Though the problems between the Slovak government and the ethnic Hungarian minority are quite real, it is important to remember that these have comprised only one of the political problems confronting Slovakia. Slovakia was not included in the first round of states invited to join either NATO or the EU in 1997, largely because of its poor democratic credentials. This lack of democratic credentials reflects the main cleavage in Slovak society, which is intra-Slovak, rather than Slovak-Hungarian. This cleavage is based on cultural, and especially urban-rural differences about the nature of the state, and it has far-reaching implications for the country's future. Will it choose Western values and standards, or continue to move, as it did under Meciar's leadership in the last few years, toward a more authoritarian model, either isolated in Europe or aligned with states to the east?[66]

Western Efforts to Decrease the Likelihood of Conflict

Western efforts to lessen the possibility of conflict in Slovakia fall into two broad categories: mediation and economic assistance. Two main groups have attempted to mediate in Slovakia: the Council of Europe, and the Organization for Security and Cooperation in Europe, through its High Commissioner on National Minorities. In addition to these mediation efforts, several Western actors have offered technical assistance and aid to Slovakia to promote market reforms and democratization. One aim of these programs is to help stabilize the country politically and economically, which should ease tensions between minority groups.[67]

The Council of Europe

The Council of Europe established a series of assistance programs beginning in 1989, with the aim of promoting European integration and democratic security (meaning a pluralist, parliamentary democratic system), respect for human rights, and the rule of law. The two central goals of the assistance programs since their inception have been the consolidation and acceleration of democratic reform in Central and Eastern Europe, and the integration of these countries into European structures, especially the Council of Europe. Accordingly, the council has initiated programs in the areas of institution building, training of justices and lawyers, and grassroots democracy building. The Council of Europe has worked jointly with the European Commission (of the European Union) in some of these areas, particularly in its activities in Albania, the Baltic states, Russia, and Ukraine.[68]

Following the breakup of Czechoslovakia, the Hungarian government attempted to block Slovakia's inclusion in the Council of Europe until the latter guaranteed the rights of its ethnic Hungarian minority, in particular by accepting that minorities had the right to establish autonomous territorial units. This outraged Slovakia and caused friction between Hungary and the Czech Republic, since Hungary's Prime Minister Antall tried to enlist Prime Minister Klaus's support for Hungary's position in this effort. It also raised concern in the West because the Council of Europe wanted to admit the Czech Republic and Slovakia simultaneously, as the two successor states to Czechoslovakia.[69] This controversy led the secretary general of the Council of Europe to propose that, together with the CSCE, the council should help deal with the minority question through confidence-building measures and by appointing an ombudsman to monitor minority rights.[70] Slovakia was admitted to the Council of Europe along with the Czech Republic on June 29, 1993; the Hungarian delegation abstained from voting on its entry.[71]

Since then, the Council of Europe has conducted training programs and provided educational materials and documents on human rights, legal co-operation, and various aspects of civil society. It has also carried out study visits to examine the protection of the rights of minorities and Slovakia's adherence to international and bilateral agreements in this area.[72]

The OSCE High Commissioner on National Minorities

The Conference on Security and Cooperation in Europe (CSCE, now the OSCE) established the post of High Commissioner on National Minorities (HCNM) in 1992, in recognition that ethnic conflict had become a major cause of violence and potential violence in Europe. The HCNM's function is to identify incipient ethnic tensions and warn the OSCE about potential conflicts, and to try to attenuate them before they result in conflict; he is "an instrument of conflict prevention at the earliest possible stage."[73] The HCNM operates independently, with the aim of promoting dialogue and cooperation, and finding compromises acceptable to all parties in a potential conflict. Particularly important for the HCNM's mission is the guarantee of confidentiality surrounding his efforts. This is intended to facilitate compromise between groups that might not be willing to show flexibility in more public statements.

The HCNM became involved in Slovakia when it appeared that regular third-party involvement could be a useful confidence-building measure between Hungarians and Slovakians in Slovakia, and to defuse tension with neighboring Hungary. A team of experts was established in 1993 to analyze impartially the situation of Hungarians in Slovakia and Slovakians in Hungary, based on CSCE (OSCE) principles. The experts were appointed for a two-year period, with the right to conduct up to four study visits to both countries. Following these visits, the experts submitted advice and recommendations to the HCNM, who passed this information on to the governments of Slovakia and Hungary in the form he considered to be appropriate. This advice was nonbinding.[74] The expert team paid four visits to Slovakia and Hungary between October 1993 and June 1995, and the HCNM, Max van der Stoel, also visited Slovakia to consult with the Slovak government and members of the Hungarian minority on the government's planned administrative reforms.

The team's investigations varied over time, as it examined planned administrative reforms and their consequences for the Hungarian minority; education issues such as the question of instruction in the Slovak language in Hungarian schools, training Hungarian teachers, and the creation of alternative bilingual education; the adoption of laws on bilingual road signs; the development of instruments of dialogue between the Slovak majority and the Hungarian minority; the government's cultural policy, especially the principles of the proposed Slovak language law; and the ratification of a Slovak-Hungarian treaty.[75] In his official recommendations to the governments of Slovakia and Hungary, the HCNM frequently cited international standards that these governments had agreed to uphold, and suggested further consultations on legislative drafts with both the Council of Europe and the OSCE, and with members of the minority communities.[76]

Slovakia's response to the mediation efforts of both the Council of Europe and the OSCE has been mixed. As noted above, the Slovak language law passed in November 1995 left the legality of minority languages, previously protected, in doubt. Both the European Commission and the HCNM continue to urge the Slovak government to pass a law protecting the use of minority languages, pointing out both that Slovakia agreed to European standards of minority rights, and that its efforts to join the EU will be damaged by its failure to submit a minority language law.[77] That these efforts have had some effect is clear from statements by Slovak officials that a minority language law is under preparation. The main obstacle to this legislation was the government of Prime Minister Meciar, which used language as an instrument to promote Slovak national identity. This was part of the government's nationalist cultural orientation, and its less than democratic approach to opposition groups of all sorts within Slovakia.[78] Ironically, the fact that the government restricted the free press and attempted to oversee interpretations of Slovak culture by controlling the Slovak National Theater, among other things, meant that the Hungarian minority could not feel singled out by the government for mistreatment on the basis of nationality. Yet this was hardly a long-term solution, and Western mediation efforts are likely to continue.

The European Union's Phare Program

The aims of the Phare program are to "build a larger family of democratic nations" in Europe. By providing training in a variety of areas such as private sector development, infrastructure, agricultural restructuring, and institutional reform, the Phare program aims to support both economic restructuring and the transition to democracy in Central and Eastern Europe.[79] In the long run, this should speed these countries in their goal of joining the European Union. It is also intended to help ensure that they sustain stable pluralist political systems in the interim, which is in the EU's interest.

American Aid to Slovakia

American aid to Slovakia has been distributed through three separate programs: the Support for East European Development (SEED) assistance program, the International Military Education and Training (IMET) program, and the Warsaw Initiative, or Partnership for Peace (PFP) funding. Each program has distinct aims, though all intend to promote stability and democratization in Slovakia and elsewhere in Eastern Europe. The SEED program, initiated throughout Central and Eastern Europe in January 1992, is meant to help the Slovak republic create a functioning market democracy; to promote Slovakia's good relations with its neighbors and integration with Euro-Atlantic political and security organizations; and to encourage it to promote responsible export and nonproliferation policies, given its substantial arms industry.[80]

The objectives of IMET are to bring military justice systems into agreement with international human rights norms; to expand understanding of key elements of the American democratic system, including the judicial system, the two-party system, the role played by a free press, unions, and educational institutions; to improve civil-military relations in participant countries; and to help shape existing civil-military systems to suit a country's particular circumstances.[81] Though it has come to be associated with NATO expansion, the PFP was originally intended as a mechanism to put off discussion about possible expansion of the alliance, while at the same time deepening political and military ties between NATO and the countries of Eastern Europe and the former Soviet Union. Its activities include joint exercises between NATO and partner countries, discussion of issues such as civilian defense oversight and military budgets, and planning for inter-operability of military equipment between NATO and PFP countries. The PFP remains distinct from the issue of NATO enlargement, and will continue, since its aim of ensuring continued cooperation and stability in the region continues to be pertinent.[82] Moreover, NATO spokesmen insist that the first group of states invited to join in 1997 will not be the last, so the PFP remains crucial as a mechanism for helping other states achieve the attributes of democracy and stability viewed as necessary for NATO membership.

The European Bank for Reconstruction and Development

The European Bank for Reconstruction and Development (EBRD) was created after the collapse of communism in Eastern Europe, to aid in the transition to market economies in these states (and later the former Soviet Union) by investing in projects in the region, and thereby encouraging private banks and businesses to do so as well. It has concentrated on support for private-sector projects, or equity investments in individual companies that are either in the process of privatizing or are restructuring after privatization, in the case of voucher privatization. The EBRD was active in

Czechoslovakia prior to its collapse, and the projects it had underway were continued once the country split. Since then, the EBRD has granted loans and funded investments in twenty projects in Slovakia.

The World Bank

Slovakia joined the World Bank and the International Development Association (IDA) in January 1993, after the breakup of Czechoslovakia. It received a portion of the structural adjustment loans that the bank had allocated for Czechoslovakia, and has received some assistance through the bank's Global Environment Facility (GEF) to phase out ozone-depleting substances and to protect biodiversity.

Costs of Conflict Prevention to International Actors

Costs to outside actors include international organizations' efforts to mediate disputes between Slovakia and Hungary as well as between the Slovak government and the ethnic Hungarian minority in Slovakia, and aid and assistance to promote economic and political restructuring in Slovakia after the dissolution of Czechoslovakia (see table 8.1).

Council of Europe Costs

The Council of Europe's expenditures in Slovakia cover its support for assistance and cooperation programs. The total budget for its 1996 assistance programs to Central and Eastern Europe was estimated at 70 million French francs, or $12,287,000; of this, roughly 1 million French francs, or $175,530, was allocated for programs in Slovakia.[83] A similar sum was appropriated for 1997.[84] Assuming that roughly equal funding was allocated from 1993 to 1995 for programs in Slovakia, the Council of Eu-

TABLE 8.1
Slovakia: Mediation Costs ($U.S. Millions)

Council of Europe	1.05
OSCE High Commissioner on National Minorities	0.75
TOTAL	**1.80**

Sources: Assistance with the Development and Consolidation of Democratic Security: Cooperation and Assistance Programmes with Countries of Central and Eastern Europe, Annual Report 1996 (Strasbourg: Council of Europe, 1997), 149, 175. Max van der Stoel, "The OSCE High Commissioner on National Minorities," *OSCE ODIHR Bulletin,* 3 no. 3 (1995), 40–41.

rope's total expenses for mediation and education in Slovakia would be about $1 million for this six-year period.

Costs of the OSCE High Commissioner on National Minorities

The OSCE budgeted roughly $1 million to the High Commissioner on National Minorities in FY1997 to cover management, travel for the commissioner, and for reporting to the OSCE headquarters in Vienna. The HCNM's activities in Slovakia presumably are included in the accounting for each of these categories.[85] The HCNM's activities in Slovakia are linked with those in Hungary, where he is monitoring the Slovak minority. These two are among twelve situations that the HCNM was monitoring in 1995.[86] Assuming that the HCNM's budget was allotted in equal portions to each project, this means that two-twelfths of the budget would go to the Slovak-Hungarian projects.[87] Thus, roughly $167,000 would be available to the HCNM for work in Slovakia and Hungary in FY1997.

Since the HCNM's mediation efforts began in late 1993, we can assume it incurred roughly similar costs in 1994, 1995, and 1996, and approximately half of these costs in 1993. Thus, total expenses by the HCNM for mediation between Slovakia and Hungary can be estimated at $750,000.

Aid and Assistance Costs

From 1990 to 1994, the European Union's Phare program allocated 80 million ECUs, or $92.64 million, to projects in Slovakia, out of a total expenditure of 4,248.5 million ECUs.[88] Calculating from its overall budget for 1995 of 964 million ECUs, expenditure in Slovakia at a similar ratio of the total would equal 18.15 million ECUs in FY1995, or about $21 million.[89] With estimated overall expenditures in 1996 of 1,037 million ECUs, the expenditure for Slovakia would be 19.5 million ECUs, or $22.6 million. Total Phare expenditures from 1990 through 1997, then, are about $136.3 million.

American aid costs include SEED money, IMET, and the PFP program. In FY1995, the SEED money allocation to Slovakia was $27,334,000; the estimate for FY1996 was $16 million, and the projected estimate for FY 1997 was $15 million.[90] IMET expenditures in Slovakia were $253,000 in FY1995; they were estimated at $530,000 in FY1996, with $600,000 requested for FY1997. Funding for Slovakia under the PFP program was $3,550,000 in FY1996, and is projected at $6 million for FY1997; no expenditure was made in this area in 1995.[91] Total American aid to Slovakia in these areas, then, is $69,267,000.

By the end of 1996, EBRD had allocated $550 million, cumulatively from 1991, to projects in Slovakia. Eighty-seven percent of this funding went to private-sector projects.[92] Slovakia also received commitments totaling $135 million from the World Bank after Czechoslovakia dissolved (see table 8.2).[93]

Estimated Costs of Conflict

The absence of violent conflict in Slovakia, or between Slovakia and Hungary, makes it impossible to compare actual costs of a war there, or of international intervention should this have become necessary. Yet it is possible to approximate the costs of either a peacekeeping operation or an intervention following a full-scale war in the region, based on the costs of similar operations undertaken elsewhere in this region.

The population of Slovakia is 5.3 million; the ethnic Hungarian minority is 580,000, or about 11 percent of the total population.[94] Ethnic Hungarians make up 90 percent of the population in the south and southeastern parts of the state where they live. The total population in this region, the area that would require policing in the event of any external involvement, is then approximately 644,000.

Estimated Costs of Peacekeeping

A peacekeeping operation in Slovakia would probably be similar in structure to the peacekeeping effort undertaken by the United Nations in Macedonia, UNPREDEP. The population of Macedonia is about 2 million.[95] The forces involved in UNPREDEP include 1,106 troops, 35 military observers, and 26 civilian police. The estimated cost of this peacekeeping operation was $38 million in 1995, and $50 million in 1996;[96] over four years, its cost has been estimated at $204 million.[97]

The population of the predominantly ethnic Hungarian region of Slo-

TABLE 8.2
Slovakia: Aid and Assistance Costs ($U.S. Millions)

Phare	136.27
American Aid	69.27
European Bank for Reconstruction and Development	550.00
World Bank	135.00
TOTAL	**890.54**

Sources: Slovak Republic: Country Overview, available at www.worldbank.org/html/etrdr/offrep/eca/svkcb.htm; *What Is Phare? A European Union Initiative for Economic Integration with Central and Eastern European Countries* (Brussels: European Commission, 1996). U.S. Department of State, *Congressional Presentation for Foreign Operations, Fiscal Year 1997* (Washington, D.C.: Congressional Information Service, 1996), 309.

vakia is roughly one-third of Macedonia's population. We can assume that only the region with a substantial minority, near the border with Hungary, would need to be patrolled by a peacekeeping mission if such an operation were undertaken, rather than the entire Slovak state. Therefore, an observer force for this region would be about one-half to one-third the size of that necessary for Macedonia; the cost (given higher start–up costs than maintenance) would be about half that of expenditures in Macedonia, or $25 million per year.

The Costs of Intervention after the Outbreak of Conflict

Given geographic and cultural similarities, the UN peacekeeping operation in Eastern Slavonia, Baranja, and Western Sirmium (UNTAES) is probably comparable to what would be necessary in southern and southeastern Slovakia to restore and maintain the peace if a violent conflict broke out within the predominantly ethnic Hungarian region of Slovakia. UNTAES involved 4,481 troops, 99 military observers, and 257 civilian police, and cost an estimated $383.5 million over eighteen months.[98]

There are two possible models for internal policing (in terms of ratio of troops to population): low-level policing, such as the standard American police force in an urban area, and high-level policing, of the type conducted by British security forces in Northern Ireland. High-level policing, such as the Northern Ireland case, requires a ratio of 20 troops per thousand of population. For high-level policing, at a ratio of 20 per thousand, 12,893 officers would be required.[99] This suggests that the number of troops necessary to conduct an operation similar to UNTAES in the portion of Slovakia inhabited primarily by ethnic Hungarians would be about 12,900 total troops, observers, and military police. This force would be 2.58 times as large as the UNTAES force. Assuming comparable costs of introduction and maintenance, such a force would cost roughly 2.58 times as much, or $659 million per year. Both the Bosnian operation and UNTAES will continue (in some form) for a minimum of two years; thus, such an operation in southern Slovakia would cost the international community over $1 billion for two years (see table 8.3).

TABLE 8.3
Slovakia: Estimated Costs of a Conflict and Postconflict Intervention ($U.S. Billions)

Military policing	.66
Humanitarian costs	.60
TOTAL	**1.26**

Humanitarian and refugee costs would raise this figure. The humanitarian costs incurred by a variety of UN agencies during the Bosnian operation were around $2 billion per year.[100] The costs of similar efforts in Slovakia, with about one-third the population of Bosnia, can be estimated at roughly one-third of this total, or $600 million per year. Refugee costs would also be significant, though primarily for Hungary and Slovakia itself; ethnic Hungarians would be likely to flee across the border to Hungary, while Slovaks seeking to avoid the conflict would be expected to emigrate internally. Estimates of the costs to these two countries are not available. But since private and nongovernmental organizations provided about $200 million to help address refugee costs to Germany and other states due to the violence in Bosnia, an additional $50–$100 million would probably be required to aid refugees in Hungary and Slovakia in the event of a conflict.[101]

Conclusions

Mediation in Slovakia has cost roughly $1.8 million. Additionally, Western organizations have spent about $890 million for both democratization assistance and investment in Slovakia to aid the shift to a market economy. This adds up to a cost of less than $1 billion spent by the international community over seven years to mediate internal and external disputes in Slovakia, to aid in economic reconstruction and development, and to promote democracy.

If the international community concluded that a preventive force in southeastern Slovakia was necessary to preclude the outbreak of conflict, this could cost roughly $25 million per year, a substantially higher figure than the total expenditure of $1.8 million on mediation over the last six years. Yet preventive peacekeeping would be far cheaper than intervention to quell a violent conflict in Slovakia, which could be expected to cost about $1.2 billion per year between military and humanitarian expenditures.

In the final analysis, this study illustrates that mediation efforts are not only far cheaper than prevention or intervention efforts, but they have probably played a useful role in preventing tensions from escalating into conflict in Slovakia, or between Slovakia and Hungary. Yet it must be noted that mediation was beneficial in this case because of the overriding interest both Hungary and Slovakia have in joining Western institutions. This preoccupation far outweighs issues that might otherwise have aggravated relations between these two states; indeed, Slovakia's continued interest in the EU and NATO is especially telling, since it was not part of the first group of states invited to join either organization. Moreover, this preoccupation with the West has had a strong influence on the behavior of both states, though this is more apparent in Hungary's case. Their interest in joining the West has abetted Western efforts to advocate an international standard for treatment of minorities, while at the same time ruling out the option of border revisions.

The implications of this are not necessarily promising for other cases, since the greater interest Slovakia and Hungary share in achieving Western standards results from their proximity to both NATO and the EU, and the realistic likelihood that they may join these institutions in the not-too-distant future. This geographic advantage is not easily transferable to other states.[102] Nonetheless, the absence of conflict in Slovakia, a state with a significant ethnic minority and a history of grievances between the majority and minority groups, suggests that it is worth considering what external inducements might be able to do to mitigate conflict elsewhere.[103] The combination of mediation plus the prospect of greater inclusion in economic and political organizations that would enable improvements in the quality of life in a given state may provide a useful model of conflict prevention in other regions.

Part Three

Mid-Course Prevention

9

Cambodia

Andrea Kathryn Talentino

Case Preview

CAMBODIA'S HISTORY HAS BEEN MARKED by invasion, civil war, genocide, and regional turbulence. The first round of civil war started in the late 1960s when popular discontent with Prince Norodom Sihanouk's government turned to armed struggle, waged primarily by the fledgling Communist Party of Kampuchea (CPK) and assisted by the Vietnamese. In 1970 Sihanouk was overthrown in a bloodless coup and replaced by General Lon Nol, an American-backed conservative of Sihanouk's government. The CPK continued its struggle in the jungles. Five years later the Communist guerrillas, called the Khmer Rouge and led by Pol Pot, overthrew Lon Nol's government and began a four-year run of societal reorganization infamous for its brutality. The atrocities of Pol Pot's Khmer Rouge government were brought to an end by neighboring Vietnam, which invaded in December 1978 and installed a new government in Phnom Penh in early 1979, creating the People's Republic of Kampuchea (PRK).

The three ousted factions—Sihanouk's National United Front for an Independent, Neutral, Peaceful, and Cooperative Cambodia (FUNCINPEC), the conservative Khmer People's National Liberation Front (KPNLF), and the Khmer Rouge—formed a government in exile, the Coalition Government of Democratic Kampuchea (CGDK), and waged a war against the PRK throughout the 1980s. Vietnam and the Soviet Union served as the PRK's main patrons. The United States, its Western allies, and China formed an uneasy alliance behind the CGDK, making ideology the defining feature of each side's legitimacy, or lack thereof, and precluding coordinated international efforts to end the violence. The end of the Cold War opened the door for a resolution of Cambodia's divisions by inspiring Vietnam and China to seek a compromise to avoid diplomatic isolation. Vietnam's 1989 decision to remove all its troops by the end of the year allowed the first real steps toward peace.

In March 1992 the United Nations Transitional Authority for Cambodia (UNTAC) was deployed to close the curtain on decades of civil war and build a foundation for democracy. This operation arrived late in the context of the overall war, but took advantage of improving international relations and a quiet period in the civil conflict itself to intervene to prevent more violence in the future. Its mandate was extensive and its goals ambitious, including the demobilization of all armed parties, direct supervision over various areas of civil administration, protection of human rights, the organization and monitoring of elections, and the economic and social rehabilitation of the nation. Its mandate ended on September 24, 1993, after successful elections resulted in a new government, a new constitution, and the restoration of Prince Sihanouk to the throne he had abdicated over thirty years earlier. The Military Component of UNTAC completed its withdrawal in November, and the last administrative personnel left the country in May 1994.

The cost of the conflict thus far to the international community has been approximately $14.9 billion. This figure includes the cost of UNTAC, economic and military aid provided to the various governments prior to the initiation of peace talks in 1990, and humanitarian assistance provided for the conflict's refugees and displaced persons during the Cold War. Since collective intervention was effectively precluded prior to 1989, the total figure includes costs that could not have been prevented given the politics of the Cold War. Excluding costs incurred during that period, the cost of the conflict to international actors was $11.9 billion. Costs incurred during the Cold War will be dealt with in a separate section of this case study because they could not have been prevented due to the international system at the time. The $11.9 billion figure includes all military, humanitarian, and rehabilitation costs incurred since 1990, which marks the earliest year in which collective intervention would have been possible.

Since then the conflict has subsided. After some renewed violence and political instability in July 1997, the Khmer Rouge now appears to have lost strength. Thousands of its guerrillas mutinied and defected in March 1998, allowing government forces to take over their traditional stronghold of Anlong Veng. With the subsequent death of Pol Pot and the insurgency on the wane, Cambodia's chances for peace may improve dramatically.

Cambodia presents a case where the costs of an actual intervention can be compared against the costs of the actual conflict. Admittedly, the intervention occurred late in the civil war and was in some sense not entirely preventive. Prior to 1990, however, intervention had been impossible due to the ideological divisions of the Cold War. Intervention did occur at the earliest possible point, taking advantage of a lull in the fighting to attempt a mission aimed to prevent violence in the future. The international community had to rebuild the basic political and economic systems that decades of war had destroyed. The eventual intervention was intended as both conflict resolution and conflict prevention, seeking to end the hostilities while at the same time rebuilding society so as to break, permanently, the twenty-five-year cycle of war. As a result, the costs of the intervention are much higher than those the international community would have faced if action could have been taken to prevent the conflict from breaking out. The UN operation was highly effective in some areas, and the basic electoral and economic reforms that UNTAC began have not been retrenched since the mission's withdrawal. Although Cambodia's future is still somewhat shaky, UNTAC was a critical first step toward peace.

The mission did, however, fall somewhat short of its goals, leaving room for speculation on what a more effective mission might have entailed. This study will therefore analyze two interventions: the UNTAC mission that actually took place, as well as a more aggressive mission that could have been launched but was not. Both missions would have been cost-effective, although a more aggressive mission might have traded some higher operational costs for greater long-term savings by more decisively and effectively ending the conflict and solidifying the reforms that would prevent it in the future.

The cost of international intervention in the Cambodian conflict from 1991 to 1995 was $1.7 billion. The UNTAC mission involved 15,000 troops and civilian personnel divided among seven components, which encompassed the entirety of military and civil rehabilitation and were intended to be preventive of future violence. Cambodia's legacy of civil war indicated peace would be difficult to obtain, and UNTAC's wide-ranging mandate aimed to rebuild from the violence of the past and guard against potential violence in the future. This goal remained elusive at UNTAC's end. It did establish some basic elements of democracy and presided over a fair election, but armed insurgency continued. Lack of cooperation among the Cambodian factions severely compromised UNTAC's ability to carry out its military mandate of cantonment and demobilization. Of its seven components only the electoral division was successful in achieving its goals. The situation in Cambodia improved during UNTAC's tenure, but remained unstable and prone to violence at its departure. The bloody coup in July 1997 showed just how tenuous UNTAC's reforms were.

International intervention probably could not have come much sooner than it did, particularly since it followed rather immediately on the heels of negotiations that made it acceptable to all parties. But a very strong argument exists for undertaking a more aggressive intervention that could have resolved the conflict more decisively. UNTAC's comprehensive mission addressed too many problems over too short a time, and its powers of enforcement were weak. When confronted with noncompliance it had to abandon the military component of its mission, the very part most critical for demobilizing the belligerent armies. The conditions of civil violence are not markedly changed in Cambodia, except for the fact that the externally backed government has been ousted. Even that is debatable, according to the Khmer Rouge, which still exists in a state of weak but persistent opposition. The Khmer Rouge initially signed the peace accords but withdrew entirely from the political process and declared its intention to continue the civil war when UNTAC proved incapable of meeting its demobilization timetable or of compelling the various factions to honor their commitments. What UNTAC needed was not necessarily more troops but a more heavily armed military division with a more active mandate. An incident in which UNTAC representatives attempting to cross a Khmer Rouge zone were turned aside by a single bamboo pole barring the way illustrates the weakness of the mission's military mandate.[1] UNTAC would coax rather than compel. Part of the operation's problem was also its tight timetable, which forced it to proceed with elections before the requirements for demobilization and disarmament had been met. UNTAC did, however, help to stop an all-out civil war and provide the security and logistics necessary for a successful election.

The mission as established cost approximately $1 billion per year, and lasted eighteen months. A mission with similar troop levels but expanded enforcement powers and the necessary heavy weaponry would have cost $1.5 billion per year at the most. Expanding its length of operation to three years, combined with an active mandate, would have allowed the mission to achieve the demobilization that was so critical to ending the actual violence. This expanded version of UNTAC, operating at full strength for three years, would have cost $4.8 billion, still far less than the $11.9 billion post–Cold War cost of the conflict to the international community, and would have had a much better chance of ending the war.

This case study is organized into four parts. The first two will describe the origins of the conflict and then the conflict itself. The third part will analyze the costs of the conflict to regional and international actors, taking into account military, humanitarian, and economic costs. A subdivision of this section will discuss the costs paid in humanitarian assistance and aid to the various factions during the Cold War. Although intervention was an impossibility, these costs are part of the whole and important to consider when analyzing the cost-effectiveness of intervention. The fourth part will discuss the costs of UNTAC and estimate the costs of a more forceful mission and why a more forceful mission was needed. The chapter will conclude with a cost summary and calculation of savings, analyzed in the context of both the UNTAC mission as it was constituted and a cost summary based on a hypothetical, expanded mission.

Cambodia's independent history can be divided into two periods of civil war, one of which started gradually during the 1960s and the second of which began with the establishment of the Vietnamese-backed government in 1979. The first period, which ended with the installation of the Khmer Rouge regime in 1975, was a critical prelude to the latter and is treated here as the origin of the second war. This second period of war was altered somewhat by the peace agreements of 1991 and the subsequent UN mission, during which factional alliances shifted, but is essentially an extension of the war that originated in opposition to the PRK in 1979.

Origins of the Conflict

Prince Sihanouk was instrumental in achieving independence from France in 1954, and he assumed the throne as the very embodiment of Cambodian sovereignty. Though he abdicated a year later to wage the political struggle as a private citizen, for the people of Cambodia he continued to be the personification of Cambodia. Elevated to the premiership in 1957, he practiced a style of rule based on personality, symbol, patronage, and the monopolization of power. This was a successful tactic in the first heady years of independence. Most Cambodians regarded Sihanouk as a quasi-mystical ruler, and opposition was infrequent. In the early 1960s, however, the country began to experience economic and political difficulties, partly as a result of the escalating war in neighboring Vietnam. Several young Cambodians inspired by Mao began to spread their message in the countryside, suggesting to the poverty-stricken peasants that a more equitable form of social organization was possible. Discontent became increasingly vocal in urban areas as well, where low-level protests became more common. Within the government, opposition to Sihanouk's policies became more frequent as officials became frustrated by his mercurial and personalistic rule.

Sihanouk seemed increasingly unable or unwilling to halt the economic downslide or bring the country's fractious political landscape under control. In the face of declining agricultural exports, stagnant rice yields, declining wages, and rising inflation, the government began the nationalization of exports in 1963. This policy proved profoundly unpopular with people who could earn higher prices selling to the Vietnamese on the black market than the government offered them, and the soldiers entrusted with enforcing the policy proved increasingly brutal as time went on. The import-export business and related enterprises fell entirely into the hands of Sihanouk's cronies, who got richer while the plight of the average Cambodian remained unchanged by the reforms. The nationalization of the banks, also part of the reforms, led to the collapse of the Bank of Phnom Penh, which started the alienation of Cambodia's economic elite.[2]

The war in Vietnam had a profound effect on both Cambodia's economy and politics. Chinese military aid to the North Vietnamese was shuttled through Cambodia beginning in 1964, leading to the enrichment of Cambodia's officer corps, which skimmed off 10 percent.[3] Sihanouk repeatedly denied any connection to the Vietnamese, but by 1966 more than 25 percent of Cambodia's rice crop was sold illegally to the Vietnamese insurgents, unbalancing the national budget, which relied heavily on export taxes for revenue.[4] North Vietnamese and Vietcong forces were allowed to camp along Cambodia's eastern border beginning in the early 1960s, and by 1969 they exercised undisputed control over large tracts of eastern Cambodia. Critiques of Cambodian society also became increasingly frequent, spurred by Sihanouk's declining popularity, the corruption of the government, and the Chinese revolution, which impressed many among the urban elite. The expansion of educational facilities, one of Sihanouk's reforms that began in the late 1950s, also worked to his detriment by creating a more alert and informed citizenry frustrated by the social problems of the country. At the same time, anti-Americanism and anticapitalism became increasingly prevalent, and demonstrations against such Western influences occurred more frequently in the capital. Sihanouk broke ties with the United States and maintained alliances with North Vietnam and China, but the loss of American aid exacerbated the increasing indebtedness of the nation, and the government's inability to provide necessary services alienated the rural population, which continued to struggle with stagnant crop yields and low prices.

Despite Sihanouk's tilt toward socialism, the radical left remained a primarily clandestine organization, spearheaded by French-educated intellectuals frustrated by the cultish and socially ineffective rule of Sihanouk. In early 1963 Saloth Sar was named secretary of the Worker's Party of Kampuchea (WPK) central committee. Sihanouk's ideology was defined most by expediency and an aversion to any sort of opposition. By May 1963 government repression against the left forced Sar to leave Phnom Penh with his first lieutenant, Ieng Sary, and set up headquarters in the forests of eastern Cambodia under the protection of Vietnamese insurgents. At this point the WPK still had little influence over Cambodian politics, but

Sihanouk's distrust for any organization outside his direct control led to a policy of repression somewhat at odds with the strength of the Communists, and, in the long run, providing justification for their opposition. In the capital the left-wing press was censored and periodically shut down, and schools and universities were under constant supervision by the government. Government-sponsored terror against radicals increased throughout the 1960s, and the climate of repression and fear led many young people, and students in particular, to join the Communist movement.

Sihanouk's interest in ruling seemed to decline as the country's problems increased, and in 1965 he turned his energies to filmmaking, which did little to endear him to the people. Opposition politicians began to gain greater recognition. Candidates running without Sihanouk's endorsement won seats in the 1966 national election for the first time, even though four of the winners had been explicitly targeted as enemies of the regime. Sihanouk managed to regain the initiative, however, by assembling a counter-government to Prime Minister Lon Nol's proposed cabinet, which was composed of people unsupportive to Sihanouk.

The factionalism of Cambodian politics increased throughout 1966. Sihanouk's power declined and that of the left rose as the gap between rich and poor continued to widen, agricultural exports continued to fall, and government expenditures increased to fund Sihanouk's films, magazines, and projects such as luxury hotels. In areas bordering Vietnam, day-to-day administration was in the hands of Vietnamese National Liberation Front (NFL) cadres. Sihanouk's insistence on monopolizing political life alienated many Cambodians, as did the lack of jobs and falling wages. The retooled WPK, now the CPK, placed all the blame for Cambodia's woes on Sihanouk and his cronies. Students protesting in the capital in early 1967 demanded the dissolution of Lon Nol's government.

Discontent became violent in March 1967, when an antigovernment rebellion broke out in the Samlaut region of western Battambang province. Inspired by injustices, lack of social change, and corruption, the uprising was exploited, though not initiated, by the CPK, which used the evidence of open discontent to promote its own social vision among the rural population. The dispatch of eight battalions of soldiers calmed the situation by May, but forced the resignation of Lon Nol. Student-led demonstrations continued to take place in the provinces of Kandal and Kompong Cham, but without violence, while inside the capital, Sino-Khmers, mesmerized by the reforms in China, declared themselves loyal to Mao. This should have been good news to Sihanouk, who had a personal alliance with China, but the cult of personality and monopolization of power he encouraged in Cambodia made any connections to other leaders potentially threatening. He therefore increased government repression against urban radicals while providing assistance to the countryside in order to ameliorate the disenchanted rural population. He instituted public works programs in Samlaut, and offered a reward to every CPK member who joined his party. At the same time, urban intellectuals who felt threatened by the government's crackdown fled to the mountains and joined the CPK throughout 1966–67.

The picture became further complicated by the events of the Vietnam War. A major buildup of Vietnamese Communist forces occurred in eastern Cambodia in 1967, in preparation for the Tet offensive of 1968. The eastern border was also one of the main areas of CPK activity, and the Vietnamese presence encouraged increased insurgency in the Samlaut region and unrest in the tribal areas of the northeast. The dynamics of the situation were somewhat convoluted—the Cambodian armed forces were simultaneously providing support to the North Vietnamese and the Vietnamese Communist guerrillas while fighting the Khmer Rouge, which was supported by those same Vietnamese elements. The government repression that followed the increased guerrilla activity prompted the CPK to inaugurate an official policy of armed struggle, although at the time it had fewer than 5,000 poorly trained guerrillas scattered around the country.[5] As a result of these sparse numbers the insurgency was regionally varied, with the fiercest fighting, at least early on, in Battambang and the northwest, where the CPK central committee stayed close to its Vietnamese protectors.

Government-sponsored violence increased consistently through the late 1960s, aimed against a shadowy enemy that was still very dispersed and operating without a coordinated plan. The most intense fighting shifted to the northeast of the country, where rebel bands pinned down government troops in Kompong Cham, Svay Rieng, and Kompong Speu. Vietnam continued to occupy the border zones, and the bizarre assistance triangle also continued. A drought worsened the economic situation in 1968, lowering exports further and leading to a rising deficit. The pitiful economic conditions in the countryside helped the rebels' cause, and made their message of drastic reorganization increasingly attractive. Sihanouk's declining fortunes reached their nadir in March 1970, when he was ousted in a bloodless coup and General Lon Nol took over the government. This did little to quell the insurgency in the countryside, since the conservative Lon Nol was no more palatable to the Khmer Rouge than the monomaniacal Sihanouk. Lon Nol withdrew most of the army from the northeast in late 1970, conceding the area to the Vietnamese and Khmer Rouge.

The Cambodian army, Vietnamese forces, citizens, and CPK guerrillas clashed throughout 1970, with fighting even reaching the outskirts of Phnom Penh. Thousands of students joined the army, answering the call to drive out the Vietnamese. Sihanouk continued to wield influence from afar, and many peasants heeded his call to join the guerrillas and drive out the Americans, the main sponsor of Lon Nol's coup. Also at this time, large numbers of Vietnamese-educated Cambodians returned home to join the resistance. Demonstrations in the rural areas were brutally suppressed. Anti-Vietnamese sentiment intensified in Phnom Penh with the increasing number of deaths among the student volunteers, who were poorly equipped and wholly untrained and quickly ripped apart by Vietnamese forces. The army took out its frustrations on Vietnamese citizens, and reports told of soldiers gunning down children, and corpses floating down the Mekong.[6] The worst fighting with guerrillas occurred in the northeast, where rebel bands pinned down government troops and temporarily took control of Kompong Cham province.

The American–South Vietnamese invasion of Cambodia in April–June 1970 increased Lon Nol's problems by forcing the Vietnamese Communist units deeper into Cambodia, and encouraging South Vietnamese units to continue operations against them throughout 1971. The security situation was by this point truly bewildering, with at least six different groups of forces present in Cambodia, three of whom were not Cambodian and were merely using the country as a staging ground for their own conflict while also maintaining alliances with various combinations of the indigenous factions. A major military offensive undertaken by the government in September 1970 proved moderately successful for Lon Nol, but its follow-up in 1971 was disastrous. CPK and Vietcong forces attacked the Cambodian army, forced it into retreat, killed many of its best soldiers, and sent huge numbers fleeing through the countryside.[7]

The CPK's numbers had increased since 1970, with perhaps 10,000 members under arms, but it still lacked training and discipline. Rival political parties were vying for control in Phnom Penh, and the uncertainty in the capital, combined with the cycles of pursuit and destruction practiced in the countryside by assorted Vietnamese and CPK units, made the rebels' presence more unsettling than, on paper, it might have seemed. The military situation was stabilized with the help of American military aid, which was provided to Lon Nol's government in massive amounts during this period, as well as the American bombing of enemy supply lines and positions. Khmer Rouge victories on the ground could be easily neutralized by American assaults from the air. But the huge increase in American aid made government service synonymous with getting rich, which increased opposition to the government further. Although North Vietnamese troops left in 1972, Lon Nol's power continued to decline. By the end of 1973 he controlled only 25 percent of Cambodian territory, though the CPK's advance was slowed by the continued bombing.[8] In December 1973 the CPK began an artillery barrage on the capital, and in March 1974 it succeeded in capturing Udong, a former royal capital just north of Phnom Penh.

The CPK then began a protracted resistance program aimed at educating the populace by pointing out the glories of socialism and the flaws of the government. The government regained some ground during this educational period, but on New Year's Day 1975 the CPK opened an all-out assault on Phnom Penh, choked off the Mekong supply line, and forced closure of the airport. By March electric power operated for only four hours, every other day. On April 17 the Khmer Rouge took over Phnom Penh and declared the state of Democratic Kampuchea (DK), led by the number one "ghost" of the CPK, Saloth Sar, now known as Pol Pot.

The killing fields of Pol Pot's socialist vision became internationally known as among the most egregious examples of brutality in human history. In Pol Pot's first official acts he evacuated the cities, closed the markets, suspended salaried employment, and decreed the abandonment of money. Execution was the normal punishment for opposition, no matter how mild: Purges and executions were common, and between one and two million people were killed. Living conditions declined further, with the peasant's marginal existence now supplemented by constant terror and the fear of death. Pol Pot had by now broken with his former protectors, and war broke out with Vietnam in 1977 after repeated border incursions on both sides. From this point on, Pol Pot's rule was doomed by its own brutality and the threat of attack by its neighbor. The regime collapsed in December 1978. Vietnamese forces invaded that same month and on January 7, 1979, captured Phnom Penh, installed a new government, and declared the People's Republic of Kampuchea.

The first civil war in Cambodia effectively ended when the Khmer Rouge took control in 1975. A new chapter opened in 1979, however, when the PRK was declared and the ousted Khmer Rouge was sent again into hiding to resume its guerrilla war. The great powers continued to play a role in the conflict, but now arrayed in an unlikely coalition with the varied Cambodian factions, encompassing left- and right-wing rebels alike. The United States and China backed the rebels and eventual CGDK alliance, and their unlikely partnership reflected the wide-ranging coalition itself, which contained both Maoist and anti-Communist elements united in opposition to the imposition of a Vietnamese puppet state in Cambodia. The conflict beginning after the PRK's creation in 1979 represents the civil war that led directly to UN intervention in the 1990s.

Overview of the Conflict

Civil war and diplomatic efforts at resolution occurred concurrently throughout the 1980s. On the ground in Cambodia, the assorted ousted factions waged low-level insurgencies, each controlling some zone of territory, but the PRK controlled most of the territory and was assisted in operations against the rebels by Vietnamese troops. The Khmer Rouge occupied small areas of the country, mainly around the Thai border, where refugees also congregated, and this continued throughout the decade. Officials of the ousted Khmer Rouge government continued to occupy the UN seat, a somewhat troubling fact to the United States in light of the regime's brutal legacy. Technically it had no more claim to the seat than the PRK, since Democratic Kampuchea was also imposed by force. Apparently a murderous Cambodian government was preferable to a Vietnamese-backed regime of any stripe, however, and the Khmer Rouge continued to be the legitimately recognized government of Cambodia in the eyes of the West, in spite of controlling negligible amounts of the country. When the international community held a conference in New York in July 1981, under the auspices of the United Nations, to resolve the problem of Cambodia, the sitting regime in Phnom Penh was not invited. The Khmer Rouge was, by virtue of its continuing UN membership, and in response Vietnam boycotted the proceedings, substantially limiting the possibilities for any resolution. With several key players absent and the remainder of the Cambodian factions and their patrons reaching no consensus on any of the key problems, the conference dissolved with little to show for its efforts except annual condemnations of the situation in the General Assembly.

The situation on the ground did not change much, due to the PRK's superior firepower and external backing. In July 1982 the United States succeeded in forming a tripartite coalition between the three rebel factions—the Khmer Rouge, FUNCINPEC, and the KPNLF. Allied in the new CGDK, this group collectively held the UN seat, thereby making the Khmer Rouge's presence in opposition to the PRK marginally more palatable to the West, and presenting a viable Cambodian alternative to the sitting government. The CGDK coalition contained the three main strands of Cambodian politics—the royalist, republican, and social revolutionary—and therefore claimed to speak for all Cambodians. The armed insurgency also became a coordinated effort of the three factions, who pooled their human and financial resources to oppose the Phnom Penh regime.[9]

This situation continued unchanged throughout most of the 1980s, with the CGDK seated at the United Nations and its guerrilla factions continuing resistance in isolated areas, the PRK controlling the country, and the Vietnamese army providing support where needed. The unlikely turning point came with Mikhail Gorbachev's rise to power in the Soviet Union in 1985. The thawing of the Cold War and retrenchment of Soviet resources led to a decrease in Soviet support for Vietnam. By early 1987 Vietnam had moved toward economic restructuring and committment to reform based on market principles, but its access to the international economy was blocked by the isolation imposed due to its role in the Cambodian conflict. Sihanouk and FUNCINPEC were by this point weary of war, and entered negotiations with Phnom Penh in 1987. Nothing concrete came of these talks, but they did catalyze the commitment of the Association of Southeast Asian Nations (ASEAN) to undertake a regional effort at settlement. The insurgent war was suspended while a diplomatic resolution was sought.[10]

Talks were held in Jakarta starting in July 1988 but fell apart because of internal divisions within the CGDK and because Prime Minister Hun Sen of the Phnom Penh government refused to accept the Khmer Rouge as an equal party to a political settlement. From Phnom Penh's perspective, the government was a legitimate one formed by dissident Cambodians determined to overthrow a genocidal regime. From the CGDK's perspective, the government was blatantly illegal and imposed by the intervention of an outside power without regard for Cambodian preferences. A break came in April 1989 when mounting economic problems and external pressure forced Vietnam to offer the unconditional withdrawal of its forces in Cambodia by September. This overture provided the opportunity for the first Paris Conference in July, chaired by France and Indonesia.

Several intractable problems remained. The CGDK coalition demanded the replacement of the Phnom Penh regime, but could not resolve the problem of interim power sharing among its own factions. The PRK, supported by Vietnam, objected to a UN role unless the Cambodian seat was declared vacant. The conference suspended its talks in August. The CGDK then resumed the war in order to test Hun Sen's staying power without the military support of Vietnam. As it turned out, the government exerted considerable autonomous control and was not quite the Vietnamese facade many had considered it. This made it clear to the CGDK that military victory would not be easy to achieve, and helped convince all factions to continue in negotiations.

Fortunately, the continued thawing of Sino-Soviet and Sino-Vietnamese relations prevented the loss of international initiative for a peace settlement. The major powers worked at an agreement suitable to all parties, and eventually resolved the major disagreements by planning an interim UN administration and creating a twelve-member Supreme National Council (SNC), composed of six members of the Phnom Penh regime and two each from the factions of the CGDK, which would embody national sovereignty and assume the seat at the United Nations. The Paris Agreement was concluded on October 23, 1991, with all parties signing. The one thing the agreement did not do was dismantle the Phnom Penh regime, and this would become one of the major flaws of the settlement and a direct catalyst for the resumption of the war.[11]

The UN mission agreed on in Paris was the most comprehensive to date, and was granted extraordinary powers during the transition period. Established on February 28, 1992, UNTAC's mandate included traditional peacekeeping duties, such as monitoring the cease-fire and the withdrawal of foreign forces, as well as the cantonment and demobilization of the Cambodian factions.[12] But the heart of its mission lay in its civilian responsibilities, which included: direct control over various parts of the civil administration and supervision over the whole; organizing and conducting national elections, which meant making electoral laws and establishing a democratic process; training and supervising a civilian police force; and providing support and assistance for the repatriation and rehabilitation of refugees and displaced persons as well as former guerrillas.

The most far-reaching of UNTAC's divisions was the Civil Administration Component, which had direct control over existing administrative structures in foreign affairs, national defense, finance, public security, and information. Any areas of government that had been or could be used by the sitting government to help its electoral cause or prolong the war were intended to be administered by UNTAC in a neutral fashion and with an eye toward establishing genuinely democratic processes. The SNC could advise UNTAC, and if fractured, Sihanouk, the chairman, could speak for the council. UN Special Representative Yasushi Akashi retained final authority to decide whether Sihanouk's and SNC's recommendations furthered the purposes of the mission. If they did not, UNTAC could act on its own.

The established timetable expected 70 percent of the existing armies of all factions to be cantoned and disarmed by September 1992.[13] The entire operation was designed to be concluded within eighteen months. Even with the full cooperation of all parties, this was an impossible goal, made all the more so because full cooperation was notably absent. Fighting continued throughout the duration of the operation, occasionally including the kidnapping of UN personnel and theft of their equipment. The PRK, now the State of Cambodia (SOC), continued to use the state apparatus to advance the fortunes of its own Cambodian People's Party (CPP) during the election season and to intimidate its opponents. The Civil Administration Component's central goal thus remained unrealized. The Khmer Rouge responded to SOC transgressions by refusing to allow UNTAC entry into areas under its control and neglecting to provide information on the number of its troops and equipment. It justified its intransigence by claiming that Vietnamese forces had not been entirely withdrawn, and that real power had not been transferred from the Phnom Penh government, which used the state for its own ends. This latter claim was certainly true. The former was not, unless the Khmer Rouge defined "Vietnamese forces" as any ethnic Vietnamese residing in the country. In the face of Khmer Rouge obstinancy, the SOC and other factions that had partially cantoned refused to demobilize or disarm their soldiers, and then dispersed the soldiers on so-called "agricultural leave."[14]

Because of the lack of cooperation, UNTAC completely abandoned the demobilization program in the fall of 1992, and at the September target date only 5 percent of troops had been cantoned.[15] The continued violence prevented the effective operation of most of UNTAC's civil mandate, which meant that its human rights and repatriation components were also severely hindered. By December 1992 its multifunctional mandate had been reduced to the single task of conducting a free and fair election. To accommodate this, the Military Component shifted from a zonal deployment designed for cantonment to a provincial deployment designed to support the organization of the election. In 1993 the SOC intensified its policy of violent intimidation of the other parties, carried out by means of fusing its security structures with the CPP. The offices of opposition parties were attacked, ransacked, and burned; opposition members were beaten, kidnapped, and killed. Various towns became subject to shelling, which continued right up to the election, scheduled for May 23–27.

Deaths, injuries, and abductions numbered in the hundreds between March and May, with FUNCINPEC and KPNLF in particular being harassed while campaigning and targeted for violence by the SOC. In April the Khmer Rouge withdrew entirely from the peace process, claiming it had abandoned hope of a free and fair election and would continue to put its faith in armed struggle. It did not say it had no faith in elections, merely those conducted in an atmosphere of violence and intimidation, and with that qualifier it stepped up its own attempts to sabotage the electoral process. It undertook several large-scale attacks in early May, particularly in the provinces of Siem Reap and Kompong Thom, where 300 polling sites were closed because of the violence.[16] In Kompong Thom voters were shelled on their way to the open polling sites.

In spite of this intimidation, 90 percent of the eligible electorate turned out to vote in the generally peaceful May 1993 elections, making the Electoral Component of UNTAC an unqualified success.[17] FUNCINPEC won 45.4 percent of the vote and 58 of the 120 seats in the assembly, with the CPP getting 38.23 percent and 51 seats. The third party was an offshoot of the KPNLF, gaining just 3.8 percent of the vote.[18] The results were endorsed by the UN Security Council in June, and on September 21, 1993, the new assembly approved a democratic constitution and reinstated the monarchy. Sihanouk, who had resigned from all parties, resumed the throne as a constitutional monarch, with his son Prince Ranariddh, now the leader of FUNCINPEC, and Hun Sen of the CPP as the first and second prime ministers, respectively. UNTAC's mandate officially ended on September 28, when the constitutional assembly became the national assembly, and its last forces were withdrawn by November 15, 1993.

The success of the election and its portent for peace were tempered, however, by the continuing civil war, with the Khmer Rouge again the lone opposition, pitted against its former colleagues of the CGDK, now in alliance with the former PRK in a new Cambodian state. Two ministers of the CPP tried to mount a secessionist movement in the east immediately after the election, but the movement crumbled when most CPP leaders withheld their support and endorsed the election results. Throughout the summer, however, the western border of Cambodia was the scene of violent battles between the Khmer Rouge and the integrated militaries of the non-Communist parties and the Phnom Penh party, the Royal Cambodian Armed Forces (RCAF). The Khmer Rouge also launched a diplomatic initiative in an attempt to convince the new government that it must be given a share of power in order to achieve peace, an interesting proposition in light of its electoral boycott, and one quickly rejected. In August the RCAF launched a concerted offensive against Khmer Rouge strongholds in Banteay Meanchey and Kompong Thom provinces, capturing a major logistical base of the guerrillas.

Government forces had success in the early part of 1994, and reclaimed several areas, but the Khmer Rouge continued its effort to sever the northwest part of the country and rejected the government's January 1994 demand to demobilize. RCAF forces seized the Khmer Rouge stronghold at Anlong Veng in February, but were routed by the guerrillas three weeks later. In March RCAF began an offensive against Pailin, the gem and logging center of northwest Cambodia and the Khmer Rouge's main base and source of income. Some 7,000 RCAF troops took control of the region and sent 25,000–30,000 refugees heading to Thailand, which initially denied access to international aid organizations and turned the refugees back into Cambodia. One month later, the Khmer Rouge retook Pailin, even though vastly outnumbered by the government.

During the 1994–95 dry season, the Khmer Rouge adopted new tactics, engaging in the destruction of homes and rice fields, looting, rape, and occasionally kidnapping Westerners. Fighting and peace talks waxed and waned throughout the summer as the Khmer Rouge pressured peasants in conflict areas into joining its ranks, and kidnapped many to work on roads and fortifications. Casualties in the conflict zones rose dramatically. An attempted coup in July 1994 was thwarted by Hun Sen, and five days later legislation was passed outlawing the Khmer Rouge. The coup attempt solidified the alliance between CPP and FUNCINPEC moderates, but exacerbated the situation in the countryside, where the Khmer Rouge proclaimed its own government.

With no legal opportunity to participate in the government, and encouraged by its successful campaigns at Pailin and Anlong Veng, the Khmer Rouge intensified its military efforts. It engaged in wholesale destruction of the government's administrative structures at the village, commune, and district levels; forced the civilian population to move behind Khmer Rouge lines, bringing their rice harvest with them; and imposed forced labor in the conflict zones. It drove the population out of entire districts in the northwest provinces and, according to Human Rights Watch, had established at least two concentration camps in Battambang province by February 1995, for the reeducation of captured government administrators.[19]

Apparently the Khmer Rouge hoped to hold its zones in the jungle and wait for the government's failings to turn people in its direction.[20] Similarly, the government tried to encourage defections by passing an amnesty law. On the last day of the amnesty period, January 15, 1995, Khmer Rouge units launched systematic attacks on villages throughout Battambang, resulting in massacre of citizens and razing of villages. The government proved little better, however, as official corruption, waste, and violence increased throughout 1995. The army, which was poorly trained, engaged in wide-ranging abuses of citizens, including abduction, torture, and the random firing of automatic weapons into crowds. This situation held through 1996, with the government still fragile and dominated by the CPP, due to its continuing control over the armed forces and police, and the Khmer Rouge still operating a competing government in the northwest. In 1998 the situation changed for the better and the Cambodian government now controls much of what was previously Khmer Rouge territory.[21]

Costs of the Conflict to International Actors

The costs of the conflict to international actors can only be estimated and are certainly underestimated, due to the impossibility of obtaining cost figures from several key Cold War players, such as Vietnam and China. The analysis here includes an estimation of military, economic, and humanitarian costs to the international community throughout the length of the war. The humanitarian costs appear quite low in spite of a large number of refugees because many operations were included in the human rights and repatriation components of UNTAC, which was designed to be an all-inclusive operation. In contrast, the costs of economic reconstruction are enormously high and reflect the attempt of the international community to rebuild Cambodian society in order to prevent future violence. The commitment of regional actors is particularly indicative of this effort. The costs of the conflict during the Cold War era, prior to efforts at settlement, are presented in a subsection incorporating all available information on humanitarian, economic, and military aid.

UN Costs

The costs of all UN efforts in Cambodia are presented together in table 9.1, since UNTAC encompassed a wide range of mandates that included the cost of its Military Component as well as the activities of the United Nations High Commissioner for Refugees (UNHCR) and other UN aid offices.[22] The United Nations Advance Mission in Cambodia (UNAMIC), established in October 1991 immediately after the signing of the peace agreements, cost $20 million, and the liaison team, which stayed six months after UNTAC's departure, until May 1994, cost $1 million.[23] UNTAC itself operated from March 1992 to November 1993 and cost $1.7 billion, which included the cost of the limited refugee assistance and repatriation it was able to undertake through UNHCR.[24] Importantly, much of the Electoral Component's work was done by highly dedicated volunteers, which meant that the most successful of UNTAC's mandates was also its least expensive.

Direct Economic Costs to Outside Powers

Cambodia has been one of the poorest countries in the world throughout its history, and remains so, although the outlook is improving. Most statistical data on its economy was not readily available prior to 1990 due to its close association with Vietnam, but its GNP has risen and its 1994 growth rate of 5 percent had improved from an estimated 0 percent in 1990.[25] This rise is the result of massive doses of economic assistance poured in by the international community beginning in this decade. Efforts to rebuild Cambodia began even before the deployment of UNTAC—in 1991 Western nations pledged the first $90 million worth of development aid. From the outset, aid disbursements reflected the ambitious nature of the international effort and were aimed at far more than stopping the war. Between 1991 and 1995 approximately 19 percent of

TABLE 9.1
Cambodia: UN Missions ($U.S. Millions)

UNAMIC	20.0
UNTAC	1,700.0
Military liaison	1.0
TOTAL	**1,721.0**

Sources: UNDPI, *The United Nations and Cambodia 1991–1995* (New York: United Nations, 1995). UNDPI, *Yearbook of the United Nations 1993* (New York: Martinus Nijhoff), 375–78. Trevor Findlay, *Cambodia: The Legacy and Lessons of UNTAC,* Stockholm International Peace Research Institute Report No. 9 (New York: Oxford University Press, 1995).

external aid went to technical assistance, 34.5 percent to investment project assistance, 19 percent to budgetary and balance of payments assistance, and the remaining 27 percent to food and emergency relief.[26] Much of the multilateral aid was pledged at a series of international conferences held solely on the subject of Cambodia's reconstruction. Regional actors played a particularly important role, with the ASEAN and the Asian Development Bank (ADB) contributing development funds and investment. Overall, gross investment in Cambodia increased from less than 10 percent of GDP at the start of 1992 to over 14 percent in 1993 and 19 percent in 1994.[27]

The International Conference on the Reconstruction of Cambodia (ICORC) and the Ministerial Conference on the Rehabilitation of Cambodia resulted in $2.6 billion worth of pledges made over three meetings.[28] Four trust funds, administered by the United Nations but established by voluntary contributions and maintained separately from UNTAC, added approximately $13 million, earmarked primarily for human rights and demining activities.[29] Assorted nongovernmental organizations contributed to rehabilitation and humanitarian assistance, led by the Cooperative for Assistance and Relief Everywhere (CARE), and international multilateral organizations, such as the World Bank and its International Development Association (IDA), and members of the Organization for Economic Cooperation and Development (OECD) provided emergency rehabilitation funds for programs aiding health, education, transport, and public utilities.[30] For a summary of the economic aid provided to Cambodia, see table 9.2

Economic Opportunity Costs to Outside Powers

The civil war did not prevent lucrative trade ventures with the West prior to 1990 because Cambodia's economy was so poor to begin with and

TABLE 9.2
Cambodia: Economic Aid ($U.S. Millions)

International Conference on the Reconstruction of Cambodia	2,600.00
Asian Development Bank	74.0
NGOs	5.0
UN Trust Funds	13.2
International Development Association	75.0
OECD Members	952.0
TOTAL	**3,719.2**

Sources: United Nations, *World Economic and Social Survey 1996,* 192–94, available from www.info.usaid.gov/pubs/cp97/countries/kh.htm. *Yearbook of the United Nations 1993,* 377–78, www.interaction.org. UNDPI, *The United Nations and Cambodia 1991–1995* (New York: United Nations, 1995), 297–300. *Development Cooperation: Efforts and Policies of the Members of the Development Assistance Committee* (Paris: OECD, 1996).

because it was closely allied with Communist nations. The rising level of foreign investment, particularly by the ASEAN, suggests that business and investment ventures were lost for the regional economy as a whole due to the instability of the war. The country's shaky history has undoubtedly resulted in lost tourist revenue. More important, and more costly, is the legacy left by the country's 10 million land mines, which have drastically reduced agricultural productivity and crippled many people. Under each square mile of land in Cambodia lie approximately 143 mines, precluding farming across most of the country and giving it a mine density per mile second only to that of Bosnia.[31] It costs approximately $300–$1,000 to remove one mine. At the minimum, therefore, it would cost $3 billion to clear the country of mines. The Cambodia Mine Action Center (CMAC) requires $10 million each year to field forty platoons of deminers, and expects to need at least five to eight years of operation with full funding in order to clear key agricultural areas. Donations thus far have not come even close to the need. Said one UNHCR representative, "the only demining going on now is when people tread on them."[32]

The social and economic costs of mining are enormous, giving Cambodia the highest percentage of physically disabled inhabitants in the world, and forcing fields, from which 90 percent of Cambodians derive their livelihood, to remain fallow (see table 9.3).[33] Tremendous revenue has already been lost, in a country that can ill afford to lose it, due to decreased agricultural production. Money has also been taken from other necessary projects in order to aid the mine victims. If the international community comes up with more money, at least $50 million will be required for the CMAC. If it does not, it will provide far more in agricultural subsidies, food aid, and health assistance for a generation of crippled citizens.

Additional Costs to Individual Nations

Bilateral aid increased substantially after 1990, separate from contributions made through multilateral organizations or the conferences specifi-

TABLE 9.3
Cambodia: Mine-Clearing Costs ($U.S. Millions)

Cambodia Mine Action Center	50
Clearing cost (estimated)	3,000
TOTAL	**3,050**

Sources: UNICEF: www.unicef.org/sowc96pk/hidekill.htm. Mats Berdal and Michael Leifer, "Cambodia," in *The New Interventionism 1991–1994: The United Nations Experience in Cambodia, Former Yugoslavia, and Somalia,* ed. James Mayall (Cambridge: Cambridge University Press, 1996).

cally on Cambodia.[34] Some of this aid was intended strictly for reconstruction costs, while some of it went toward humanitarian assistance programs. Beginning in 1993, Japan became Cambodia's largest bilateral donor.[35] Foreign direct investment (FDI) also increased in an attempt to jump-start Cambodia's economy.[36] Members of ASEAN in particular became heavily involved through FDI, which they concentrated in sectors with high immediate returns, such as tourism and financial services.[37] By 1995 the amount of overall bilateral development aid extended to Cambodia had increased by 400 percent from 1991.[38] The costs of bilateral aid between 1991 and 1996 are summarized in table 9.4.

Because of the continuing security problems in Cambodia, the government continues to spend large sums on military and defense—29 percent of the proposed budget for 1996—crowding out investment in critical areas such as education, health, and rehabilitation of infrastructure. Significantly, however, there has been no reversal of economic reforms since UNTAC's departure.[39]

Cold War Costs

The cost of the war prior to 1990 is difficult to determine, largely because information cannot be obtained on several of the main providers of aid, such as China and Vietnam. By the end of 1987 the international com-

TABLE 9.4
Cambodia: Bilateral Aid ($U.S. Millions)

Japan	131.6
United States	130.0
Australia	65.0
France	33.7
Netherlands	30.3
Italy	27.1
Sweden	18.5
Germany	17.4
North Korea	15.0
Indonesia	3.0
Foreign Direct Investment	3,000.0
TOTAL	**3,471.6**

Sources: Japan's Office of Development Assistance, ODA Annual Report 1995 (Tokyo: Association for the Promotion of International Cooperation), 304, and *ODA Annual Report 1994* (Tokyo: Association for the Promotion of International Cooperation), 289–91. Frank Gibney Jr., "The Trials of Living in Peace," *Time* (November 27, 1995). United Nations, *World Economic and Social Survey 1996* (New York: United Nations, 1996). *Development Cooperation: Efforts and Policies of the Members of the Development Assistance Committee* (Paris: OECD, 1996).

munity, mainly through the UNHCR and associated agencies, had contributed $1 billion in relief operations to the Cambodian people, particularly refugees trapped on the Thai-Cambodian border.[40] The United States provided nearly $2 billion worth of aid throughout the 1970s and 1980s, though not all of this may have been directly related to the civil war.[41] The bulk of the aid was military, which certainly was used against the Khmer Rouge. Assuming that half the aid was war related, probably an underestimation, and that the Khmer Rouge received just as much through Vietnam, China, and the Soviet Union combined, at least $2 billion worth of aid was provided to the warring parties from approximately 1968 to 1989. The estimated costs for the period 1970–1989 are summarized in table 9.5.

Total Costs

The total cost of the Cambodian conflict to the international community is $15 billion. Some $12 billion worth of this total has been incurred, or spent, since 1990 in the ongoing effort to end the war and rehabilitate the country. Since preventive action was impossible during the Cold War this study will deal primarily with comparisons to the latter number. These costs are also investments in prevention, since the aim of the rehabilitation effort is not only to rebuild from violence but to transform the economic and political structures that led to the violence to begin with. The massive amounts of economic aid poured into Cambodia thus are part of both the costs of conflict and the costs of prevention for the future. The total costs of the conflict are summarized in table 9.6.

Costs of Preventive Action

This section will present two different analyses: the cost of the actual UNTAC mission, and the cost of a more aggressive mission that could have been launched. As noted earlier, some aspects of the conflict remained unchanged at UNTAC's departure, suggesting that a more forceful mis-

TABLE 9.5
Cambodia: Cold War Aid ($U.S. Millions)

Humanitarian aid	1,000
U.S.	1,000
China/USSR/Vietnam	1,000
TOTAL	**3,000**

Sources: Yearbook of the United Nations 1986 (New York: United Nations, 1987); and www.tradeport.org/tx/countries/cambodia/bnotes.html.

TABLE 9.6
Cambodia: Total International Costs of Conflict ($U.S. Millions)

Post–Cold War costs:	
UN missions	1,721.0
Economic aid	3,719.2
Opportunity costs	3,050.0
Individual nations	3,471.7
Total costs since 1990	**11,961.9**
Cold War costs	3,000.0
TOTAL	**14,961.9**

sion would have been needed to decisively end all aspects of the civil war. UNTAC did achieve some notable successes, but also failed to meet the goals of its military component, allowing armed insurgency to continue. Alongside UNTAC's costs, therefore, this section will analyze the costs of a more forceful mission, which could have successfully demobilized the Khmer Rouge and reintegrated its members into Cambodian society.

Assessing preventive action in Cambodia proves difficult, since intervention occurred only after nearly twenty-five years of war. As noted, the Cold War prevented interventionist action prior to 1990, thus the UNTAC mission was intended as both rehabilitation and prevention. It had to reconstruct a society afflicted by over two decades of violence and seek to provide the basic security and stability in which to develop political structures in order to prevent violence in the future. Whether UNTAC's efforts actually prevented a resumption of the war remains to be seen. There is certainly recent evidence that "stable" is still a somewhat optimistic description of Cambodian politics. The problem was that UNTAC's mandate was too weak to cope with the range of tasks assigned to it and its timetable too restrictive to allow for the setbacks that inevitably took place. It never gained control over the structures for public security, although this was one of its main tasks, partly because SOC blocked it and partly because the mission was inadequately prepared. This underscored one of the major weaknesses of the Paris Agreement, which was the failure to dismantle the sitting government. The Phnom Penh regime continued to hold the upper hand through its control of state security. UNTAC had no enforcement capability, and could only solve problems "through dialogue, persuasion, negotiation, and diplomacy."[42]

UNTAC's total cost was $1.7 billion. This figure includes the costs of the UNHCR and other humanitarian agencies whose work was included in UNTAC's Human Rights and Repatriation Components. These were the more successful parts of the mission. The operation as a whole included seven components—human rights, electoral, military, civil administration, civilian police, repatriation, and rehabilitation. All together the mission included approximately 15,000 troops and 3,500 military police. Some nonmilitary components were composed of staff members of the United Nations and its specialized agencies.[43]

The early intransigence of SOC encouraged the same on the part of the Khmer Rouge, and the continued obstruction of these two parties led to the unraveling of the Military and Police Components of the mission. Operating under mandates that severely restricted their enforcement capabilities, these two components became largely bystanders, dependent on the cooperation of the Cambodian factions. If they refused to turn in their weapons or assemble at the designated cantonment points, there was little UNTAC could do. The Electoral Component functioned effectively, and certainly made a difference in the governance of the country. Although some elements of the SOC declared a secession in three eastern provinces after the election, the elected assembly began work in June 1993. In addition, by 1994 most of the 370,000 Cambodian refugees had been successfully repatriated. An argument could be made that the situation would currently be worse absent the efforts of UNTAC.

An argument could also be made, however, that more was needed, since in spite of some successes the guerrilla conflict continues. The number of troops present in Cambodia was probably sufficient, but they needed a more forceful mandate and more time in which to accomplish it to really bring the situation under control. Providing enforcement capability and the heavy weaponry necessary to support it, and doubling the length of UNTAC's mission from eighteen months to three years, would have added approximately $500 million per six months, bringing a three-year operation to a total cost of $4.8 billion. This cost envisions a military component composed of combat-ready battalions able to engage in active and, if necessary, forceful demobilization. The estimate is based on a comparison with the UN mission in Somalia, which comprised 15,000 troops and cost approximately $800 million per year.[44] UNTAC's mandate covered far more than the military situation, however, and should be expected to be more costly. Adding $500 million to its yearly cost, over half the cost of the Somali operation, to account for necessary weaponry and an expanded deployment of the Military Component seems a reasonable comparison.

Numerically, adequate personnel were probably already present in Cambodia, but they needed more military capability and more time to end the war. The total of $4.8 billion envisions a force of approximately 15,000 heavily armed troops prepared to undertake peace enforcement, as well as the civilian and humanitarian operations of UNTAC, operating at full strength for a period of three years. In order to emphasize the generous nature of this estimate, it is worth noting that only the UN mission in the former Yugoslavia, which included nearly 40,000 troops spread out over a much wider area, was more expensive than the hypothetical mission proposed here.

The progress of peace in Cambodia since UNTAC's withdrawal suggests that a more robust operation was sorely needed in order to truly prevent future violence. While some of UNTAC's mission was accomplished, the weakness of its military component allowed guerrilla groups to pursue their goals outside of the peace process, thus undermining the potential success of the new government. An operation such as the hypothetical force proposed above would have been able to successfully complete the critical task of demobilization, forcing opposition groups to seek influence through political rather than military means.

But a more robust mission would have benefited the nonmilitary components as well. The success of the elections obviously brought that component of the mission to its conclusion, allowing for a redistribution of its limited finances to the other components for the remaining eighteen months. Given a longer timetable, the Human Rights Component, which undertook education of the citizenry and investigation of complaints, both time consuming, might have been more successful. And given greater enforcement powers, the Civil Administration Component could have fulfilled its role rather than trying to cajole the SOC into honoring the agreement it signed in Paris.

Conclusions

The war in Cambodia has cost the international community $11.9 billion since 1990 alone. Adding the costs of bilateral and humanitarian aid incurred during the Cold War, when intervention was impossible, the total comes to $14.9 billion. The operation launched by the United Nations, which was intended to both resolve the conflict and prevent future violence, cost $1.7 billion. Allowing for UNTAC's shortcomings and proposing a more aggressive and more costly force, the price of prevention would have been $4.8 billion. Excluding Cold War costs, the savings would have been $7.1–$10.2 billion. Based on the total costs, the international community could have saved $10.1–$13.2 billion.

In the very worst case, assuming an expanded military operation and excluding Cold War costs, the difference between the cost of war and the cost of a combined rehabilitation and prevention effort was $7.1 billion. The cost-effectiveness of prevention is clear. Even when proposing a hypothetical operation with enhanced military capabilities, its costs are far less than the costs of years of conflict. What is more, the more limited mission in Cambodia was effective in helping the society transform the fundamental problems that led to violence. UNTAC did make progress, and its initiation of a democratic process in Cambodia is the first step toward preventing conflict in the future. It also stabilized conditions enough so that the international community could begin to rebuild Cambodia's economy and civic institutions. The enormous international and regional support extended to Cambodia in this regard demonstrates the interest all nations share in making it a stable and contributing member of the regional and global economy.

After renewed violence and political instability beginning in July 1997, the Khmer Rouge now appears to be losing strength. Thousands of its guerrillas mutinied and defected in March 1998, allowing government forces to take over its traditional stronghold at Anlong Veng. With Pol Pot dead and the insurgency on the wane, Cambodia's chances for peace may improve dramatically.[45] The hypothetical mission included in this study, however, demonstrates that more forceful action earlier would have been more effective, while remaining cost-effective to the international community. Cambodia's history provides a lesson in two ways—it shows how devastating and how costly protracted civil war can be for the international community, and it shows how effective and relatively inexpensive even comprehensive preventive action can be.

10

El Salvador

Andrea Kathryn Talentino

Case Preview

EL SALVADOR'S CIVIL WAR has no precise starting date. The country spiraled slowly toward violence for years, but it was in January 1980 that the varied opposition groups combined to form a unified front, with the Democratic Revolutionary Front (FDR) spearheading the political opposition and the Farabundo Marti National Liberation Front (FMLN) heading the military command structure. From this point on, violence and terror became a fact of life in El Salvador, enduring for twelve years until the signing of a peace agreement and the arrival of a UN mission in 1991. Over the course of those twelve years the fortunes of both the government and opposition forces alternately waxed and waned, with each offensive and takeover of territory by one side counteracted by the other. Citizens became the targets of random violence, arbitrary detention, death squad killings, and abduction. By the end, an estimated 75,000 people had been killed, and at least 1 million became refugees or internally displaced persons.[1]

Members of the international community were involved from the outset of the war, due to the socialist ideology of the dominant elements in the rebel coalition, which made El Salvador a stage for superpower conflict by proxy. The United States viewed El Salvador as one more piece of the East-West jigsaw; its government a beachhead against the Communist infiltration of Latin America. Beset by the fear of Marxism in its own hemisphere, the United States provided enormous amounts of aid to the right-wing military government (later a civilian government substantially backed by the military) whose only saving grace, even by American standards, was its anti-Communism. The United States justified its aid on the grounds that "Communist powers" were funding and arming the rebels in equally massive amounts. The amounts are debatable, but Cuba, Nicaragua, and the Soviet Union did provide the FMLN with arms and political support, and helped cultivate the organization's ideological development.[2] Independent groups in places such as West Germany also helped raise funds for the FDR-FMLN, which contained Christian and social democrats in its coalition and, therefore, exerted considerable appeal beyond Marxism.[3]

Serious international efforts to stop the violence did not begin until late 1989–90, when the end of the Cold War, the exhaustion of the belligerent parties, and the realization that no military end was in sight led both sides to seek the assistance of the United Nations in reaching a negotiated settlement. In September 1989 the government of El Salvador and the FMLN agreed to begin a dialogue in order to end the conflict by political means. This agreement was ultimately derailed by a massive resumption of fighting in November, but the February 1990 defeat of the Sandinista government in Nicaragua, one of the FMLN's main supporters, and the peaceful transfer of power in that country convinced the Salvadoran parties that there were better alternatives to fighting. Peace talks continued intermittently, resulting in an agreement signed in Mexico City in April 1991. The United Nations Observer Mission in El Salvador (ONUSAL) was established in May, and formally launched throughout El Salvador on July 26, 1991.

The cost of this conflict to the international community has been approximately $8.1 billion. This figure covers the entirety of the war and subsequent peace operations, from 1980 to 1995, and is a very conservative estimate since it can only include a rough estimation of the aid provided to the FMLN throughout the conflict by the Soviet Union and Cuba. Some of the costs, much like the conflict itself, derive from the Cold War. Excluding the costs incurred during that period, the cost of the war to the international community was $2.4 billion. This figure accounts only for money spent from 1990 on, and includes the cost of the UN mission, rehabilitation aid provided by individual nations and multilateral organizations to rebuild and reform El Salvador's infrastructure and institutions, and humanitarian assistance costs, not covered under ONUSAL, paid by regional and nongovernmental organizations. Although small in comparison to the total cost, the post–Cold War cost is still far greater than the cost of intervention. The greatest task for the international community has been economic rehabilitation—a dozen years of violence preceded by decades of mismanagement caused enormous economic and social dislocation, both a cause and effect of the war.

El Salvador is a useful case in analyzing the cost-effectiveness of prevention because it allows for a comparison between the costs of an actual intervention and the costs of the actual conflict. Protracted civil war had a devastating effect on El Salvador's society and economy, a cost amply reflected in the sums paid by the international community since the peace agreement to rebuild all aspects of Salvadoran society. The total costs of rehabilitation will be juxtaposed in this case study with the costs of the actual intervention. The total costs of the war from its inception to the present will not be used as the main baseline of comparison, since prior to 1990 intervention was not possible. Instead, the cost-benefit analysis will be conducted using only the costs incurred since 1990. The UN force in El Salvador undertook a broad program of conflict resolution combined with societal rehabilitation intended to prevent future violence. It has been highly successful, and ONUSAL's total cost was only a fraction of the cost of conflict. Some of the economic aid costs paid in El Salvador are also undoubtedly part of the preventive operation, since the international community used the aid to transform some of the political and economic structures that had caused the violence. Rehabilitation and prevention are thus distinct yet connected in El Salvador's case, since prevention was also inherent in the act of rebuilding.

ONUSAL operated from July 1992 to April 1995, at a total cost of $107 million. Authorized to include approximately 1,000 military and police observers and 100 civilian staff, it undertook an ambitious program of reforming the country's institutions in order to build a fledgling democracy, in which it proved highly effective.[4] The mission's mandate included military tasks, as well as the transformation of the government's approach to state security, human rights, and economic structures. Perhaps its most significant feature was that it established and staffed its human rights offices even before a cease-fire took effect, a move that signaled its seriousness and commitment to the citizens, and assisted in securing their good faith in its offices. Although this occasionally led to expectations for the mission that were too high, it also prevented the belligerent parties from labeling it ineffective.

Part of its success lay in the exhaustion of the warring parties and their mutual request for a settlement to the conflict. The cooperation of the belligerents also helped keep the mission's costs low. Nonetheless, ONUSAL's success underscores the cost-effectiveness of preventive action. The international community took action as soon as it was possible, and succeeded in providing rehabilitation for the effects of the past conflict while helping to reform political and economic institutions. The wide-ranging mandate of the mission was as much an attempt to end a civil war as an attempt to prevent one in the future. El Salvador's history of unrest and discontent spans over a century. The difficulty of ONUSAL's task lay not so much in how it would end the violence but in how it would transform the basic structures of a country for which violence was the most familiar form of politics. Rebuilding a society costs billions. The effort to create stable political, economic, and social institutions is still ongoing, and requires the continued financial commitment of the international community.

This case study is organized into four parts. The first two sections will present the historical origins and an overview of the conflict. The third section will analyze the costs of the conflict to international actors, taking into account humanitarian, military, reconstruction, and aid costs. The fourth section will discuss the preventive mission deployed by the United Nations, which occurred after already a decade of conflict but was preventive to the extent that it undertook to rebuild societal institutions in order to prevent future violence. The chapter concludes with a cost summary and comparison of the cost-effectiveness of preventive efforts.

Origins of the Conflict

El Salvador's saga of violence developed from its historic reliance on a monocrop economy that concentrated the majority of the land in the hands of a few. The dependence on first cacao and then indigo in the 1700s gave rise to a plantation system that was essentially feudal, and allowed landowners to control political life by the end of the century. In the mid-1800s coffee became the major crop, requiring an even greater concentration of land and the transferal of communal properties into private hands. The peasantry resisted this transfer in a series of popular uprisings starting in 1872, but with little success. Their most significant result was the creation of state security forces in the pay of the landowners. In 1881 a new legal order recognized only private property and completely abolished the peasant's traditional communal ownership, dispossessing a majority of the rural population from their homes and livelihood.[5] The commitment of land to coffee crops also necessitated the importation of basic foodstuffs, a further problem for peasants, who could not pay. By the end of the nineteenth century the majority of land was in the hands of "Los Catorce" ("the Fourteen"), the dominant group of families from which also came the presidents of the republic.[6] Though the oligarchy did number somewhat more than fourteen, the name captures the inequality created by socioeconomic realities.

In narrow economic terms the reforms that abolished the communal lands were a success. The wealth of the nation and of its coffee producers increased enormously, with the value of coffee exports increasing from

$2.9 million in 1881 to $21.9 million in 1916.[7] But the concentration of land and income in the hands of a few prevented the development of a strong market, resulting in a thriving export industry existing alongside a poverty-stricken rural domestic sector. A cycle of underdevelopment afflicted the nation, literacy rates remained abysmal, and peasants were forced to travel in search of work, causing social dislocation in the countryside. The world financial downturn between 1914 and 1922 increased the problem by driving the smaller coffee farms out of business and incorporating their holdings into the plantation of the oligarchy.[8]

As early as 1896 the government realized the severity of the social problem it faced, as evidenced by the series of rebellions, but continued dependence on coffee exports and the control of the oligarchy meant little could be changed.[9] Instead, the judicial system was revamped to meet the needs of landlords, allowing them to expel tenants and squatters and turning local civil and military authorities into agents of enforcement. Therein lay the origins of the death squads that would later become such a familiar part of the political landscape. By the late 1920s coffee constituted 92 percent of the country's exports, one family had dominated the presidency from 1913 to 1927, force was applied openly in rural areas to dispossess peasants, and all so-called political parties were organized around competing coffee families.[10]

El Salvador was essentially two countries throughout the 1920s. In the cities, the tremendous profits from coffee exports activated the urban economy, where working-class organizations and limited democratization could be found. In the countryside, peasant dispossession and increasing political repression resulted in extreme poverty and underdevelopment. The onset of the depression lowered the demand for and price of coffee, which meant that the peasants working on the coffee plantations were put out of work, losing their meager wages and last means of subsistence. In 1931 the last of the presidents selected by the Melendez-Quinonez family held "free" elections, but the elected president failed to pay military salaries and was deposed nine months later by a group of officers, and power quickly devolved to the top level of the military.[11] A minor peasant rebellion occurred in the western part of the country in 1932, and the landlords responded by sending in military and police forces as well as White Guards, the vicious security forces of the landowners, massacring up to 30,000 and ushering in a new era of military control.[12]

A repressive and brutal military dictatorship ruled from then until 1944, when it began to promote modernization and the diversification of exports. Although the military formally held government power, it clearly ruled with the interests of the oligarchy in mind. The high price of coffee on world markets helped the success of economic improvements, and unions and political parties were allowed to organize in cities. The modernization was economically successful, like reforms of the past, and both industry and urbanization grew remarkably. In 1964, for the first time since 1931, opposition representatives took seats in the national assembly. But the living conditions of 75 percent of the population remained stagnant and miserable. The diversification of export agriculture into cotton and sugar led to another phase of land concentration and peasant dispossession. Cotton production was particularly problematic, since the majority of peasants were deliberately left homeless and jobless so that they would be dependent on the spotty employment of its picking season. Population growth and decreased food production meant increasing dependence on food imports and increasing misery for peasants. By 1975, 40.9 percent of families were landless, compared to only 11.8 percent in 1961. Most egregiously, only 1.8 percent of families held land of more than 10 hectares. The result of the modernization was to leave over 50 percent of the rural labor force unemployed for more than 60 percent of the year.[13]

Industrialization increased throughout the 1950s and 1960s as a result of aid incentives provided through the Alliance for Progress and the UN Economic Commission for Latin America (ECLA), but in a confused fashion. American insistence on free markets and private national and foreign investment contradicted the ECLA's emphasis on balanced growth and the establishment of regional industries. As a result, the industrial growth rate averaged 8.1 percent through the 1960s, and vastly increased employment, but most of the growth occurred in San Salvador. At the same time, the increased share of foreign investment in the economy created problems by leading to the increase of repatriated profits and a dependence on imported raw materials, thereby increasing the country's dependency on exports. The state revenues pouring into the industrial and urban sectors took capital from other programs, and further isolated the countryside. Approximately 75 percent of the population lacked the income to consume the goods produced, which in turn blocked further industrial expansion.[14]

The oligarchy compounded those problems by investing their profits abroad, further impoverishing the country and creating an urban, consumer culture that showed a marked preference for imported goods, which then took more money out of the domestic sector. Some sense of an urban working class did develop and they were allowed to organize unions, but the rulers held a strong sense of anti-Communism and cracked down on worker independence and student associations. In the 1960s, workers began to organize outside government control more effectively, although the government continued to control a large segment of urban labor and co-opted workers with material rewards. Force and intimidation remained the rule in the countryside. The military was organized in a caste-like fashion in which advancement depended entirely on the political power of officers in each academy class, and had no connection to merit. The army and the death squads that it clandestinely promoted operated on a system of booty and patronage, and thrived on corruption.

Beginning in 1964 the military did organize relatively free elections for the Legislative Assembly and municipalities, in which, much to the military's surprise, the Christian Democratic Party (PDC), formed just four years earlier, won thirty-seven mayoralties (including that of San Salvador) and fourteen assembly seats. In the 1968 elections the opposition won twenty-five seats to the government's twenty-seven, a matter for some concern since the electoral system had been allowed to function on the implicit understanding that the opposition would not win. The four-day "Soccer War" with Honduras in July 1969, so named because it followed a series of tense soccer matches between the two countries, exacerbated El Salvador's problems by sending a large influx of Salvadoran refugees back across the border. Their sudden arrival in the countryside forced the issue of agrarian reform and led to increased political activity in the rural areas. A vague program of agrarian reform was announced within the month, as the administration desperately tried to gain support. The Legislative Assembly took its own initiative and convoked a National Agrarian Reform Congress for January 1970.

The opposition's standing was increased enormously when the church, long considered a symbol of national loyalty, also joined the call for reform. The new year did not look good from the administration's point of view, since it opened with unions organizing strikes, opposition parties winning elections, and the church defending the rights of peasants. The Popular Forces of Liberation (FPL) was founded in April 1970, and adopted a concept of "prolonged population war," involving grassroots political work and a guerrilla army. The People's Revolutionary Army (ERP) followed in early 1971, founded with a short-term view of struggle and the need to use guerrilla action to incite popular rebellion. Throughout the early 1970s these groups carried out "ajusticimientos," which meant literally "bringing to justice," or more specifically the beating, kidnapping, and occasional assassination of local government officials.[15]

The 1972 presidential campaign brought an unprecedented level of popular involvement, most of it on the side of the National Opposition Union (UNO), a coalition of three opposition parties promoting anti-oligarchic reform. UNO's candidate, José Napoleon Duarte, defeated the government candidate by a ratio of two to one in San Salvador and the large cities, after which the media stopped reporting the results. The government solved its problems by doing some quick calculating and declaring its own candidate the winner, thanking Duarte for his participation by means of arrest, beating, and exile to Venezuela. This blatant fraud accelerated the radicalization of the opposition and discouraged participation in the political system. The government cracked down on the opposition, particularly the PDC, after the elections, engaging in mass execution of opposition protestors in February 1978 and forcing most of its leaders into exile. The focus of political conflict shifted to the countryside, where the church's defense of peasant interests made clerics the targets of extreme violence throughout the 1970s. The military and security forces operated by occupying towns and villages, searching houses, and arresting and beating hundred of citizens. The mayor of San Salvador explained, "The purpose of these operations is not crime prevention, but rather to instill terror in the population as a whole."[16]

The increasing repression strengthened popular organization as well as the opposition's ties to the populace, and increased support behind the guerrilla organizations. Even so, until the elections of 1977 most opposition politicians were not ready to endorse the rising number of popular protest organizations, much less the guerrillas, as an alternative to electoral opposition. UNO withdrew briefly from the political process in 1975 but returned to advance the cause of democracy in the 1977 election, during which the extent of fraud reached incredible levels, even by Salvadoran standards. Local officials were told to stuff ballot boxes. Military and paramilitary groups assaulted and intimidated voters and evicted UNO supervisors. Where votes were honestly counted, UNO led three to one.[17] Five days later the Central Election Council declared the government's candidate victorious.

Protests involving 50,000–70,000 participants exploded in the capital and lasted several days. Strikes, work stoppages, and land seizures became the norm throughout the year. Society began to break down socially and economically, as the disruptions slowed industrial growth to only 3 percent in 1978 and caused exports to fall by 10.5 percent.[18] A coup d'état on October 15, 1979, brought an apparently reformist military-civilian junta to office, which demonstrated its new spirit by inviting Duarte to participate in the government as a civilian member. Its early reforms looked promising when it reduced the price of food staples, set a minimum wage for agricultural workers, nationalized the coffee export structure, disbanded the main paramilitary group, and established a committee to investigate the fate of political prisoners. But the military High Command, distinguished by totalitarian and anti-Communist tendencies, showed little regard for the authority of the junta by continuing to use the security forces for brutal repression. By the time Duarte was named junta president in December 1980, the real power had been appropriated by the military, represented by the hard-right vice president, Colonel Gutierrez. The popular organizations and guerrilla groups increased their activities, allowing the High Command to demand the restoration of law and order and an increase in repression.

The civilian members of the junta were never allowed to exercise power and turned out to be mostly reformist cover to hide the repression from the rest of the world. Most had resigned by January 1980 in protest of the increasing violence and rampant brutality of security forces and paramilitary organizations in the countryside. The progressive officers of the junta were driven into exile, and power was controlled by the hard-line senior members of the military. In response, the popular organizations and guerrilla groups began to unify and coordinate their military action in January 1980. The civil war was at hand.

Overview of the Conflict

The opposition groups reorganized themselves into the Democratic Revolutionary Front, the head of political opposition, and the Farabundo Marti National Liberation Front (FMLN) served as the command structure for the guerrilla units. Violence quickly increased, with 2,000 people dying each month due to increasing engagements between guerrilla units and the armed forces, and the brutality of the army in carrying out agrarian reforms. Government-sponsored death squads and wholesale government attacks on rural areas where the FMLN operated also accounted for a large number of deaths. A state of siege was declared, under which the armed forces assumed sole implementation of the reforms, which they carried out by terrorizing peasant organizations and invading settlements.

On March 24, 1980, Archbishop Oscar Arnulfo Romero was killed by a government sniper as he celebrated mass in San Salvador. During his funeral a bomb exploded outside San Salvador Cathedral and the panicked crowd was machine-gunned by government forces, leaving thirty dead.[19] The assassination of Romero, head of the Salvadoran church and a symbol of the nation, was a milestone, polarizing society further and catalyzing opposition to the government. Clerics continued their efforts at social education in the countryside, begun in the late 1970s, in spite of increasing repression, and their work with the peasants was a significant factor in simultaneously expanding and consolidating the opposition.

Throughout the summer the army engaged in battles with the FMLN, particularly in the northern provinces of Chalatenango and Morazan, and around the Guazapa volcano in San Salvador province. As the conflict wore on, the army wreaked havoc on the countryside as a means of eliminating the insurgency, adding massacre to its list of accomplishments. By September 1980, 6,000 people were dead.[20] Another 5,000 died by the end of the year. Cities were not exempt. Between January 1 and July 13, 1980, the Legal Aid Office of the church identified 77 army raids and sackings of union and student organizations, democratic institutions, and offices of the church. It also documented 128 machine-gunning and dynamite attacks on the same offices.[21]

In December the junta was reconstituted. Duarte, rehabilitated and returned from exile, was named its largely figurehead president, with a hard-line colonel as his vice president. In January 1981 the FMLN conducted its first major offensive, increasing the territory under its control and testing, reasonably successfully, the unified command structure. One of the offensive's most significant results was the desertion of large numbers of soldiers from the military barracks in Santa Ana, El Salvador's second-largest city. Death squads roamed the country, controlled by officers and functioning as an integral part of the armed forces. The economy continued to decline due to the increasing violence, with GNP dropping 9.5 percent in 1981. Massive capital flight occurred, and export revenues declined. Government forces destroyed entire villages, starting a refugee crisis as peasants fled the army.

The FMLN launched its second offensive in July 1981, and averaged three offensives of 1,500–4,500 troops per month through December. The government was by this time entirely dependent on American military aid, which was probably the only reason the government forces did not succumb entirely to the FMLN's campaign. Some Salvadoran units, including several that engaged in attacks clearly aimed at civilians, were trained at Fort Bragg, North Carolina. The U.S. Army's School of the Americas trained military officers for Latin America, and the training manual it used throughout the 1980s advocated use of "fear, payment of bounties for enemy dead, beatings, false imprisonment, executions, and the use of truth serum," according to a Department of Defense summary. One of the school's graduates was Roberto D' Aubuisson, leader of the Salvadoran death squads.[22]

During the elections in 1981 the FMLN laid siege to the city of Usulatan for two weeks, preventing voting in four eastern areas. In January 1982 it attacked the Ilopango air base, destroying 70 percent of the air force. In June it started a devastating offensive that captured Perquin and San Fernando in Morazan, and after a brief autumn break continued the attack until declaring a unilateral cease-fire for the Pope's visit in March 1983.

By 1982 the Honduran army and air force were regular collaborators with the El Salvadoran government in large operations by the border, supplemented by American Green Berets and a CIA-established training center.[23] Although technically present only as advisers, the presence of American personnel in the field meant that they were occasionally caught in combat situations, while some were more directly engaged in flying helicopters and attack aircraft. As the presence of American trainers and advisers became more widely known, the FMLN advertised several of its attacks beforehand by announcing that they were intended to kill American personnel. The American "advisers" in El Salvador countered by sponsoring the National Campaign Plan (NCP), which was intended to hunt down guerrillas and protect the civilian population. Its pilot project began in San Vicente, an area of major guerrilla activity, in June 1983. It was initially successful, but the FMLN launched an offensive in the eastern zone in September 1983 that wiped out several government battalions by the end of November. The FMLN attack lasted until January 1984, and required the redeployment of military units to that area. The remaining civil defense plan could not protect the San Vicente area, and the guerrillas attacked the towns and garrisons, stalling the NCP.

By early 1984 the FMLN controlled large areas of eastern, central, and northern El Salvador. The army regained some control prior to the March 1984 presidential elections, but the embassy cables, referred to as "grimgrams" for their reports on the climbing totals of the dead and disappeared, were not encouraging. Almost 7,000 people were dead and at least 2,300 had disappeared.[24] Violence escalated in 1984, when the FMLN undertook a forced recruitment policy that created an exodus of 1,500 refugees in April and May, and was quickly discontinued. The air war conducted by the government with the assistance of the United States led to increasing civilian casualties. Indiscriminate bombing and artillery attacks resulted in massacre and destruction of entire communities in an effort to deprive the guerrillas of their means of survival. But death squad activity decreased from 1983 to 1987, perhaps as a result of the American attempt to "professionalize" the Salvadoran military and security forces beginning in the early 1980s.[25]

The ongoing violence did force a political change. Throughout the 1980s the democratic left gradually returned from exile, coordinating the urban opposition and demanding focus on the political process. Presidential elections were opened to the opposition in 1984. Duarte won the election, becoming the first civilian president in fifty-three years, and taking the post twelve years after being denied his first electoral victory. He met with the FMLN in October of that year, but rejected its proposal for peace a month later. From 1985 on, the war claimed 50 percent of the national budget.[26]

In 1985 the FMLN adopted a new tactic, making every guerrilla into a political officer and concentrating on selling its policies to the populace. It also began sending guerrillas out in small, self-sufficient units, thus allowing expansion into all fourteen provinces and establishing regional operations in thirteen of them. In January 1986 the army began Operation Phoenix around the Guazapa volcano—a combined onslaught of elite forces, continual operations, and massive air bombardment to clear the zone of guerrillas and their supporters. By 1990 at least thirteen of these operations had been undertaken, but the FMLN had not retreated from the area and it continued its insurgent operations.

From 1987 to 1988 an equilibrium of attack and counterattack defined the situation on the battlefield, with neither side able to win or lose. In 1989 the FMLN offered to renounce armed struggle, reorganize as a party within the political process, and recognize a single army, in return for military reforms. The military party rejected the offer. Election day was bloody, as firefights occurred throughout the country and the FMLN blacked out San Salvador and 80 percent of the country, ordering a four-day transportation stoppage. Alfredo Cristiani, candidate of the Nationalist Republican Alliance Party (ARENA), the party historically associated with the military and oligarchy, assumed the presidency on June 1, 1989, and immediately called for talks with the FMLN, a sentiment gaining popular acceptance due to the enormous social and economic costs of the war. Peace talks began in September, but the government continued the bombings of rebel zones and union offices, and the FMLN launched a new offensive in November of that year. The rebels were very successful against the army on the ground, and were only kept from victory by means of the American-sponsored air war, which strafed neighborhoods and towns of guerrillas and civilians alike.[27]

By the end of the year the situation was clear to all sides. The government could not match the rebels on the ground. The rebels could not match the government in the air. Neither side could win. Neither side would fold. At the request of both sides, the United Nations initiated talks in early 1990. Initially just a sponsor, the United Nations became an active mediator in late October when the FMLN demanded disbandment of the armed forces, the government refused, and the target date for a cease-fire passed. The guerrillas launched a new series of coordinated attacks in November and December 1990, which included the humiliation of a U.S.-trained battalion that retreated after forty hours of combat. The air force refused to provide air support, and the army that had just a year earlier minimized the guerrillas' capability now exaggerated their strength, largely to encourage peace negotiations.

No progress was made in early 1991, though talks continued. The impasse was broken during the summer, and a peace accord appeared closer when the FMLN accepted incorporation into the new national police rather than the army, and participation in the peace commission. The accords were signed on January 16, 1992, in Mexico City, and the cease-fire became formal on February 1. The National Committee for the Consolidation of Peace (COPAZ) also became active on that date, and for the first time FMLN members and their supporters were allowed to go public. The accords committed the signatories to end the armed conflict, promote democratization, guarantee respect for human rights, and reunify Salvadoran society. The Human Rights Division of ONUSAL began its work immediately after the signing of the initial step of the peace accords in the fall of 1991. All other divisions were deployed once the cease-fire took effect. The Electoral Division, however, was not authorized until May 1993, and began its work later that year in preparation for the March 1994 elections.[28] By the end of the year, the FMLN was a legal political party.

Costs of the Conflict to International Actors

The cost of the conflict to outside actors includes military, humanitarian, economic, and rehabilitation costs that resulted from the war. An estimation of the costs incurred during the Cold War is calculated separately. This portion of the analysis is necessarily rough due to the difficulty in obtaining information from countries such as the Soviet Union, Vietnam, and Cuba, which backed the FMLN and provided aid throughout the 1980s.

UN Costs

The ONUSAL mission lasted from July 1992 to April 1995 and cost $107 million. Unlike other peace missions, it sought to go beyond ending the military conflict in order to address its root causes. The key elements of the mission included the separation of forces; the dismantling of the military structure of the FMLN and reintegration of its members into society; reduction of the army by 50 percent; abolition of the Treasury Police and National Guard; investigation of human rights violations; and UN verification of all activities.[29] It was composed of 380 military observers, 315 police observers, and approximately 140 civilian staff. Although both sides failed to concentrate their forces within the initial proscribed time, and numerous delays arose in various areas, the cease-fire was not broken. Even the discovery of an illegal FMLN arms cache in early 1993 did not derail the peace process. By the end of 1992, 60 percent of FMLN combatants had been demobilized, the armed forces were being reduced on schedule, and ONUSAL was able to reduce its own military division accordingly.[30]

Humanitarian Costs

By the scale that has recently become the norm, El Salvador's refugee crisis was never very acute. Nonetheless, several hundred thousand people were either refugees or displaced persons, and mining of the countryside proved an ongoing problem requiring the assistance of humanitarian organizations. The international community turned its attention to these problems after the peace accord was signed, and table 10.1 represents costs incurred between 1992 and 1996. Much of the humanitarian costs were targeted for education on human rights issues to reverse the climate of abuse that had become the primary tactic of government officials and the expectation of citizens. The International Conference on Central American Refugees (CIREFCA) channeled $420 million from donor governments to projects in El Salvador, and was also instrumental in early efforts to assist refugees.[31] Nongovernmental organizations contributed $77 million to give ex-combatants vocational training and provide medicine and surgery for the wounded.[32] UNICEF contributed $287,000 for the training of teachers and health care personnel on mine awareness, and the Norwegian Refugee Council and European Union added funds for medical and vocational assistance.[33]

Direct Economic Costs

El Salvador's economy remained dependent on its agricultural exports, despite attempts at diversification, and coffee constituted 60 percent of its exports by the end of the 1980s. As a result, the cost of its imports was more than double the value of exports, leaving the country with a large foreign debt. In addition, economic losses due to guerrilla sabotage totaled approximately $2 billion by 1990, and the continued strain of maintaining an enormous military restricted the government's capacity to provide essential social services.[34] A decade of civil war had thus seriously crippled the economy, preventing investment and restructuring during the course of the war and requiring massive reconstruction after.

The bulk of the costs of war to international actors, therefore, resulted from the attempt to rebuild El Salvador's economic and social institutions and fundamentally transform a society that had been governed throughout

TABLE 10.1
El Salvador: Humanitarian Costs ($U.S. Millions)

International Conference on Central American Refugees	420.0
NGOs	77.0
UNICEF	0.29
Norway	0.09
European Union	0.05
TOTAL	**497.43**

Sources: United Nations High Commissioner for Refugees: www.unhcr.ch/world/amer/camerica.htm. U.S. Agency for International Development: gopher.info.usaid.gov. International Committee of the Red Cross: www.icrc.ch/icrcnews/2396.htm and web.so.no/nrc-no/anurep.95.htm#america. UNDPI, *The United Nations in El Salvador 1992–1995* (New York: United Nations, 1995).

its history by corruption and violence. The World Bank and its International Finance Corporation (IFC), the Inter-American Development Bank (IDB), and the European Union (EU) have all given substantial sums (see table 10.2). These funds went toward the provision of basic social services, infrastructure projects, and a land transfer program.[35]

The land transfer program was one of the most critical and most contentious parts of El Salvador's rehabilitation. The concentration of land in the hands of a few, and the consequences of such a policy for the bulk of the population, were at the very heart of the FMLN's opposition. The attempt to distribute land equitably among the peasants and former insurgents reversed a long trend of dispossession for those same populations. The international community thus funded reforms that sought nothing less than a transformation of the basic character of El Salvador's social structure, which was predicated for nearly 200 years on keeping land out of the citizens' hands. They also attempted to assist agrarian reforms that would be successful in reintegrating former soldiers and guerrillas, providing them with an alternative to a career of violence. All such programs could only begin after the signing of the peace accords, and the reconstruction efforts discussed in this section cover the period from 1992 to 1996.

Economic Opportunity Costs

El Salvador's economy suffered for decades due to mismanagement and then civil war. Since the onset of peace and the restructuring of society, it has shown great potential. The average rates of growth between 1992 and 1995 were 6.5 percent, with inflation staying low, dropping to 10 percent in 1995. Manufactures replaced coffee as the major export earners, at last relieving the land pressures the country had faced for centuries. A stock market started in 1992, and the country received its first Standard and Poor's rating in August 1996, which called its banks "among the most efficient in Latin America." The privatization of business, particularly industry, real estate, and the financial sector, has progressed smoothly and suc-

TABLE 10.2
El Salvador: Economic Aid ($U.S. Millions)

World Bank (excluding IFC)	370.0
International Finance Corporation	72.0
Inter-American Development Bank	170.0
European Union	87.6
TOTAL	**699.6**

Sources: World Bank: www.worldbank.org. Eurostat, *Europe in Figures* (Luxembourg: Office for Official Publications of the European Communities, 1995), 414.

cessfully.[36] El Salvador's quick financial turnaround suggests that opportunities existed for restructuring of the economy and its integration as a thriving member of the regional economy, but were lost due to the continued war and the stranglehold of the oligarchy. Although the financial sector continues to be dominated by members of the oligarchy, it has also expanded and diversified, aligning more with the market than repression. Potential business and investment revenues can only be a matter of speculation, but El Salvador clearly holds economic potential, the realization of which was delayed for years. This lost opportunity constitutes an important but immeasurable cost to outside powers.

Additional Costs to Individual Nations

The United States has provided the bulk of the aid for El Salvador's reconstruction, outside of multilateral organizations (see table 10.3). Between 1993 and 1996 it contributed substantial sums through the Agency for International Development (USAID), as well as $463 million in debt forgiveness.[37] In 1997 USAID provided an additional $35.5 million for development assistance.[38] The second- and third-ranking bilateral donors are Japan and Germany, respectively.[39] Japan's aid level doubled between 1992 and 1993, though such a marked increase is not matched by other donors. Although El Salvador on the whole continued to receive a small percentage of total world development aid throughout 1995, its share of the American total jumped from 1 percent in the 1980s to 4.1 percent in 1994, and has remained roughly constant since.[40]

TABLE 10.3
El Salvador: Costs to Individual Nations ($U.S. Millions)

United States	866.00
Germany	85.98
Japan	38.45
Italy	35.90
Netherlands	33.06
Spain	8.70
TOTAL	**1,068.09**

Sources: World Bank: www.worldbank.org. UNDPI, *The United Nations in El Salvador 1992–1995* (New York: United Nations, 1995), 488–506. U.S. Agency for International Development: www.usaid.gov. International Committee of the Red Cross: www.icrc.ch/icrcnews/2396.htm. *Japan's Official Development Assistance, ODA Annual Report 1994,* 425–27. *ODA Annual Report 1994* (Tokyo: Association for the Promotion of International Cooperation), 449–50. *Development Cooperation: Efforts and Policies of the Members of the Development Assistance Committee* (Paris: OECD, 1996), A82.

The modest increase in aid levels to El Salvador is largely due to the success of the ONUSAL-managed elections, which produced a relatively stable government that committed its personnel and finances to rebuilding the country. The government of El Salvador has initiated several development projects and committed start-up funds to others, thereby encouraging expanded support from multilateral financial institutions rather than massive infusions of bilateral aid. Its long-term commitment is somewhat questionable, however.

Cold War Costs

Throughout the 1980s the Cold War prevented collective intervention from taking place in El Salvador because the FMLN's Marxist ideology transformed the war from a struggle for social justice and equality into a component of the worldwide struggle between the Soviet Union and the United States. The United States supported the El Salvadoran government while the Soviet Union, Vietnam, and Ethiopia supported the rebels, ensuring the continuance of the struggle and costing the international community substantial amounts. These costs are important to analyze in order to better understand the value of preventive action.

American aid is the most staggering figure, totaling $4.4 billion between 1981 and 1991 (see table 10.4).[41] Other Western countries added, collectively, just over $300 million in aid to the government, though West German citizens, who had sympathy for social democrats, donated $1 million to the FMLN through a voluntary "Arms for El Salvador" campaign.[42] The contributions of socialist countries to the FMLN can only be guessed at, since they do not make such information available, particularly when the aid was extended to guerrilla organizations. One billion dollars is a conservative estimate for the economic and military support rendered by

TABLE 10.4
El Salvador: Cold War Costs ($U.S. Millions)

United States	4,400.0
West (non-U.S.)	300.0
West German citizens' voluntary contributions to FMLN	1.0
USSR & allies (estimated)	1,000.0
Humanitarian	39.0
TOTAL	**5,740.0**

Sources: www.sirius.com/~isthmus. Douglas Farah, "Death Squads Flex Muscle," *Washington Post* (October 13, 1996), A42. UNDPI, *Yearbook of the United Nations 1984* (New York: United Nations, 1985). Central Intelligence Agency, *World Factbook 1990* (Washington, D.C.: CIA).

the Soviet Union, Vietnam, and Ethiopia over the course of the decade. This estimate is one-quarter of the known volume of American aid, and projects aid of only $100 million per year collectively from the FMLN's Marxist supporters. Some humanitarian assistance was also provided through UN channels in the 1980s, but is not generally distinguished in UN accounting from the assistance given to the region as a whole; $3.9 million of food aid was provided in 1984, which suggests that perhaps $39 million worth of humanitarian assistance was provided over the course of the decade.[43] These figures make the enormous costs of war clear, as well as the paucity of support for its victims.

Total Costs

The total cost of El Salvador's civil war to the international community was approximately $8.1 billion, as illustrated in table 10.5. The bulk of these costs were incurred during the 1980s, prior to attempts to end the war and when the Cold War fueled much of the aid giving.

Costs of Preventive Action

ONUSAL was in one sense not preventive, since it commenced after eleven years of war. In another sense, however, it was designed with the purpose of reshaping the social and economic face of El Salvador so as to prevent future violence. Separating and even demobilizing combatants without an accompanying social mission would have ensured the resumption of violence in the not-so-distant future. Instead, ONUSAL conducted a vigorous campaign of education, investigation, and demobilization that sought to alter the fundamental causes of the conflict.

Because of its dual role in conflict resolution and prevention, ONUSAL is both a cost of the war and the actual cost of prevention. Obviously, Cold

TABLE 10.5
El Salvador: Total International Costs of Conflict ($U.S. Millions)

Post–Cold War costs:	
UN operations	107.0
Humanitarian aid	497.4
Economic aid	699.6
Individual nations	1,068.0
Total costs since 1990	2,372.0
Cold War costs	5,740.0
TOTAL	**8,112.0**

War politics prevented international intervention prior to 1990. The inability of the international community to take action in the late 1970s or 1980s made ONUSAL necessary to end the conflict and demobilize its participants. At the same time, it sought to rebuild the social and economic institutions that had been destroyed by the war, making its costs as a preventive mission much higher than if action could have been taken before the war broke out. In both roles, however, ONUSAL seems to have been successful. The country has stabilized, the economy is expanding and noted among the stronger in the region, and the former warring parties are working within the political process without a return to violence.

The Human Rights Division of ONUSAL began work in the fall of 1991. The complete operation was deployed from July 1992 to April 1995, with a total cost of $107 million. It undertook reconstruction partially through education, which was intended to alter the country's fundamental approach to economic organization and human rights. It was composed of approximately 700 military and police personnel, 170 international civilian staff, and 187 local staff, divided into four components, the Human Rights, Military, Police, and Electoral Divisions.[44]

Perhaps the most important component of ONUSAL, and the biggest, was the Police Division, which had the task of assisting in the creation of a new Salvadoran police force, the National Civil Police (PNC), to replace the old public security structures that had been so implicated in the civil war. The Police Division supervised and instructed an auxiliary police force that functioned during the transition period, and closely monitored the program and functioning of the new National Public Security Academy, which would provide the ranks of future police. When the PNC began its deployment in March 1993, the Police Division worked closely with the force to evaluate performance and provide logistical and technical support. The Police Division was also a critical support to the Human Rights Division, conducting special inquiries when necessary and providing security for former rebel leaders, although some tensions developed between the divisions regarding the success of operations in rooting out human rights problems.

The Human Rights Division did its part to transform society by working with the Supreme Court of Justice to oversee the training of judges and magistrates and to develop a new doctrine for the armed forces and a human-rights oriented curriculum for the military academies. Although violations of human rights still occurred, the division undertook extensive educational programs to develop a regard for justice and constitutional law among the citizens and security forces.

The Police and Human Rights Divisions may have been the most critical parts of the mission in terms of preventing future violence. For over a century El Salvador had been governed by dictatorial leaders, a brutal military, and ruthless death squads who ruled together through repression and blatant disregard for human or civil rights. ONUSAL began to reverse this trend, and its emphasis on education rather than condemnation was a critical part of El Salvador's reform. Though abuses exist still, so too do the means by which to bring offenders to justice. This is hardly meant to suggest that all problems have been solved and that the mechanisms of justice work flawlessly, but the mechanisms do exist, a notable difference in the country's approach to law.

As a result of ONUSAL's work, the elections of March 1994 progressed reasonably freely and fairly. No candidate in the presidential voting received an absolute majority, and the coalition brought Armando Calderon Sol of the ARENA, the former government party, to the presidency. The ARENA led in legislative voting as well, with thirty-nine of the eighty-four seats, to twenty-one for the FMLN, eighteen to the PDC, and four to the PCN.[45] ONUSAL's mandate was slated to end in December 1994, but was extended until April 30, 1995, in order to ensure the continued transition to democracy, particularly in the continued reform of the police force and judicial and electoral systems, economic reintegration programs, and extension of public services to former conflict zones. When ONUSAL withdrew in April 1995, the prospects for continued stability and peace looked promising.

Conclusions

The total cost of the war to the international community was $8.1 billion. Excluding the costs incurred during the Cold War, when intervention was impossible, the cost to the international community was $2.4 billion, incurred mainly in reconstruction costs begun after the signing of the peace accords. Although the sum may seem relatively small, the cost of intervention was only $107 million. The ONUSAL mission was, therefore, highly cost-effective, totaling only 4.6 percent of the non–Cold War costs. It was also highly effective at transforming the problems that had led to violence, leaving behind a stable government and expanding economy at its departure. This clearly illustrates that even an expansive interventionist mission designed to restructure the very foundations of a society is more cost-effective than war. As both resolution and prevention, ONUSAL was both highly effective and highly cost-effective from the standpoint of the international community.

Part Four

Conclusion

11

The Case for Conflict Prevention

Michael E. Brown and Richard N. Rosecrance

IN THIS STUDY, WE HAVE TRIED to determine whether conflict prevention makes sense in selfish cost-benefit terms for international powers and the world community in general. We recognize that the initial and main impact of conflict falls on the participants themselves. But outsiders are affected by it, and in the conflicts we have studied, outside powers ended up paying a large part of the bill.

Our main conclusion can be stated straightforwardly. In every case we examined—which included different kinds of conflict and diverse international responses—conflict prevention actually cost or would have cost the international community much less than the conflicts themselves. In some cases the cost difference is truly staggering—in short, conflict prevention is cost-effective. We therefore reject the null hypothesis that early conflict prevention would have made no political, economic, or military difference to the outcome.

In this concluding chapter, we summarize our findings and discuss their policy implications. Our view is that the case for conflict prevention is a compelling one. This is partly because internal costs of conflict frequently and generally become international costs. When internal conflicts break out, the interests of regional and outside powers are almost always engaged. Deadly conflicts—even within states—are rarely hermetically sealed. Moreover, the costs of prevention efforts are much lower than the costs that actual conflicts impose on outside powers, such as refugee costs, direct economic costs, economic opportunity costs, military costs, and the costs of conflict resolution, reconstruction, and rehabilitation. It is significant that many of these costs are ultimately paid for by the world's leading powers, including the United States. In the future, we believe, the burden of proof against intervention should reside with policymakers opposed to conflict prevention efforts.

It is not surprising that there has been, until now, a worldwide disposition to neglect important intervention or conflict prevention tasks. The remembered impact of Vietnam and other episodes predisposes decision makers to hesitate when confronted with deadly internal conflicts. One should recall, however, that Vietnam occurred during the height of the Cold War. It was fed by both sides of that broader conflict. There was no general agreement, shared by all great powers, that it should rapidly be brought to a close. The intervening parties to the conflict therefore did not enjoy well-recognized legitimacy, internally or internationally. Involvement did not anticipate the conflict or take place in the early stages of its gestation. The intervention was regarded by many as a one-sided attempt to thwart well-developed nationalist sentiments on the part of a mobilized Vietnamese population. Intervention in Vietnam also did not have the stable support of public opinion in the United States or other nations over the period. Public opinion fluctuated and then came to oppose American action.

The conflicts we have studied suggest, per contra, that leadership can bring a hesitant public to support conflict prevention so long as it does not involve large casualties or proceed over too long a time. We realize that this is an imprecise standard, but it would be foolish to aim for a false and possibly evanescent concreteness in such matters. Conflict prevention in Haiti, and later, Bosnia, was initially opposed by the U.S. population, but when it was shown that these interventions were limited ones, public opinion shifted to approve them. Public tolerance for such involvement is also buttressed by international community acceptance and sanction. This lends further support for our conclusion that early efforts supported by international agreement are more effective and cheaper than later ones.

We recognize that some reject this conclusion. A few observers believe that internal conflict will not generally be governed by outside powers even when international legitimacy is on their side. There are always sources of support, they say, fueling such conflicts. Private sources have helped to finance extremist groups in neighboring and noncontiguous nations. Automatic rifles and bomb-making equipment are readily available on the world market. According to this view, conflicts create their own international constituencies even in the absence of the Cold War. They cannot be completely shut down.

Acknowledging these claims, we nonetheless contend that the task of conflict prevention is much easier than it has been typically portrayed to be in the aftermath of Vietnam. Few disputes represent potential quagmires for international conflict resolution and prevention efforts. With Russia and China on board, a more or less unified stance could be and has been developed toward North Korea. With South Africa in the hands of the African National Congress, conflict in Namibia, Angola, and Mozambique moderated. Conflict prevention and resolution also became more feasible as the parties came to recognize the opportunity costs they were paying for indulging in unlimited local conflict. Both Israel and the Arab states have paid an exceedingly high price for continued strife. This has not yet led to success of the Oslo Accord. In regard to Northern Ireland, there has been agreement between the British government, the Dublin government, and the contending parties in Belfast. In all these cases, conflict continues to unroll when international leadership flags. UN peacekeepers cannot be expected to perform miracles when key great powers stand aside. When they are active and in agreement, however, the local situation changes radically, and for the better. We again claim that early conflict prevention efforts will be far more effective than they have in the past been expected to be.

Findings

We acknowledge that analyzing the cost-effectiveness of conflict prevention is a difficult task. The main problem is that if conflict prevention efforts are successful, we cannot know what armed conflict might have cost: those latter costs never materialize. By the same token, if conflict prevention efforts are not launched or if they fail and war breaks out, we cannot be sure what the costs of successful prevention might have been. We can therefore make only indirect comparisons of the costs of prevention and the costs of armed conflict, as pointed out above. There are three ways around this problem.

First, we can engage in counterfactual analysis by comparing the costs of *actual* conflicts to *estimates* of what it would have cost to prevent these conflicts from taking place. In this case, we identify a moment when international action could have been taken to prevent the dispute from escalating to violence, then ascertain what kinds of international actions would have been needed to prevent violence from breaking out.

Second, we can engage in counterfactual analysis by comparing the costs of *actual* conflict prevention efforts to the *estimated* costs to regional and international powers of conflicts that might have taken place. To engage in this kind of counterfactual analysis, we need to make assumptions about how conflicts might have escalated and spread. Here we need to examine alternative scenarios.

Third, we can compare the costs of *actual* conflicts to the costs of the *actual* conflict resolution and conflict prevention efforts that followed. Although these efforts are usually characterized as conflict resolution efforts because they aim to resolve conflicts that have already taken place, they are also conflict prevention efforts because they seek to keep war from breaking out again. This is a hard case for conflict prevention because the international community is helping to rebuild political and economic systems that have been torn apart by years of war. These costs are higher than the costs the international community would have paid to prevent these conflicts from breaking out in the first place.

In this study we have employed all three of these methodological options, thus minimizing the chance of bias skewing the final results. First, Andrea Talentino and Mike Blakley compared the costs of actual conflicts to the estimated costs of conflict prevention efforts that could have been, but were not, taken. They analyzed five conflicts: Bosnia, Rwanda, Somalia, Haiti, and the Gulf War. Second, Bradley Thayer and Renée de Nevers compared the costs of actual prevention efforts in Macedonia and Slovakia, respectively, to the estimated costs of conflict that might have taken place. Third, Andrea Talentino compared the costs of the conflicts in Cambodia and El Salvador to the costs of the conflict resolution and conflict prevention actions that followed. The findings from these case studies are summarized in table 11.1. In each of these cases, conflict prevention cost or would have cost the international community far less than the conflicts themselves. As noted above, the cost difference in some cases is truly enormous.

It is also important to note that in some respects we have understated the costs of violent conflicts to outside powers. For example, the economic opportunity costs generated by conflicts are undoubtedly great, but they are difficult to measure and are consequently downplayed in our calculations. In addition, violent conflicts often undermine regional stability, international organizations (like the United Nations), international norms, and international order in general. It is hard to place a dollar value on these costs, but they are real, and they are paid by every actor in the international system. Unless they are stopped, regional conflicts frequently beget other conflicts.

Policymakers in distant capitals would like to think that the costs of local conflicts are paid mainly by local and regional powers. It is certainly true that many refugee costs and economic costs fall on nearby states. It is also true that a wide range of direct economic costs, opportunity costs, economic reconstruction costs, and costs associated with both military intervention and conflict resolution missions are paid for by the leading powers. The United States, which is geographically isolated from most of the

TABLE 11.1
Summary of the Effectiveness of Conflict Prevention Efforts: Total Costs of Intervention ($U.S. Billions)

Case	Cost of Conflict to Outside Powers	Cost of Conflict Prevention	Difference
Bosnia			
Actual conflict	53.7		
Possible intervention		33.3	20.4
Rwanda			
Actual conflict	4.5		
Possible intervention		1.3	3.2
Somalia			
Actual conflict	7.3		
Possible intervention		1.5	5.8
Haiti			
Actual conflict	5.0		
Possible intervention		2.3	2.7
Gulf War[a]			
Actual conflict	114.0		
Possible intervention			
Small		10.0	104.0
Intermediate		30.0	84.0
Macedonia			
Possible conflict			
Intermediate	15.0		14.7
Large	143.9		143.6
Actual intervention		0.3	
Slovakia			
Possible conflict			
Intermediate	1.3		0.4
Large	15.0		14.1
Actual intervention		0.9	
Cambodia[b]			
Actual conflict	12.0		
Possible intervention		1.7	10.3
El Salvador[b]			
Actual conflict	2.4		
Possible intervention		0.1	2.3

[a]Costs to the Western powers only [b]Costs incurred since the end of the Cold War

world's violent struggles, nonetheless pays a disproportionate share of the costs generated by these conflicts. Because of its economic position, the United States is often deeply involved in economic reconstruction efforts, for example. And because it stands alone as the world's only military superpower, the United States plays a leading role whenever multilateral military operations are undertaken: the Gulf War, Haiti, and Bosnia are cases in point. In short, violent conflicts impose high costs on both neighboring states and distant lands, and the United States often pays a high price sooner or later.

Lessons

Although neighboring states and regional powers often become involved in local conflicts—usually for reasons of self-interest—distant powers are generally reluctant to do so. Policymakers in Washington and other Western capitals deploy three main arguments in defense of inaction.

First, it is often said that the interests of international powers are not engaged by conflicts in far-off lands. Why, Western decision makers say, should we care about what happens half a world away? The answer is that local conflicts almost always have important regional ramifications, and regional turmoil—even in far corners of the world—affects the interests of major powers. In addition, failure to prevent deadly conflicts from breaking out undermines the credibility of the United Nations, international law, and international norms of behavior, as well as the international reputations of the great powers. In indirect but nonetheless important ways, failure to act also affects the interest of these states. Moreover, according to the UN Charter, the five permanent members of the UN Security Council—the United States, the United Kingdom, France, Russia, and China—are formally obligated to safeguard international peace and security. This is the price they have agreed to pay in exchange for their special status in the United Nations system.

Western policymakers would like to think that their interests are not engaged by violent conflicts in remote parts of the globe and that they can avoid the problems they cause. However, as we have seen time and again—precisely because their interests are likely to be involved—the United States and other leading powers become embroiled in violent conflicts anyway. However, their involvement often comes at a later stage when the costs of international engagement are high. This study suggests that many local conflicts impose high costs even on distant powers.

Second, it is said that even if international powers would like to launch more conflict prevention efforts, they do not know what to do because they cannot predict where conflicts will break out. But as we have shown, international powers have often received timely warning of impending trouble. It was widely recognized in the first few months of 1992, for example, that Bosnia was about to plunge into chaos. Similarly, it was widely understood in late March and early April 1994 that the situation in Rwanda was moving toward violence. Early warning was not lacking in these cases, and it is not, more generally, an insuperable barrier to preventive action.

Third, it is often said that the international community lacks the capacity to engage in large numbers of conflict prevention efforts. U.S. officials, in particular, insist that the United States cannot afford to become the "world's policeman." This, in our view, is a particularly specious argument. It is of course true that the United States and the international community cannot become involved in conflicts everywhere. It does not follow, however, that they cannot take action anywhere. The United States and the community of nations clearly have the capacity to project tremendous military capabilities over long distances, as they proved during the Gulf War. The United States currently spends far more on defense than any other country in the world—more, in fact, than the next ten countries combined. If, given this level of investment, the United States is incapable of deploying comparatively small numbers of soldiers to places where genocide is being committed and where no great power stands in opposition (Bosnia and Rwanda come to mind), then the competence of those in charge of the U.S. defense establishment has to be called into question. Nor did U.S. public opinion shifts in Haiti or Bosnia appear to bar the way to purposeful U.S. leadership.

Conflict prevention in any event involves more than military responses to impending crises. It also includes long-term efforts to promote political and economic development in potential trouble spots, before violence emerges. The international community clearly has the capacity to engage in large-scale development efforts, if it is so inclined. It often launches economic reconstruction and rehabilitation efforts after wars have come to an end, when those costs are comparatively high. Bosnia, El Salvador, and Haiti are cases in point. If the world can support economic reconstruction after wars have taken place, it can surely afford (much cheaper) development efforts before violence breaks out.

If national interests are often engaged, early warning frequently available, and operational capabilities robust, why are distant powers reluctant to become involved in regional trouble spots? The answer is that domestic political considerations strongly influence intervention. Western policymakers have five main political fears. Yet each is unfounded in respect to conflict prevention efforts.

First, decision makers fear that international actions will lack public support. This fear is particularly strong in policy circles in the United States.

Polls confirm that Americans do not want the United States to become the world's policeman. But the question is whether the public will support selective engagement in a comparatively small number of places. The United States has become involved in peace operations in Haiti, Bosnia, Macedonia, the Middle East, and elsewhere, and these operations have been supported by the U.S. public. The key, as always, is for the executive to make a strong and explicit case on interest or moral grounds for the United States to be involved. We believe that officials in particular underestimate the extent to which latent public support exists for preventive engagement, and for the means at the disposal of the president to create public support after the fact.

Second, policymakers fear that international operations will cost too much economically. This is a legitimate concern for wars that have already broken out. However, as the case studies of this volume have shown, the costs of preventive actions are far more modest. Decision makers who worry about justifying the economic costs of their policy decisions should place more emphasis on comparatively inexpensive and cost-effective prevention efforts.

Third, Western policymakers fear that their soldiers will be killed or wounded in international military operations. It is right and proper that high officials should care deeply about the soldiers under their command who could be placed in harm's way. Conflict prevention operations, however, are comparatively low-risk undertakings. The preventive UN military deployment in Macedonia, for example, has so far accomplished its mission without major incident. It is far riskier to send troops into war (as coalition leaders did in the Persian Gulf) or into situations where brutal conflicts have raged for years (as they did in Bosnia) than to use them in prevention efforts. The Somalia episode shows that when intervention is both too little and too late, the consequences can be serious in terms of both public opinion and policy. But it is also worth underscoring the key point that conflict prevention involves a wide range of economic and nonmilitary activities that do not involve the deployment and stationing of troops.

Fourth, policymakers say that they do not want to make open-ended commitments in far-off places. U.S. officials in particular worry about getting "bogged down in another Vietnam"—a military quagmire that drags on without resolution. As a result, American leaders insist on an "exit strategy" before they agree to "enter" the regional conflict. In most cases these exit strategies are not strategies at all, but merely timetables for withdrawal. U.S. President Bill Clinton's 1996 decision to keep American troops in Bosnia was linked to a timetable to pull them out by the summer of 1998, though this commitment has now been changed in favor of an indefinite deployment. We believe that policymakers can distinguish between long-term involvement in open military hostilities (another Vietnam) and commitments to low-risk, low-cost, largely nonviolent operations, designed to prevent conflict. The latter might involve long-term military deployments (such as the UN peacekeeping missions in Cyprus and the Middle East), but this is not necessarily a dangerous outcome. The UN force in Cyprus has already kept the peace on the island for over two decades. There has been no permanent resolution of the conflict, but such successful operations lead to the conclusion that policymakers would be fortunate to have another Cyprus or two on their hands. Such long-term commitments, moreover, are not anachronistic. Western nations have just decided to bring new members into the NATO alliance, an action that increases and extends the commitments of previous members. If these kinds of open-ended commitments can be made over the long term, long-term commitments to conflict prevention can also be made.

Finally, decision makers fear failure, for obvious domestic political reasons. One advantage of early conflict prevention efforts is that they are more prone to succeed than later interventions. International efforts in Cyprus, Macedonia, and Slovakia have helped to stabilize volatile regions. We thus suspect that conflict prevention efforts are more likely to be successful than late-term interventions in ongoing wars. Conflict prevention is more feasible than conflict management or resolution.[1] If this is true, conflict prevention should be in the primary armory of policy leaders.

It is simply a fact of life that policymakers will be influenced by domestic political factors when they make foreign policy decisions. They will be reluctant to launch high-cost, high-risk, long-term international missions. But peacekeeping and conflict prevention should not be lumped under this catch-all category. Timely intervention may be a comparatively low-cost and low-risk undertaking.

The Burden of Proof

The analytical case for conflict prevention is a compelling one. Its costs are much lower than the costs that actual conflicts impose on outside powers. Although distant powers have managed to keep some conflicts at arm's length (Portuguese Timor and Sudan, for example), they usually become involved in one form or another over time. The question is not whether distant powers and international organizations will become involved in trying to stop deadly conflicts, but when and how. All too often international powers wait until violence has already broken out and conflicts have escalated. They need not do so.

The political case for conflict prevention is also persuasive. Conflict prevention efforts will generally enjoy public support if policymakers are careful to distinguish prevention from riskier types of operations and if the case for engagement is enunciated carefully. As this study seeks to demonstrate, conflict prevention operations are generally cost-effective undertakings. The burden of proof should henceforth be on decision makers who oppose conflict prevention activities.

The Significance of Conflict Prevention Efforts

In every case we examined—involving several different kinds of conflict and three different methodological approaches—conflict prevention through early intervention would have cost the international community far less than the costs generated by the conflicts themselves. In some cases, like the Gulf War, the cost differential between prevention and conflict is absolutely staggering.

This is true even though we have significantly underestimated the costs of conflict in general terms. We have focused centrally on the costs to outside powers and neglected the human and material costs to the participants themselves. These are enormous. In addition, the economic opportunity costs generated by conflicts are undoubtedly great, but they are difficult to assess, and they are, if anything, underestimated in our calculations. The ensuing regional instability that comes from unregulated conflict (note the history of the contemporary Middle East) is very great. Yet instability cannot be measured. When conflicts escalate into major wars, the costs are massive. Genocide and 800,000 deaths took place in Rwanda. Tens of thousands were killed in Bosnia, and Cambodia suffered more than 1 million deaths during its travail under Pol Pot.

Norm and Action in Conflict Prevention

One of the factors that importantly assists international conflict prevention efforts is the growing consensus around key norms in international politics. As one example, NATO will not admit countries that have not settled disputes with their neighbors. This pressure brought Slovakia and Hungary together; it also forced Romania and Hungary to settle their differences over Transylvania. The European Union will not take in countries that are domestically unstable, undemocratic, or have distorted, closed, or subsidized economies. The European Union insists that countries treat their minorities in a humanitarian way. Admission to the key clubs of international politics requires eschewing involvement in domestic or international conflict.

It is not enough, however, to espouse such norms at the theoretical level. International practice must follow international precept. Unfortunately, domestic leaders are still not fully aware of the leeway they enjoy in launching conflict prevention measures. This study suggests the following.

1. Conflict may be engendered by international inaction.
2. Successful conflict prevention can dampen and even eradicate the recrudescence of local conflict.
3. Successful conflict prevention is not expensive economically as compared to the costs of unregulated conflict.
4. Successful conflict prevention is not expensive politically as compared to the costs of unregulated conflict.
5. Conflict prevention is successful. Action in Macedonia successfully took place even though domestic politics by no means mandated such action. With the great powers of the Security Council agreed, costs will be low.
6. Conflict prevention is far less risky than intervening in a civil or international war. Preventive military deployments usually involve far lower risks to troops than entering active hostilities. In addition, many of the elements of conflict prevention do not involve troops at all but rather mediation, economic aid/sanctions and technical assistance.
7. The United States is clearly a principal actor in the success of prevention efforts, especially if military action is being considered. Also, the United States often ends up paying a large proportion of the costs when conflicts among parties escalate.

This study contends that the United States, the United Nations, and key decision makers should adopt a policy of early conflict prevention in world politics. The world is not now in a situation like that of the 1920s when norms were propounded that generated no national response. The world is not now in a situation like the 1930s when actions by international organizations were resisted and even thwarted by key aggressive countries. The world is not now in a situation like that of the Cold War, in which international intervention to prevent local conflict only applied to one side of the bipolar division of world politics, and where efforts by one side could be and often were canceled by actions of the other. International action today requires agreement of the five permanent members of the UN Security Council. Securing this agreement means that action will be prompt, successful, and far less costly than it has been in the past. In fact it may be asserted that the decision makers of most important countries lag behind the actual state of international affairs. They display a hesitancy to intervene that stems from inapplicable Cold War analogies. They believe intervention causes rather than stems conflict. If the findings of this study become more generally recognized, however, an opposite conviction can gain strength. In that instance, the burden of proof will be on decision makers in key countries to explain why they did not intervene when they could have both prevented conflict and expense by doing so. In the United States, the Haiti case already focuses attention on this unnecessary delay. In Europe, Germany, and Japan, leaders understand that forces have to be ready to perform this function. In international conflict as well as many other realms of human activity, an ounce of prevention is worth a pound of cure.

Notes

Chapter 1

1. Boutros Boutros-Ghali, *Supplement to An Agenda for Peace—Position Paper of the Secretary-General on the Occasion of the Fiftieth Anniversary of the United Nations,* S/1995/1, 1995. This is not to say that early warning problems are nonexistent in this context. For a discussion of these problems, see Michael S. Lund, *Preventing Violent Conflicts: A Strategy for Preventive Diplomacy* (Washington, D.C.: U.S. Institute of Peace Press, 1996), 108–21. For a discussion of the ways in which these and other problems are underestimated by some advocates of preventive action, see Stephen John Stedman, "Alchemy for a New World Order: Overselling 'Preventive Diplomacy,'" *Foreign Affairs* 74 (May/June 1995): 14–20.

2. Indeed, senior officials in the Clinton administration instructed spokespeople to avoid using the word "genocide" in describing what was happening in Rwanda, fearing that this would push the administration into taking actions they dreaded for domestic political reasons. See Douglas Jehl, "Officials Told to Avoid Calling Rwanda Killings 'Genocide,'" *New York Times* (June 10, 1995). See also Holly J. Burkhalter, "The Question of Genocide: The Clinton Administration and Rwanda," *World Policy Journal* 11 (Winter 1994): 44–54.

3. For more details on this operation, see chapter 7 by Bradley Thayer.

4. Corollaries to the null hypothesis are (1) that the timing of intervention is irrelevant (early intervention is as difficult as mid-course or late intervention), and (2) that intervention has no effect on the outcome of civil conflicts.

5. See Susan L. Woodward, *Balkan Tragedy: Chaos and Dissolution after the Cold War* (Washington, D.C.: Brookings Institution, 1995).

6. See James D. Fearon, "Counterfactuals and Hypothesis Testing in Political Science," *World Politics* 43 (January 1991): 169–95.

7. Personal communication with John Mueller, University of Rochester, Department of Political Science, Sept. 1, 1998.

8. See H. R. Trevor-Roper, *History: Professional and Lay; An Inaugural Lecture Delivered before the University of Oxford on 12 November 1957* (Oxford: Clarendon Press, 1957).

9. See David Reynolds, "Churchill and the British 'Decision' to Fight on in 1940: Right Policy, Wrong Reasons," in *Diplomacy and Intelligence during the Second World War: Essays in Honour of F. H. Hinsley,* ed. Richard Langhorne (Cambridge: Cambridge University Press, 1985).

10. For more details on these operations, see UN Department of Public Information, *The United Nations and El Salvador, 1990–1995* (New York: United Nations, 1995); UNDPI, *The United Nations and Mozambique, 1992–1995* (New York: United Nations, 1995); UNDPI, *The United Nations and Cambodia, 1991–1995* (New York: United Nations, 1995); Marc Chernick, "Peacemaking and Violence in Latin America," in *The International Dimensions of Internal Conflict,* ed. Michael E. Brown (Cambridge: MIT Press, 1996), 267–307; Michael W. Doyle, *UN Peacekeeping in Cambodia: UNTAC's Civil Mandate* (Boulder: Rienner, 1995); Trevor Findlay, *Cambodia: The Legacy and Lessons of UNTAC,* Stockholm International Peace Research Institute (SIPRI) Report No. 9 (Oxford: Oxford University Press, 1995). See also chapters 9 and 10 on Cambodia and El Salvador by Andrea Talentino in this volume.

11. On Haiti, see UNDPI, *The United Nations and Haiti* (New York: United Nations, forthcoming), and chapter 5 by Mike Blakley in this volume. On Bosnia, see Spyros Economides and Paul Taylor, "Former Yugoslavia," in *The New Interventionism, 1991–1994: United Nations Experience in Cambodia, Former Yugoslavia, and Somalia,* ed. James Mayall (New York: Cambridge University Press, 1996), 59–93; Ivo H. Daalder, "Fear and Loathing in the Former Yugoslavia," in *The International Dimensions of Internal Conflict,* ed. Brown, 35–67; and chapter 2 by Andrea Talentino in this volume.

12. See Lawrence Freedman and Efraim Karsh, *The Gulf Conflict, 1990–1991* (London: Faber and Faber, 1993), and chapter 6 by Mike Blakley in this volume.

13. For a discussion of the methodological problems associated with counterfactual analysis, see Philip E. Tetlock and Aaron Belkin, eds., *Counterfactual Thought Experiments in World Politics: Logical, Methodological, and Psychological Perspectives* (Princeton: Princeton University Press, 1996), and Fearon, "Counterfactuals and Hypothesis Testing," 169–95.

14. For more on peace operations in general, see Alan James, *Peacekeeping in International Politics* (New York: St. Martin's Press, 1990); William J. Durch, ed., *The Evolution of UN Peacekeeping: Case Studies and Comparative Analysis* (New York: St. Martin's Press, 1993); Paul Diehl, *International Peacekeeping* (Baltimore: Johns Hopkins University Press, 1993); Donald C. F. Daniel and Bradd C. Hayes, eds., *Beyond Traditional Peacekeeping* (New York: St. Martin's Press, 1995); Mayall, ed., *The New Interventionism.* For discussions of the differences between traditional and multifunctional peacekeeping, see Chantal de Jonge Oudraat, "The United Nations and Internal Conflict," and Dan Lindley, "Collective Security Organizations and Internal Conflict," in *The International Dimensions of Internal Conflict,* ed. Brown, 489–535 and 537–68. For more details on the peace operations in Cambodia and El Salvador in particular, see chapters 9 and 10 by Andrea Talentino in this volume.

15. True conflict prevention was not an option in these five cases because the international system's leading powers could not agree on joint courses of action

during the Cold War. Indeed, the international competition between Washington, Moscow, and Beijing played a key role in sparking and driving these five conflicts as well as many others.

16. See Michael E. Brown, "Internal Conflict and International Action," in *The International Dimensions of Internal Conflict,* ed. Brown, 603–27. For a different breakdown of the conflict prevention problem, see Lund, *Preventing Violent Conflicts,* appendix A.

17. This discussion is based on Michael E. Brown and Chantal de Jonge Oudraat, "Internal Conflict and International Action: An Overview," in *Nationalism and Ethnic Conflict: An International Security Reader,* ed. Michael E. Brown, Owen Coté, Sean Lynn-Jones, and Steven E. Miller (Cambridge: MIT Press, 1997).

18. See Stephen Van Evera, "Hypotheses on Nationalism and War," *International Security* 18 (Spring 1994): 5–39.

19. This discussion is based on Brown and de Jonge Oudraat, "Internal Conflict and International Action," in *The International Dimensions of Internal Conflict,* ed. Brown.

20. For more on mediation, see Stephen John Stedman, "Negotiation and Mediation in Internal Conflict," in *The International Dimensions of Internal Conflict,* ed. Brown, 341–76; Roy Licklider, ed., *Stopping the Killing: How Civil Wars End* (New York: New York University Press, 1993); I. William Zartman, *Ripe for Resolution: Conflict and Intervention in Africa* (New York: Oxford University Press, 1989).

21. Promoting transparency will not help when groups have malign intentions toward one another, but it will dampen escalatory spirals when groups are driven to strengthen themselves by fears of the unknown. For more on confidence-building measures, see Joanna Spear, "Arms Limitations, Confidence-Building Measures, and Internal Conflicts," in *The International Dimensions of Internal Conflict,* ed. Brown, 377–410.

22. For more on traditional peacekeeping operations, see UNDPI, *The Blue Helmets: A Review of United Nations Peace-keeping* (New York: United Nations, 3rd ed.); UN Institute for Disarmament Research (UNIDIR), "Peace-keeping, Peacemaking, Peace Enforcement," *UNIDIR Newsletter* 24 (December 1993); Mats R. Berdal, *Whither UN Peacekeeping?* Adelphi Paper No. 281 (London: Brassey's, for the International Institute for Strategic Studies, 1993); Lori Fisler Damrosch, ed., *Enforcing Restraint: Collective Intervention in Internal Conflicts* (New York: Council on Foreign Relations Press, 1993); Daniel and Hayes, *Beyond Traditional Peacekeeping*; Durch, *The Evolution of UN Peacekeeping.*

23. For more on multifunctional peacekeeping operations, see Durch, *The Evolution of UN Peacekeeping.*

24. See Spear, "Arms Limitations, Confidence-Building Measures, and Internal Conflicts," in *The International Dimensions of Internal Conflict,* ed. Brown.

25. For more on arms enbargoes, see Spear, "Arms Limitations, Confidence-Building Measures, and Internal Conflicts." For more on economic sanctions, see Elizabeth Rogers, "Economic Sanctions and Internal Conflicts," in *The International Dimensions of Internal Conflict,* ed. Brown, 411–34.

26. For more on the use of military force, see Anthony Clark and Robert J.

Beck, *International Law and the Use of Force* (London: Routledge, 1993); Laura W. Reed and Carl Kaysen, *Emerging Norms of Justified Intervention* (Cambridge, Mass.: American Academy of Arts and Sciences, 1993); Richard N. Haass, *Intervention: The Use of American Military in the Post–Cold War World* (Washington, D.C.: Carnegie Endowment for International Peace, 1994); Ivo H. Daalder, "The United States and Military Intervention in Internal Conflict," in *The International Dimensions of Internal Conflict,* ed. Brown, 461–88; Damrosch, *Enforcing Restraint.*

27. Few analysts have attempted to estimate the costs of violent conflicts. Among those who have are John M. Richardson Jr. and S. W. R. de A. Samarasinghe, "Measuring the Economic Dimensions of Sri Lanka's Ethnic Conflict," in *Economic Dimensions of Ethnic Conflict,* ed. S. W. R. de A. Samarasinghe and Reed Coughlan (London: Pinter, 1991), 194–223; Michael Cranna, ed., *The True Cost of Conflict: Seven Recent Wars and Their Effects on Society* (New York: New Press, 1994). Neither of these studies focused on the costs of conflicts to outside powers, our main concern in this study.

28. For more discussion, see Gil Loescher, *Refugee Movements and International Security,* Adelphi Paper No. 268 (London: International Institute for Strategic Studies, 1992).

Chapter 2

1. U.S. State Department *Fact Sheet* prepared by the Bureau of European and Canadian Affairs, *Implementing the Dayton Peace Agreement: The Contribution of the U.S. and International Community to Economic Revitalization* (cited August 12, 1996); for more information, see www.state.gov/www/current; and "Preliminary Plan of Needs of Bosnia and Herzegovina in the Process of Reconstruction and Rehabilitation," available from www.bosnianembassy.org/bih/ak0002.htm.

2. The CIA predicted in November 1990 that Yugoslavia would break apart within the next 18 months and that "this [was] likely to be accompanied by ethnic violence and unrest which could lead to civil war." A U.S. official stated, "I think you can almost write the death certificate now." Deputy Secretary of State Lawrence Eagleburger, who had been an ambassador to Yugoslavia, reportedly shared the CIA's pessimistic view of the country's future. See "Evolution in Europe: Yugoslavia Seen Breaking Up Soon," *New York Times* (November 28, 1990).

3. John Mueller, "The Rise, Decline, and Shallowness of Militant Nationalism in Europe," prepared for presentation at the Rochester-Jagiellonian Conference, May 30–31, 1997.

4. "Bosnia: Too Little, Too Late?" *U.S. News and World Report* (May 17, 1993); estimates as high as 400,000 have also been made, but these came primarily when fighting had already begun and intervention would have entailed rolling back Serb gains.

5. Warren Zimmermann, *Origins of a Catastrophe* (New York: Times Books, 1996), 212–14.

6. The information in this section is taken from several sources: Mark Almond, *Europe's Backyard War: The War in the Balkans* (London: Heinemann, 1994);

David Owen, *Balkan Odyssey* (London: Gollancz, 1995); Susan L. Woodward, *Balkan Tragedy: Chaos and Dissolution after the Cold War* (Washington, D.C.: Brookings Institution, 1995); and Warren Zimmermann, *Origins of a Catastrophe*.

7. Woodward, *Balkan Tragedy,* 51.

8. Ibid., 54–55.

9. This is the perspective of Warren Zimmermann, the last U.S. ambassador to Yugoslavia, and a recurring theme of his book. See Zimmermann, *Origins of a Catastrophe*.

10. Woodward, *Balkan Tragedy,* 133.

11. Ibid., 143.

12. Zimmermann, *Origins of a Catastrophe,* 145.

13. Woodward, *Balkan Tragedy,* 146.

14. Ibid., 173.

15. Both Lord Owen and Warren Zimmermann suggested that, particularly early on, most Serbs outside of Milosevic and Karadzic were not convinced of their "historic" mission and could have been easily deterred by a Western army (Owen, *Balkan Odyssey,* and Zimmermann, *Origins of a Catastrophe*).

16. Owen, *Balkan Odyssey,* 263.

17. United Nations, *Information Notes, United Nations Peace-keeping* (New York: United Nations, 1994), 69.

18. James B. Steinberg, "International Involvement in the Yugoslavia Conflict," in *Enforcing Restraint, Collective Intervention in Internal Conflicts,* ed. Lori Fisler Damrosch (New York: Council on Foreign Relations Press, 1993), 44.

19. Ivo H. Daalder, "Fear and Loathing in the Former Yugoslavia," in *The International Dimensions of Internal Conflict,* ed. Michael E. Brown (Cambridge: MIT Press, 1996), 54.

20. Stockholm International Peace Research Institute, *SIPRI Yearbook 1995: Armaments, Disarmament, and International Security* (Oxford: Oxford University Press, 1996), 217.

21. Ibid., 221–22.

22. Ibid., 221.

23. Ibid., 222.

24. Ibid., 228.

25. "Peace at Last, at Least for Now," *The Economist* (November 25, 1995).

26. Ibid.

27. *Final Fact Sheet, Operation Deny Flight* (cited December 21, 1995), available from www.nato.int.

28. "A Chilly Peace in Bosnia," *U.S. News and World Report* (December 4, 1995).

29. The IFOR mandate is to monitor and enforce compliance with the Dayton agreement. It also supports nonmilitary tasks such as creating a secure environment for elections, assisting the UNHCR and other aid agencies, preventing interference with the movement of civilian populations, and assisting in the clearing of mine fields. It is composed of IFOR land forces, headquartered in Sarajevo with divisions in Mostar, Tuzla, and Banja Luka; IFOR air forces, exercised through the NATO operations center at Vincenza, Italy; and IFOR naval forces, provided by a

joint NATO/WEU force of destroyers, frigates, and patrol craft. Carrier-based aviation and amphibious forces are also in the region and able to provide support if necessary. Ten thousand of the available forces are provided by non-NATO nations. All information on IFOR comes from the International Institute for Strategic Studies, *The Military Balance 1996–97* (London: Oxford University Press, 1997), 303–5.

30. UNPROFOR's 40,000 troops were divided among eight sectors and the command center. Command held 7,096 troops; Sector North: 3,925; Sector South: 4,334; Sector East: 1,842; Sector West: 3,060; Sector Sarajevo: 5,043; Sector Southwest: 5,787; Sector Northeast: 2,873; and Gorazde: 477. In most cases, the troops consisted of infantry battalions with police and logistical support. International Institute for Strategic Studies, *The Military Balance 1992–93* (London: Brassey's, 1993), 249; and *The Military Balance 1994–95* (London: Oxford University Press, 1995), 274–76.

31. These operations are listed with UNPROFOR in *The Military Balance,* and are not listed separately in the *SIPRI Yearbook.* NATO Fact Sheets give no indication of cost.

32. *The Military Balance 1996–97,* 304 and 1997–98, 284; IFOR is composed mainly of combat soldiers divided into three sectors. The northeast is controlled by an American division based on Tuzla; the northwest by a British-led division based in Gornji Vakuf; and the south by a French-led division based in Mostar. The French sector includes the highly sensitive Sarajevo area.

33. *SIPRI Yearbook 1995,* 89.

34. United Nations, *Information Notes, United Nations Peace-keeping* (New York: United Nations, 1994), 104–8; United Nations Department of Public Information, *The United Nations and the Situation in the Former Yugoslavia* (New York: United Nations, 1995), 62.

35. "UN Chief Eager over Peace Plan" (cited December 1995), available from www.nando.net/newsroom/nt/1204yugo33.html; and *The United Nations and the Situation in the Former Yugoslavia,* 62–65.

36. "Thin Hope for Bosnian Refugees in Peace Planning," Reuters Information Service, December 9, 1995.

37. "Land of Slaughter," *Time* (June 8, 1992), and "War Refugees Panicked by German Moves to Send Them Back," Associated Press (cited January 12, 1996), available from www.nando.net.

38. American Council for Voluntary International Action, "Humanitarian Efforts in Bosnia," available from www.interaction.org.

39. "A Chilly Peace in Bosnia," *U.S. News and World Report* (December 4, 1995).

40. U.S. State Department *Fact Sheet,* prepared by the Bureau of European and Canadian Affairs, released by the Department of Public Information, *Implementing the Dayton Peace Agreement: The Contribution of the U.S. and International Community to Economic Revitalization* (cited August 8, 1996), available from www.state.gov/www/current/bosnia/bosnia_economic_recovery.html.

41. "Preliminary Plan of Needs of Bosnia and Herzegovina in the Process of Reconstruction and Rehabilitation," available from www.bosnianembassy.org.

42. "Economic and Infrastructure Overview for Bosnia," available from www.itaiep.doc/eebic/balkan/economic.html.

43. "Summary of Multilateral Reconstruction Programs for Bosnia and Herzegovina," available from www.itaiep.doc/eebic/balkan/opps/multi2.html; and "Donors Pledge $1.23 Billion to Help Rebuild Bosnia," available from www.europa.eu.int.

44. "Economic and Infrastructure Overview for Bosnia."

45. WEU Information Document, *The Yugoslav Conflict—Chronology of Events,* available from www.weu.int/eng.

46. "Macedonia Appeals for Help for Ex-Yugoslavia," available from www2.nando.net/newsroom/nt/425mace.html.

47. Bosnia Peace Implementation Conference (London), "Summary," *Session Five: Reconstruction and Development,* December 11, 1995, available from www.usis.lt/wireless/wf951211/95121103.htm.

48. United Nations, *Economic Survey of Europe in 1995–96* (Geneva: United Nations, 1996), 108–9.

49. "Macedonia Appeals for Help."

50. OMRI Special Report No. 1, *Pursuing Balkan Peace* (cited January 9, 1996), available from www.omri.cz/Publications/PBP/Index.html

51. *FY96 US-Funded Economic Development and Humanitarian Assistance for Bosnia-Herzegovina,* available from www.itaiep.doc.gov/eebic/balkan/opps/aid.htm. As some of this aid was channeled through private organizations such as the American Red Cross and CARE, this figure has been reduced by $200 million, the sum already counted in the humanitarian costs section.

52. U.S. State Department, *Fact Sheet* (cited August 12, 1996).

53. U.S. State Department, *Fact Sheet* (cited November 11, 1996), available from dosfan.lib.uic.edu/www/current/bosnia/bosnia_economic_recovery.html.

54. White House Fact Sheet, *Training and Equipping the Bosnian Federation,* released by the White House July 9, 1996, and distributed by the Bureau of Public Affairs (cited July 12, 1996), available from www.state.gov/www/current/bosnia/iforrole.html.

55. The information on Germany, Italy, Austria, and the Netherlands comes from *Japan's Office of Development Assistance, ODA Annual Report 1995* (Tokyo: Association for the Promotion of International Cooperation), 494; other information comes from "UK Bilateral Humanitarian Aid for the Former Yugoslavia," available from www.oneworld.org/oda/oda_yugo.html.

56. "Emergency Aid for Refugees, Internally Displaced Persons and Afflicted Persons in the Former Yugoslavia," available from www.nttls.co.jp/infomofa/press/release/emgcy_aid.html.

57. Mueller, "The Rise, Decline, and Shallowness of Militant Nationalism in Europe."

58. Ibid., 10; Zimmermann also supports this perspective, contending that the Bosnian Serb forces in particular had little commitment to their cause beyond opportunism and would melt before a show of Western resolve.

59. "Bosnia: Too Little, Too Late?" Reuters World Service, April 25, 1996.

60. This estimate is based on the IFOR cost of $5 billion per year for 60,000 troops. As such, it is a high estimate since a preventive force would not have faced

the problems with land mines, cantonment, demobilization, and refugee issues that IFOR later did.

61. Zimmermann, *Origins of a Catastrophe,* 214.

62. United Nations, *Information Notes, United Nations Peace-keeping* (New York: United Nations, 1995), 126.

63. See Mueller, "The Rise, Decline, and Shallowness of Militant Nationalism in Europe"; and Zimmermann, *Origins of a Catastrophe.*

64. "Bosnia: Too Little, Too Late?"

65. Massimo Calabresi, "Hope on the Rise," available from www.pathfinder.com/time/magazine/1998/int/980406/europe.hope_on_the-rise.9.html; Misha Glenny, "Europe's Restless Region," available from www.pathfinder.com/time/magazine/1998/int/980119/special_report_europes_14.html.

66. It is important to remember here that we are focusing solely on the Bosnian case and not on the factors causing the breakup of Yugoslavia. If a democratic Yugoslavia could have been created, the republics might not have seceded, reducing the costs for all parties, Bosnia included.

Chapter 3

1. Estimates on deaths due to the conflict vary widely. The UNAMIR site on the Internet—ralph.gmu.edu/cfpa/peace/unamir.html—estimates 500,000. In "Canada Army Chief Named to Lead Zaire Forces as Officials Map Strategy" (November 15, 1996), the *Los Angeles Times* reports 800,000 dead; reports in *U.S. News and World Report* and *Time* also cite this figure. The Internet site provided the refugee statistics that are corroborated by the UN report, *UNHCR by Numbers* (1995), which estimated the total number of Rwandan refugees to be 2.25 billion by January 1995. Information on the state of life in the refugee camps comes from "Rwanda: Dilemmas of a Total Disaster," *World Disasters Report,* International Committee of the Red Cross, available from www.ifrc.org/wdr95/ch07.htm.

2. United Nations Department of Public Information (UNDPI), *The United Nations and Rwanda, 1993–1996* (New York: United Nations, 1996), 44.

3. Nancy Gibbs, "Rwanda: Cry the Forsaken Country," *Time* (August 1, 1994), available from cgi.pathfinder.com/time/magazine/archive/1994/940801/94081.cover. html.

4. Scott R. Feil, *Preventing Genocide: How the Early Use of Force Might Have Succeeded in Rwanda* (Washington, D.C.: Carnegie Commission on Preventing Deadly Conflict, 1998).

5. United Nations, *Information Notes, United Nations Peace-keeping* (New York: United Nations, 1995), 126 and 158.

6. UNDPI, *The United Nations and Rwanda, 1993–1996,* 9.

7. Ibid., 9–11.

8. Gérard Prunier, *The Rwanda Crisis 1959–1994: History of a Genocide* (London: Hurst, 1995), 84.

9. Ibid., 87–160.

10. Central Intelligence Agency, *World Factbook 1988, 1989, 1990* (Washington, D.C.: CIA).

11. Stockholm International Peace Research Institute, *SIPRI Yearbook 1995: Armaments, Disarmament and International Security* (Oxford: Oxford University Press, 1996), 101.

12. UNDPI, *The United Nations and Rwanda,* 21.

13. Ibid., 32.

14. Ibid., 244; letter dated March 14, 1994, from the minister of foreign affairs of Belgium to the UN secretary general, Document 34.

15. *SIPRI Yearbook 1995,* 103; "The Killers Meet Their Match," *The Economist* (December 3, 1994).

16. *SIPRI Yearbook 1995,* 103.

17. Ibid., 104.

18. Ibid.

19. The story of Kibuye was reported in "From Mass Murder to Mass Amnesia," *Los Angeles Times* (November 29, 1996), A1.

20. UNDPI, *The United Nations and Rwanda,* 37; most major newspapers and newsmagazines report the latter number.

21. Ibid., 209.

22. Ibid., 46.

23. Michael E. Brown, Introduction, in *The International Dimensions of Internal Conflict,* ed. Michael E. Brown (Cambridge: MIT Press, 1996), 3; *SIPRI Yearbook 1995,* 109.

24. United Nations, *UNHCR by Numbers,* informational pamphlet of the UNHCR (New York: United Nations, 1996).

25. U.S. Agency for International Development, Office of U.S. Foreign Disaster Assistance, Situation Report #6, FY95 (July 24, 1995).

26. Gibbs, "Rwanda: Cry the Forsaken Country."

27. International Institute of Strategic Studies, *The Military Balance 1994–1995* (London: Oxford University Press, 1995), 273.

28. John Borton, Emery Brusset, and Alistair Hallam, *The International Response to Conflict and Genocide: Lessons from the Rwanda Experience. Study 3: Humanitarian Aid and Effects* (Copenhagen: Joint Evaluation of Emergency Assistance to Rwanda, 1996).

29. All figures for this section are taken from tables printed in UNDPI, *The United Nations and Rwanda,* 381, 565–68.

30. "Aid Workers Flee after Rebels Take Zairian City," *Los Angeles Times* (November 3, 1996), A1.

31. Central Intelligence Agency, *World Fact Book 1995.*

32. Ibid.

33. Central Intelligence Agency, *World Fact Book 1990, 1995.*

34. Central Intelligence Agency, *World Fact Book 1995.*

35. UNDPI, *The United Nations and Rwanda,* 607–55.

36. OECD Development Assistance Committee, *Annual Report* (Paris: OECD, 1996), A65.

37. Central Intelligence Agency, *World Fact Book 1990, 1995.*

38. This total is estimated based on economic data taken from Central Intelligence Agency, *World Fact Book 1996.*

39. "Crime and Nourishment," *The Economist* (April 1, 1995).

40. Central Intelligence Agency, *World Fact Book 1995,* 467–68.
41. "Little Rwanda," *The Economist* (July 2, 1994).
42. "You're Saying We Did It?" *The Economist* (June 3, 1995).
43. Borton, "Humanitarian Aid and Its Effects."
44. *SIPRI Yearbook 1995,* 89.
45. OECD, *Annual Report,* A65. This amount has been subtracted from the OECD Development Assistance total, which was $684 million, including Belgium's contribution.
46. U.S. Agency for International Development, Situation Report #6.
47. *SIPRI Yearbook 1995,* 105.
48. Feil, *Preventing Genocide,* 16–17.
49. United Nations, *Information Notes, United Nations Peace-keeping,* 110–26.
50. IFOR cost $5 billion per year for 60,000 combat-ready troops composed primarily of infantry battalions. The proposed operation in Rwanda would have deployed one-twelfth of the manpower and is estimated here at one-tenth of the cost. This may even be an overestimation because of the small size of Rwanda as compared to Bosnia, where troops were deployed at great distance from each other and required much more extensive communication and logistics support.
51. Feil, *Preventing Genocide,* 22.

Chapter 4

1. Michael Maren, "Spoiled," *The New Republic* (December 12, 1994), 13.
2. John L. Hirsch and Robert B. Oakley, *Somalia and Operation Restore Hope* (Washington, D.C.: U.S. Institute of Peace Press, 1995).
3. Ironically, the typical UN perspective was that the end of the Cold War would allow the United Nations to "fulfill the promise of the Charter—to save succeeding generations from the scourge of war."
4. Hirsch and Oakley, *Somalia and Operation Restore Hope.*
5. Ibid.
6. About $1.2 million was spent by UNOSOM according to the *Somalia News Update* 3 (September 14, 1994).
7. Variants of this causal mechanism are presented by Terrence Lyons and Ahmed I. Samatar, *Somalia: State Collapse, Multilateral Intervention, and Strategies for Political Reconstruction* (Washington, D.C.: Brookings Institution Occasional Papers, 1995), though they stress societal demands for better government and economic advancement.
8. J. Boyer Bell, *The Horn of Africa* (New York: Crane, Russak, 1973), 42.
9. David Rawson, *The Somali State and Foreign Aid* (Arlington, Va.: Foreign Service Institute, 1994).
10. United Nations, Development Report, *Somalia: Annual Development Corporation Report* (New York: United Nations, 1988).
11. Central Intelligence Agency, *World Factbook 1991* (Washington, D.C.: CIA), 282–83. *African Recovery* 3 (October 1989) estimates that the trade deficit

for 1985, 1986, and 1988 was $220 million, $371 million, and $380 million respectively.

12. Michael Johns, "Preserving American Security Ties to Somalia," *Heritage Foundation Reports* (December 26, 1989).

13. Lyons and Samatar, *Somalia,* 17.

14. According to Samatar, sheep prices were down 21.75%, cattle prices were down 23.95%, and camel prices were down 11.11% from pre-January 1985 levels. The lack of any substitutable export markets or exportable products imposed high costs on Somali herders.

15. United Nations Department of Public Information, *The United Nations and Somalia, 1992–1995* (New York: United Nations, 1995), Doc. 61, 285.

16. Estimates from the CIA's *World Factbook 1991* indicate that Somalia received $639 million from 1970 to 1989, or approximately $32 million per year. Other Western aid largely consisting of loans and loan guarantees during the same period amounted to $3.2 billion and much of this is reflected in the $2 billion in external Somali debt that must be written off.

17. Lyons and Samatar, *Somalia,* chapter 1, note 24.

18. Timeline information adapted and condensed from UN publications, mainly *The United Nations and Somalia, 1992–1995.*

19. "The Final Cost of a Mission of Hope," *Newsweek* (April 4, 1994): 44.

20. Tom Pfeiffer, "US Hands Over Somali Mission to New UN Peacekeeping Force," *Arms Control Today* 23 (June 1993): 28.

21. UNDPI, *The United Nations and Somalia, 1992–1995,* Doc. 110, 482–83; and www.un.org/depts/dpko.

22. Michael Maren, "Spoiled," *The New Republic* (December 12, 1994): 13.

23. UNDPI, *The United Nations and Somalia, 1992–1995,* Doc. 83, 352.

24. E. Palmer, "Putting a Price on Global Aid," *Congressional Quarterly Weekly* 51 (January 23, 1993): 186.

25. *Somalia News Update* 3 (January 7, 1994).

26. Various documents from UNDPI, *The United Nations and Somalia, 1992–1995.*

27. Ibid., Doc. 61, 295.

28. Ibid., Doc. 85, 360.

29. Central Intelligence Agency, *World Factbook 1996,* CD-ROM Edition.

30. Central Intelligence Agency, *World Factbook 1991.*

31. Pfeiffer, "US Hands Over Somali Mission," 28.

32. *Somalia News Update* (August 13, 1994).

33. Various NGOs, in cooperation with Somaliland officials, have begun widespread cattle vaccination that has been helpful in rural areas according to *Somalia News Update* (April 18, 1994).

34. Lyons and Samatar, *Somalia,* indicated that by November 1992 no preemption was possible, though they do argue that earlier intervention might have been successful (see pp. 25–26).

35. Thirteen hundred Marines quickly secured the airport during the actual operation (Hirsch and Oakley, *Somalia and Operation Hope*).

36. The 10th Mountain Infantry Division was used in Somalia and is proposed for the preemption force as well.

37. During the actual operation this goal was only specified much later.
38. Hirsch and Oakley, *Somalia and Operation Hope.*
39. Lyons and Samatar, *Somalia.*
40. Hirsch and Oakley, *Somalia and Operation Hope.*
41. This estimate is based on the costs of U.S. forces in Somalia in support of the UN operation and would initially include elements of the 25th Mechanized Division and 1st Marine Division in roughly equal brigade strength and several companies of military police. As the operations imposed an end to the fighting, and food and economic aid increased, the combat units would be withdrawn and replaced by more MP and other noncombat units that would build civil and economic infrastructure.

Chapter 5

1. Strobe Talbott, testimony before the Senate Foreign Relations Committee; cited in Senate Committee on Foreign Relations, *Implementation and Costs of U.S. Policy in Haiti,* 104th Congress, 1st session, 1995, S. Hrg. 104–52, 4.
2. Ibid., 5.
3. This summary figure is a consensus estimate and is documented below. Journalistic sources include Nina Shea, "Voodoo Diplomacy," *National Review* (June 17, 1996): 26.
4. The state-society distinction goes back at least to writings by Antonio Gramsci.
5. Sidney Mintz, "Can Haiti Change?" *Foreign Affairs* 73 (January/February 1995): 84.
6. Population pressure and how it leads to state collapse is considered in Ernest H. Preeg, *The Haitian Dilemma: A Case in Demographics, Development, and U.S. Foreign Policy* (Washington, D.C.: Center for Strategic Studies, 1996). In *Aiding Migration: The Impact of International Development Assistance on Haiti* (Boulder: Westview, 1988), Josh DeWind and David H. Kinley III also note how this led to outmigration pressure and a U.S. response that worsened the problems.
7. Adam Przeworski, *Democracy and the Market* (New York: Cambridge University Press, 1991).
8. Statement by Sam Nunn; cited in Senate Committee on Armed Services, *Situation in Haiti,* 103rd Congress, 2nd session, 1994, S. Hrg. 103–863, 32.
9. Josh DeWind and David H. Kinley III in *The Haiti Files: Decoding the Crisis,* ed. James Ridgeway (Washington, D.C.: Essential Books, 1994).
10. Ernest Preeg, testimony before the House Committee on International Relations; cited in *Haiti: The Situation after the Departure of the U.S. Contingent from UNMIH,* 104th Congress, 2nd session, 1996, H. Doc. 12/3.
11. United Nations Department of Public Information, *The United Nations and the Situation in Haiti* (New York: United Nations, March 1995), 2.
12. President Bill Clinton quoted in John Canham-Clyne, in *The Haih Files,* ed. Ridgeway, 112.
13. UN Security Council Resolution 917.
14. Including naval personnel, the force totaled 28,000.

15. Linda Robinson, "Will Haiti Have Law or Disorder," *U.S. News and World Report* (July 1, 1996).

16. Letter from Alice Rivlin included in the testimony of John M. Deutch before the Senate Armed Services Committee; cited in *The United Nations and the Situation in Haiti,* 17–19.

17. Statement by Senator Paul Coverdell, cited in *Implementation and Costs of U.S. Policy in Haiti,* 3.

18. Ibid.

19. This is roughly what current operations in Haiti cost and the correct cost allocation.

20. This information was obtained from the UN through its Internet site; available from www.un.org/Depts/DPKO/Missions/unmih.htm.

21. See the web site of the UN Department of Peacekeeping operations, www.un.org/Depts/dpk.

22. Eric Schmitt, "Pentagon Estimates It Will Cost $427 Million to Invade Haiti," *New York Times* (September 2, 1994).

23. This information was obtained from the UN through its Internet site; available from www.un.org/Depts/DPKO/Missions/unmih.htm.

24. Talbott, *Implementation and Costs of U.S. Policy in Haiti,* 5.

25. Donald Schulz, "Whither Haiti," *SSI US Army College* (April 1, 1996): 15.

26. *Implementation and Costs of U.S. Policy in Haiti,* 83.

27. "U.S. Releases Some Aid to Haitian Police," *Facts on File* 56 (February 1, 1996): 46.

28. *Macleans* 109 (July 8, 1996): 27.

29. Dominican Republic economic statistics are adapted from *The Military Balance, 1994–95* and *1995–96* (London: Oxford University Press).

30. Preeg, *Haiti,* 105.

31. See Schmitt, "Pentagon Estimates." Also see quotation by John Deutch in Pat Towell, *Congressional Quarterly Weekly Report* 52 (September 24, 1994): 2702.

Chapter 6

1. The Gulf War cost Iraq $240 billion and Kuwait $120 billion in economic losses according to Ibrahim M. Oweiss, "The Economic Impact of the War," in *The Gulf Crisis: Background and Consequences,* ed. Ibrahim M. Oweiss (Washington, D.C.: Center for Contemporary Arab Studies, 1991), 296. The damage to Kuwait has been largely repaired using Kuwaiti investment funds and oil revenue. Damage to Iraq has not been significantly addressed. In either case, the West should see no additional costs for reconstruction for Iraq or Kuwait so no estimate is included.

2. These four signals are adapted from "Kuwait: How the West Blundered; The Signals That Were Sent—and the One That Wasn't," *The Economist* (September 29, 1990): 19–22, cited in *The Gulf War Reader,* ed. Micah L. Sifry and Christopher Cerf (New York: Times Books, 1991), 99–105.

3. Lawrence Freedman and Efraim Karsh, *The Gulf Conflict: 1990–1991* (Princeton: Princeton University Press, 1993).

4. Abbas Alnasrawi, "Oil Dimensions of the Gulf Crisis," in *The Gulf Crisis,* ed. Oweiss, 38–39.

5. Freedman and Karsh, *The Gulf Conflict,* 37–39.

6. Oil prices were as low as $7 per barrel before the crisis and had risen to $14 per barrel in the weeks before the invasion. Iraq debt service and a large standing army that could not be demobilized because there were no jobs or housing for them suggested that Iraq needed around $25 per barrel to survive. This meant that even the OPEC benchmark of $18 per barrel would not have been sufficient for Iraq to manage. Alnasrawi, Sifry and Cerf, and others make this point; see also Amatzia Baram, "The Iraqi Invasion of Kuwait: Decision Making in Baghdad," in *Iraq's Road to War,* ed. Amatzia Baram and Barry Rubin (New York: St. Martin's Press, 1993). Kuwait also accounted for 75% of OPEC overproduction during the two years before the war. See Freedman and Karsh, *The Gulf Crisis,* 41.

7. Bishara A. Bahbah, "The Crisis in the Gulf—Why Iraq Invaded Kuwait," in *Beyond the Storm: A Gulf Crisis Reader,* ed. Phyllis Bennis and Michel Moushabeck (New York: Olive Branch Press, 1991), 50.

8. Ibid., 52–54.

9. Steve Niva, "The Battle Is Joined," in *Beyond the Storm,* ed. Bennis and Moushabeck, 56.

10. Baram and Rubin, *Iraq's Road to War,* x–xii.

11. Walid Khalidi, "Iraq vs. Kuwait: Claims and Counterclaims," in *The Gulf War Reader,* ed. Sifry and Cerf.

12. Baram makes this point without following through.

13. Baram, "The Iraqi Invasion of Kuwait," in *Iraq's Road to War,* ed. Baram and Rubin, 5–35.

14. Baram, in an overview of the conflict, notes the importance of the question of "Why the Whole of Kuwait? Why Not Saudi Arabia?" The answer is essentially Saddam Hussein's perception of the chances of a U.S. response.

15. Bruce W. Jentleson, *With Friends Like These: Reagan, Bush, and Saddam 1982–1990* (New York: Norton, 1994).

16. This overview relies primarily on UN sources and *The Gulf Crisis,* ed. Oweiss.

17. Oweiss, *The Gulf Crisis,* ed. Oweiss, 319, and other sources.

18. Freedman and Karsh, *The Gulf Conflict,* 67.

19. Ibid., 361.

20. These figures are from Department of Defense estimates widely reported in the press.

21. Youssef M. Ibrahim, "Gulf War Is Said to Have Cost the Region $676 Billion in 1990–91," *New York Times* (April 25, 1993), 7. An earlier estimate was $620 billion.

22. See Oweiss, *The Gulf Crisis,* ed. Oweiss.

23. K. S. Ramachandran, *Gulf War and Environmental Problems* (New Delhi Ashish, 1991), 30.

24. David R. Henderson, "The Myth of Saddam's Oil Stranglehold," in *America Entangled,* ed. T. G. Carpenter (Washington, D.C.: Cato Institute, 1991); and Ramachandran, *Gulf War,* 30.

25. Yoram Meital, "Egypt in the Gulf Crisis," in *Iraq's Road to War,* ed. Baram and Rubin, 191–99.

26. Les Aspin, *The Aspin Papers: Sanctions, Diplomacy, and the War in the Persian Gulf* (Washington, D.C.: Center for Strategic and International Studies, 1991), 88.

27. Oweiss, *The Gulf Crisis,* ed. Oweiss, 295–96.

28. Hisham H. Ahmed, "The Impact of the Gulf Crisis on Jordan's Economic Infrastructure," *Arab Studies Quarterly* 15 (Fall 1993): 33.

29. Joseph Nevo, "Jordan's Relations with Iraq: Ally or Victim?" in *Iraq's Road to War,* ed. Baram and Rubin, 135–48.

30. Mustafa B. Hamarneh, "Jordan Responds to the Gulf Crisis," in *Beyond the Storm,* ed. Bennis and Moushabeck, 228–29.

31. Tim Lake, "Chronology of the Gulf Crisis: May 1990–June 1991," in *The Gulf Crisis,* ed. Oweiss, 340.

32. David Kushner, "Turkey: Iraq's European Neighbor," in *Iraq's Road to War,* ed. Baram and Rubin, 213–17.

33. Aspin, *The Aspin Papers,* 88.

34. Freedman and Karsh, *The Gulf Crisis,* 82.

35. Ibid., 359.

36. Niva, "The Battle Is Joined," in *Beyond the Storm,* ed. Bennis and Moushabeck, 70. This same figure is reported in Oweiss, *The Gulf Crisis,* ed. Oweiss, 292–93.

37. Baram, "The Iraqi Invasion of Kuwait," in *Iraq's Road to War,* ed. Baram and Rubin, 5–35.

38. Estimates of the Iraqi loan write-offs are as high as $80 billion; see *Financial Times* (September 8, 1989) for estimates of Western exposure.

39. Ramachandran, *Gulf War,* 35–36.

40. Oweiss, *The Gulf Crisis,* ed. Oweiss, 289–91.

41. See Baram, "The Iraqi Invasion of Kuwait," in *Iraq's Road to War,* ed. Baram and Rubin.

42. B-52s from Guam were used in the actual conflict.

Chapter 7

1. Macedonia is both a region in Greece and a province of the former Yugoslavia. This study is concerned only with the former Yugoslav republic known officially as the Republic of Macedonia but recognized by most states and the United Nations as the Former Yugoslav Republic of Macedonia (FYROM). Unless otherwise noted, this study will refer to FYROM as Macedonia. This does not imply the adoption of a position in Greece's dispute with FYROM over the name "Macedonia." Also, this study will refer to the Federal Republic of Yugoslavia (which includes Serbia, Montenegro, and Kosovo) as Serbia.

2. UNPREDEP was officially established on March 31, 1995, by UN Security Council Resolution 983 to replace UNPROFOR (UN Protection Force, which also had responsibility for Bosnia and Croatia) in Macedonia. Originally, UN Res-

olution 795, adopted December 11, 1992, authorized its deployment as part of UNPROFOR. Effective February 1, 1996, UNPREDEP became an independent mission reporting directly to the UN Secretariat in New York. This study will refer to UNPROFOR and UNPREDEP consistently as UNPREDEP although it did not exist officially until 1995.

3. Bulgaria is not a viable threat to Macedonia because Bulgarian influence within Macedonia is marginal. This is due to the small number of Bulgarians within Macedonia, to the poor manner in which Bulgaria treats its Macedonian minority, and to the legacy of the two periods of Bulgarian occupation, the first from 1916 to 1918 and the second from 1941 to 1944. See Stefan Troebst, "Macedonia: Powder Keg Defused?" *RFE/RL Research Report* (January 28, 1994), 37–38.

4. For a discussion of the history and culture of Macedonia see Elisabeth Barker, *Macedonia: Its Place in Balkan Power Politics* (London: Royal Institute for International Affairs, 1950); Loring M. Danforth, *The Macedonian Conflict: Ethnic Nationalism in a Transnational World* (Princeton: Princeton University Press, 1995); Evangelos Kofos, *Nationalism and Communism in Macedonia: Civil Conflict, Politics of Mutation, National Identity* (New Rochelle, N.Y.: Aristide D. Caratzas, 1993); Steven E. Palmer Jr. and Robert R. King, *Yugoslav Communism and the Macedonian Question* (Hamden, Conn.: Archon, 1971).

5. Ivo Daalder argues that the immediate cause of the dissolution of Yugoslavia and the subsequent wars was the rise of hypernationalism in Serbia. See Ivo H. Daalder, "Fear and Loathing in the Former Yugoslavia," in *The International Dimensions of Internal Conflict,* ed. Michael E. Brown (Cambridge: MIT Press, 1996), 35–67. Also see V. P. Gagnon Jr., "Ethnic Nationalism and International Conflict: The Case of Serbia," *International Security* 19 (Winter 1994/95): 130–66. For histories of the dissolution of Yugoslavia, see Lenard Cohen, *Broken Bonds: The Disintegration of Yugoslavia* (Boulder: Westview, 1993); Robert D. Kaplan, *Balkan Ghosts: A Journey through History* (New York: St. Martin's Press, 1993); Laura Silber and Allan Little, *Yugoslavia: Death of a Nation* (n.p.: TV Books, 1995 and 1996); Susan Woodward, *Balkan Tragedy: Chaos and Dissolution after the Cold War* (Washington, D.C.: Brookings Institution, 1995); and John Zametica, *The Yugoslav Conflict,* Adelphi Paper No. 270 (London: International Institute of Strategic Studies, 1992).

6. According to the 1994 census, Macedonia's population was 1,936,877, of whom 1,288,330 (66.5%) were ethnic Macedonians; 442,914 Albanians (22.9%); 77,252 Turks (4%); 43,732 Roma (Gypsies) (2.3%); 39,260 Serbs (2%); 15,315 Torbeshi (0.07%); and 8,467 Vlachs (0.004%). The remainder are Croats, Bosnians, Bulgarians, and others (0.022%). See Duncan M. Perry, "On the Road to Stability—Or Destruction?" *Transition* 1 (August 25, 1995): 41. The 1991 census estimated Macedonia's population to be slightly over two million (2.2 million), including 65% Macedonians, 21% Albanians, 4% Turks, 3% Roma (Gypsies), 2% Serbs, 2% Macedonian Moslems, and a small number of Vlachs; cited in Danforth, *The Macedonian Conflict,* 143. Also see Woodward, *Balkan Tragedy,* 33–35. The Albanian minority boycotted the September 1991 referendum, but expressed support for an independent Macedonia in a separate referendum in January 1992 in which 90% of those eligible to vote did so and more than

99% of the participants supported independence. In this referendum they evinced strong support for the creation of an independent Albanian state: "the Republic of Ilirida." See Hugh Poulton, "The Republic of Macedonia After UN Recognition," *RFE/RL Research Report* (June 4, 1993): 24; Zlatko Isakovic, "Macedonia, Its Neighbours and Security of the Balkans," *Assocation for the Study of Nationalities Analysis of Current Events* 6 (May 2, 1995): 8; and Danforth, *The Macedonian Conflict,* 145.

7. Silber and Little, *Yugoslavia,* 200–201.

8. Danforth, *The Macedonian Conflict,* 148.

9. Ibid.

10. Ibid; for a detailed account of the cultural importance of the symbol see pages 163–74. Nikolaos Zahariadis makes the point most strongly: "The term *Macedonia* and its derivatives are an integral part of Greek national and cultural heritage, recorded in history more than ten centuries before the arrival of Slavs in the Balkans." See Nikolaos Zahariadis, "Is the Former Yugoslav Republic of Macedonia a Threat?" *Mediterranean Quarterly* 5 (Winter 1994): 88; emphasis in original. Also see Nikolaos Zahariadis, "Nationalism and Small-State Foreign Policy: The Greek Response to the Contemporary Macedonian Issue," *Political Science Quarterly* 109 (Fall 1994): 647–67.

11. "UN to Admit Macedonia; Name Will Be Negotiated," *Boston Globe* (April 8, 1993), 4.

12. Kerin Hope, "Fears Grow Over Action Against Macedonia," *Financial Times* (February 18, 1994), 3; Lionel Barber, "Greece Warned on 'Illegal' Embargo," *Financial Times* (February 22, 1994), 1; and Kerin Hope, "Embargo Strangles Macedonia," *Financial Times* (April 6, 1994), 2.

13. Macedonia was well integrated into the former Yugoslav economy, conducting more than 70% of its trade with the rest of the country. See Kevin Done, "Prospects Have Improved," *Financial Times* (November 15, 1996), 25.

14. Daalder makes this argument in "Fear and Loathing in the Former Yugoslavia," 48. Also see Henry Kamm, "Greek Prime Minister Insists Macedonia Endangers His Country," *New York Times* (April 7, 1994), A1.

15. Foreign Broadcast Information Service (FBIS), West Europe (September 25, 1991), 42, cited in Zahariadis, "Is the Former Yugoslav Republic of Macedonia a Threat?" 92. Also see Duncan M. Perry, "The Republic of Macedonia: Foreign Relations, Issues and Dilemma," *Association for the Study of Nationalities Analysis of Current Events* 6 (May 2, 1995), 3.

16. The disputes over, first, the Greek Cypriots decision to buy a Russian air defense system and, second, the Imia islets have made Greek-Turkish relations especially tense. In the second case both countries claim the islets and each had planted its flag on them only to see the other remove it. See "Guns, Not Butter," *The Economist* (January 11, 1997), 48; Kerin Hope and John Barham, "Clinton Peace Envoy Turns to Aegean," *Financial Times* (February 1, 1996), 2; Stephen Engelberg, "U.S. Is Trying To Help Cool Aegean Anger," *New York Times* (January 31, 1996), A6; and Thomas W. Lippman, "Tiny Island Stirs Tension in Aegean," *Washington Post* (January 31, 1996), A12. Also see John Barham, "Turks' 'Friendly' Snarl at Greece," *Financial Times* (June 9, 1995), 3.

17. Quoted in Eric Herring, "International Security and Democratisation in

Eastern Europe," in *Building Democracy? The International Dimensions of Democratisation in Eastern Europe,* ed. Geoffrey Pridham, Eric Herring, and George Stanford (London: Leicester University Press, 1994), 99.

18. Danforth, *The Macedonian Conflict,* 144. For a good analysis of the VMRO-DPMNE and the other major political parties in Macedonia immediately after its independence, see Duncan M. Perry, "Politics in the Republic of Macedonia: Issues and Parties," *RFE/RL Research Report* 2 (June 4, 1993): 31–37. The abbreviation for VMRO-DPMNE is also given as IMRO-DPMNE or VMRO-DPMNU.

19. Hakan Wiber, "Social Security and the Explosion of Yugoslavia," in *Identity, Migration and the New Security Agenda in Europe,* ed. Ole Weaver, Barry Buzan, Marten Kelstrup, and Pierre Lemaitre (London: Pinter, 1993), 105.

20. Anthony Borden and Richard Caplan, "The Former Yugoslavia: The War and the Peace Process," in *SIPRI Yearbook 1996* (New York: Oxford University Press, 1996), 226.

21. Michael G. Roskin, "Macedonia and Albania: The Missing Alliance," *Parameters* 23 (Winter 1993–94): 92.

22. Henry Kamm, "Macedonia Sees Its Albanians as Its 'Biggest Problem,' " *New York Times* (May 5, 1994), A4.

23. The precise size of the Albanian minority is difficult to determine. Officially, it is about 21% to 23% of the population, while the ethnic Albanian community estimates its numbers at 35% to 40% of the population. See Hans Binnendijk and Jeffrey Simon, "Preventing a Sixth Twentieth-Century Balkan War," *Strategic Forum* 9 (October 1994): 1.

24. Frank Viviano, "Next Balkan Flash Point—It Could Be Macedonia," *San Francisco Chronicle* (August 25, 1993); quoted in Zahariadis, "Is the Former Yugoslav Republic of Macedonia a Threat?" 98.

25. Zlatko Isakovic and Constantine P. Danopoulos, "In Search of Identity: Civil-Military Relations and Nationhood in the Former Yugoslav Republic of Macedonia (FYROM)," in *Civil-Military Relations in the Soviet and Yugoslav Successor States,* ed. Constantine P. Danopoulos and Daniel Zirker (Boulder: Westview, 1996), 180.

26. Michael S. Lund, *Preventing Violent Conflicts: A Strategy for Preventive Diplomacy* (Washington, D.C.: U.S. Institute of Peace Press, 1996), 63; Troebst, "Macedonia," 38.

27. Isakovic and Danopoulos, "In Search of Identity," in *Civil-Military Relations,* ed. Danopoulous and Zirker, 187; Troebst, "Macedonia," 38; Fabian Schmidt, "From National Consensus to Pluralism," *Transition* (March 29, 1995), 26; and Laura Silber, "Albanian Ministers Arrested in Macedonia Crackdown," *Financial Times* (November 11, 1993), 1.

28. Isakovic and Danopoulos, "In Search of Identity," in *Civil-Military Relations,* ed. Danopoulos and Zirker, 181.

29. Perry, "On the Road to Stability—Or Destruction?" 43.

30. Xhaferi complains that Albanians are oppressed because "Slavs want to dominate non-Slavs" (ibid). For an account of the divisions within the PPD, see Schmidt, "From National Consensus to Pluralism," 28.

31. Borden and Caplan, "The Former Yugoslavia," in *SIPRI Yearbook 1996,* 225.

32. Perry, "On the Road to Stability—Or Destruction?" 42. Also see Iso Rusi, "Averting Another Balkan Wildfire," *New York Times* (March 4, 1995), 19.

33. Schmidt, "From National Consensus to Pluralism," 29. Also see Perry, "On the Road to Stability—Or Destruction?" 42.

34. Schmidt, "From National Consensus to Pluralism," 29–30.

35. Perry notes this suspicion among the ethnic Albanians, "On the Road to Stability—Or Destruction?" 43.

36. Herring, "International Security and Democratisation in Eastern Europe," in *Building Democracy?* ed. Pridham, Herring, and Stanford, 99.

37. Poulton, "The Republic of Macedonia After UN Recognition," 24.

38. Laura Silber, "Macedonia's Albanians Fearful of Ethnic Bloodbath," *Financial Times* (November 17, 1992), 2.

39. Quoted in Perry, "On the Road to Stability—Or Destruction?" 44.

40. Poulton, "The Republic of Macedonia After UN Recognition," 25–26. However, the Albanian minority does not object to the name of the country and argues that if the country must have a new name that it be an ethnically neutral one such as the Central Balkan Republic.

41. Troebst, "Macedonia," 35.

42. Poulton, "The Republic of Macedonia After UN Recognition," 23. According to Poulton, some Serbian nationalists claim that the number of Serbs is closer to 300,000 or about 14% of the population.

43. Troebst, "Macedonia," 35.

44. Ibid.

45. Poulton, "The Republic of Macedonia After UN Recognition," 23. Also see Hugh Poulton, *The Balkans: Minorities and States in Conflict* (London: Minority Rights Group, 1991).

46. The best overview of the dispute between the churches is found in Poulton, "The Republic of Macedonia After UN Recognition," 23–24.

47. An excellent brief study of the dangers in Kosovo is Fabian Schmidt, "Kosovo: The Time Bomb That Has Not Gone Off," *RFE/RL Research Report* (October 1, 1993): 21–29.

48. It is, in fact, a low-intensity guerrilla war in which the KLA and Serbian special police units frequently take casualties. See "The Kosovo Cauldron," *The Economist* (March 14, 1998), 53–54, and "Jaw, Jaw?" *The Economist* (May 16, 1998), 55.

49. Troebst, "Macedonia," 36.

50. Both Presidents Bush and Clinton warned Serbian President Slobodan Milosevic that the United States would not permit Kosovo to be ethnically cleansed. Secretary of State Warren Christopher stated publicly that the United States has "reminded" Milosevic of U.S. determination to contain the conflict and for it not to spread to Kosovo or Macedonia: "I can tell you that we have a very strong position that the conflict shall not spread south—that it's got to be contained, tragic as it is, to the areas where it is now." Quoted in John Pomfret, "First U.S. Troops Arrive in Balkans," *Washington Post* (July 6, 1993), A1, and Jim Hoagland, "Another Brink in the Balkans," *Washington Post* (March 31, 1994), A31.

51. Lund, *Preventing Violent Conflicts,* 63–66.

52. The size of Macedonia's armed forces is only 10,400 men with 4 T-34 Main Battle Tanks (MBTs). It is overshadowed by its neighbors, even the Albanians. This compares with about 54,000 men in the Albanian armed forces, with 138 T-34s in reserve and 721 T-59 MBTs; 113,900 men and 1,360 MBTs in the Serbian armed forces; and 168,300 men and 1,735 MBTs in Greece's. International Institute for Strategic Studies, *The Military Balance 1996–97* (London: Oxford University Press, 1996), 92, 77, 102, and 59.

53. Trevor Findlay, "Multilateral Conflict Prevention, Management and Resolution," *SIPRI Yearbook 1994* (New York: Oxford University Press, 1994), 78.

54. U.S. participation in UNPREDEP has been labeled ABLE SENTRY by the Pentagon. Steve Vogel, "More U.S. Troops Join UN Macedonia Force," *Washington Post* (July 13, 1993), A1.

55. Binnendijk and Simon, "Preventing a Sixth Twentieth-Century Balkan War," 3.

56. As Macedonian Defense Minister Vlado Popovski said in July 1993 when U.S. troops arrived, the arrival "of even a token American contingent" improves the chances of war being kept from Macedonia; while Deputy Foreign Minister Risto Nikovski described the U.S. presence as creating also creates an obligation for the United States. "In case of difficulty, they cannot just flee from Macedonia." Quoted in Pomfret, "U.S. Troops Deployed in Balkan Republic," A1.

57. In addition, there were 35 UN military observers, 26 UN civilian police monitors, 73 international civilian staff and 127 locally recruited staff. UNDPI, *The Blue Helmets: A Review of United Nations Peace-keeping,* 3rd ed. (New York: United Nations, 1996), 564–66.

58. UNDPI, *The Blue Helmets,* 564.

59. In addition to UNPREDEP, there is an OSCE mission in Macedonia, the OSCE Spillover Mission to Skopje. It was established in September 1992 to report on political, economic, and social conditions in Macedonia, and to monitor elections. It consists of about 10 members. Trevor Findlay, "Multilateral Conflict Prevention, Management and Resolution," 56.

60. The cost estimate for the period January 1 to June 30, 1996, was $24,694,800. UNDPI, *The Blue Helmets,* 756.

61. In a letter from UN Secretary General Boutros Boutros-Ghali to the president of Security Council, the cost of UNPREDEP was estimated to be $29 million for six months. Letter dated February 6, 1996 (S/1996/94), available from gopher.undp.org:70/00/uncurr/sgrep/96_02/94. The costs rose slightly, by about $4 million, because the administrative, logistical, and communications services were centrally provided by UN Peace Forces Headquarters (UNPF-HQ) as theater assets, and this support ended once UNPREDEP became independent.

62. The economic costs to Macedonia have been significant, with estimates ranging from $4 billion to $7.6 billion in losses for complying with the trade embargo imposed on Serbia. See Kerin Hope, "The Macedonian Question," *Europe Magazine* (May 1994): 8, reprinted in Jessica Hobart, Miriam Lanskoy, and Robert Leavitt, comps., "After Bosnia: Conflict and Security in the Balkans," *European Security Network Working Paper* 18 (June 1994), 55; Raymond Bonner, "Balkan

Conflict's Spread to Macedonia Is Feared," *New York Times* (April 9, 1995), 1; and Perry, "On the Road to Stability—Or Destruction?" 44. In addition, Macedonia's access to the south was terminated when Greece imposed its blockade in February 1994. While these costs should not be included in the costs of conflict prevention because they were initiated by Greece, the February 1994–October 1995 economic embargo is estimated to have cost Macedonia between $840 million and about $1 billion. See Saso Ordanoski, "Balkan Stepchild," *New York Times* (September 4, 1994), E9; and Perry, "On the Road to Stability—Or Destruction?" 44–46.

63. Kevin Done, "Prospects Have Improved," *Financial Times* (November 15, 1996), 25.

64. Some $5 million was invested in 1994 and $16 million in 1995. Economic Commission for Europe, *Economic Survey of Europe in 1995–1996* (New York: United Nations, 1996), 150.

65. The Gross National Product of Macedonia was estimated to be $1.6 billion in 1995 with a 20% unemployment rate, and a 40% decline in Gross Domestic Product since 1992. The real GDP growth rate was positive for the first time since independence only in 1996. Kevin Done and Kerin Hope, "Survival Against All the Odds," *Financial Times* (November 15, 1996), 23. The GNP estimate comes from Perry, "On the Road to Stability—Or Destruction?" 44.

66. All cost information about Bosnia is drawn from chapter 2 by Andrea Talentino in this volume.

67. Even guerrilla conflicts between small states and great powers can take a long time and be extremely costly in lives and material, as demonstrated by the Chechen war, the invasion of Afghanistan, and the Vietnam War.

68. Bosnia has about 4,300,000 people in 51,129 sq. km. of territory, twice the Macedonian population (about 2 million) and territory (25,713 sq. km.). *The Stateman's Yearbook 1996–1997* (New York: St. Martin's Press, 1996), 224 and 843.

69. Done and Hope, "Survival Against All the Odds," 23.

70. All Gulf War cost estimates are drawn from chapter 6 by Mike Blakley in this volume.

71. Figures are drawn from *The Statesman's Yearbook 1996–1997*.

Chapter 8

1. It should be noted that the potential for conflict in Slovakia is assessed here as a *counterfactual* exercise. Conflict has not broken out in Slovakia, and low-level mediation has been conducted. It is useful, therefore, to examine the costs of preconflict mediation as a contrast to postconflict efforts to ease higher levels of tension elsewhere. This chapter does not presume to present a comprehensive overview of Slovak politics. Rather, it focuses on the potential for conflict either within Slovakia or between Slovakia and Hungary in order to analyze the potential costs of conflict prevention were this to be necessary. While tensions exist between the Slovak and Hungarian populations within the state, a far greater political divide

exists within the Slovak population itself. This is not geographic, but is based on culture, and especially urban-rural differences about the nature of the state and how it should be governed. This division is not elaborated here for two reasons. First, it appears less likely to produce widespread bloodshed. Second, were such bloodshed to occur, the international community would find it particularly hard to intervene promptly, as other chapters in this volume on civil war demonstrate. On intra-Slovak political tensions, see Martin Simecka, "Slovakia's Lonely Independence," *Transitions* 4 (August 1997): 14–21. For more exhaustive analyses of Slovakian history, see Joseph A. Mikus, *Slovakia: A Political and Constitutional History* (Bratislava: Slovak Academic Press, 1995); Carol Skalnik Leff, *The Czech and Slovak Republics: Nation versus State* (Boulder: Westview, 1997); Martin Butora, "The Identity Challenges of the Newly Born State," *Social Research* 60 (Winter 1993): 705–32.

2. The Warsaw Pact collapsed, for all intents and proposes, when the Communist Party rulers in Eastern Europe lost power at the end of 1989. The political/military organization was not officially dissolved until July 1991. See Raymond L. Garthoff, *The Great Transition: American-Soviet Relations and the End of the Cold War* (Washington, D.C.: Brookings Institution, 1994), 465.

3. This history draws on an earlier project done in cooperation with Istvan Szonyi at the Center for International Security and Arms Control, Stanford University, in 1991–92.

4. Vladimir V. Kusin, "Czechs and Slovaks: The Road to the Current Debate," *RFE Report on Eastern Europe* (October 5, 1990); Jiri Pehe, "Growing Slovak Demands Seen as Threat to Federation," *RFE Report on Eastern Europe* (March 22, 1991).

5. There are historical reasons for this, since Bohemia and Moravia were among the most industrialized parts of Europe early in the twentieth century.

6. On Slovak history both before and during the interwar period, see John Lukas, *The End of the Twentieth Century and the End of the Modern Age* (New York: Ticknor and Fields, 1993), 204–7.

7. "Thousands of Slovaks Protest Country's New Name," Associated Press (March 30, 1990).

8. Among them were the Independent Party of Slovaks, the Slovak National Party, the Slovak Christian Democratic Party and the National Democratic Movement. *Nepszabadsag* (August 17, 1990).

9. Ibid.

10. An early example of this was the attempt, on July 8, 1990, by several alumni of the Teacher's Training College of Banvice nad Bebravou to erect a plaque at the college honoring Joseph Tiso, founder of the college in 1934. Since Tiso had been president of the fascist Slovak state during World War II, this was met with strong protests, and the plaque was eventually removed by order of the Slovak National Council. Yet the Slovak National Democratic Movement demanded in turn that all plaques and statues commemorating Edouard Benes, a Czech and Czechoslovakia's president immediately after the war, be removed as well. "Weekly Record of Events," *RFE Report on Eastern Europe* (March 22, 1991); *MTI* (July 12 and July 21, 1990).

11. The Slovak National Party did less well in the local elections held in November 1990. However, it only contested seats in 4% of the electoral districts in Slovakia, and won 41% of these, which was an indication of support for its nationalist rhetoric. Furthermore, the Christian Democratic Movement, which led in election results, had adopted a more strongly nationalist stance at its preelection congress. *RFE/RL Daily Report* (November 8, 1990); Jiri Pehe, "The Local Government Elections," *RFE Report on Eastern Europe* (December 14, 1990).

12. Indeed, Carnogursky began to advocate a looser coalition between the Czech and Slovak republics as a way to move toward the eventual dissolution of the federated state. The clear appeal of nationalism probably also contributed to the decision by the Slovak government under Prime Minister Vladimir Meciar to establish a separate Slovak ministry of international affairs, which was in clear violation of the Trencianske Teplice agreement. Under his leadership the Slovak government also began to broach the possibility of two money-issuing centers, and thus, implicitly, of a separate Slovak currency. On Carnogursky's policies, see Pehe, "Growing Slovak Demands Seen as Threat to Federation."

13. *RFE/RL Daily Report* (November 15, 1990).

14. Like Civic Forum, Public Against Violence was not a political party but an umbrella organization of many different groups, which made it vulnerable to fragmentation as political viewpoints became more sharply delineated in Czechoslovakia. The radicalization within the PAV coincided with calls for greater Slovak autonomy outside the PAV; in late February the Slovak Christian Democrats stated that a treaty must be signed between the Czech and Slovak republics equalizing their standing within the federation before any new constitution could be signed. *Literarni Noviny* 5 (1990); *CTK* (March 6, 1991).

15. The Slovak government also insisted on the need for a state treaty between the Czech and Slovak republics before constitutional changes could be made. Tentative agreement was reached on June 15, 1991, for a state treaty to precede the constitution. A draft was finally agreed upon on February 9, 1992, and submitted to the republic and federal parliaments. The Slovak parliament's presidium rejected the treaty, however, on February 12, 1992. On these issues, see Pehe, "Growing Slovak Demands Seen as Threat to Federation," 3; Pehe, "The First Weeks of 1991: Problems Solved, Difficulties Ahead," *RFE Report on Eastern Europe* (March 8, 1991); "Weekly Record of Events," *RFE Report on Eastern Europe* (June 28, 1991); "Weekly Review," *RFE/RL Research Report* (February 21, 1992).

16. This was later shortened to simply the Movement for a Democratic Slovakia (MDS).

17. For example, on March 11, 1991, the Slovak Heritage Foundation, while supporting a call for a referendum proposed by the PAV, simultaneously urged the Slovak National Council to make an immediate declaration of sovereignty. "Weekly Record of Events," *RFE Report on Eastern Europe* (March 22, 1991), 44; *Mlada Fronta* (March 6, 1991); Reuters (March 12, 1991); Pehe, "Growing Slovak Demands Seen as Threat to Federation," 1–10.

18. Though Meciar had countered these accusations by arguing that his group only wanted to prevent the PAV from veering to the right, his actions looked like an attempt to control Slovakia with demagoguery and by promising that the eco-

nomic reforms would be less painful in Slovakia as a result. Meciar was also accused of opposing the screening of parliamentary deputies and government officials for links with the former secret police, raising questions about his own past affiliations there. *CTK* (March 4, 10, and 11, 1991); *Lidove Noviny* (March 4, 1991).

19. *CTK* (February 27, 1991).

20. *CTK* (March 11, 1991); "Weekly Record of Events," *RFE Report on Eastern Europe* (March 22, 1991).

21. A law on referendums was passed on July 19, 1991 setting out the provisions under which such a referendum could be held. Jiri Pehe, "Controversy over the Referendum on the Future of Czechoslovakia," *RFE Report on Eastern Europe* (August 30, 1991), 27–31.

22. In a March 1991 poll, for example, only 9% of the Slovak population was in favor of the country's division; 21% supported confederation, and 43% favored federation. Pehe, "Growing Slovak Demands Seen as Threat to Federation," 2.

23. There were obvious legal advantages to doing so, since this would then put the onus on Slovakia to obtain international recognition as an independent state, and to work out new treaty and trade arrangements. Jiri Pehe, "Bid for Slovak Sovereignty Causes Political Upheaval," *RFE Report on Eastern Europe* (October 11, 1991), 13.

24. Jiri Pehe, "Czech and Slovak Leaders Deadlocked over Country's Future," *RFE Report on Eastern Europe* 2 (November 28, 1991), 7–13; see also Jan Obrman, "President Havel's Diminishing Political Influence," *RFE/RL Research Report* (March 13, 1992), 18–23.

25. Indeed, before the debate over Slovak independence became so heated, Slovak leaders such as Meciar and Carnogursky had acknowledged that an independent Slovak Republic would not be viable. *Smena* (October 11, 1990). See also Peter Martin, "Slovakia: Calculating the Costs of Independence," *RFE/RL Research Report* (March 20, 1992), 33–38.

26. Other strains existed as well; not only had isolated incidents of anti-Semitism emerged, but Moravia and Silesia began, in 1991, to press for greater autonomy within the federal state. The Jewish cemetery in Nitra was defaced with swastikas and offensive drawings in November 1990, and fascist slogans and anti-Jewish attacks were found on walls in Bratislava. *RFE/RL Daily Report* (November 8, 1990); Pehe, "The First Weeks of 1991: Problems Solved, Difficulties Ahead," 9; Jan Obrman, "The Issue of Autonomy for Moravia and Silesia," *RFE/RL Report on Eastern Europe* (April 12, 1991), 13–22.

27. On August 26, 1992 the two leaders formally agreed on the division of Czechoslovakia as of January 1, 1993. See *Strategic Survey 1992–1993* (London: Brassey's for the IISS, 1993), 103–5 and 228–29.

28. "Check, O Slavakia," *The Economist* (June 27, 1992): 55.

29. Sharon Fisher, "Making Slovakia More 'Slovak,'" *Transition* 2 (November 29, 1996): 14.

30. Indeed, Carnogursky stated in October 1990 that Slovak independence was unlikely, both because international recognition would be difficult to obtain (especially at a time when the Western powers were insisting on the importance of honoring existing borders within the provisions of the CSCE accords) and because a

Slovak government would not be able to guarantee Slovak territorial integrity. *Smena* (October 11, 1990).

31. The Hungarian Students' Federation was formed in November 1989; the Federation of Hungarian Teachers in January 1990; the Association of Hungarian Writers in December 1989; and the Hungarian Journalists' Association in January 1990. Edith Oltay, "Hungarian Minority in Slovakia Sets Up Independent Organizations," *RFE/RL Report on Eastern Europe* (March 16, 1990).

32. *Nepszabadsag* (April 2, 1990).

33. Its affiliation with the Communist government made the alliance vulnerable to charges of collaboration. Yet with 97,000 members and over 500 local offices throughout the state, it remained a major organization. After the Communist regime collapsed, Csemadok reshaped its profile and presented itself as democratically inclined. It also expanded its concerns to political as well as cultural affairs. *Uj Szo* (December 8, 1989).

34. *Nepszabadsag* (February 8, 1990).

35. One of the examples they raised was the televising of an interview with a member of the coexistence movement. See ibid. (May 29, 1990).

36. This was seen in the emergence of scattered demonstrations in southern Slovakia, which attacked politicians who favored minority rights, and called for the establishment of a pure Slovak state. *Mogyar Hirlap* (March 2, 1990).

37. Coexistence and the HCDM had held discussions with the FMK, which had reshaped itself as a political party, the Hungarian Civic Party (HCP) in January 1992, about creating a coalition. But they failed to reach agreement, since the HCP refused to leave the Slovak government prior to the elections. This led Coexistence and the HCDM to accept the HPP, a far smaller group, in the three-way coalition.

38. The election law passed in Czechoslovakia in January 1992 stipulated that individual parties must gain 5% of the vote to win representation in parliament, while coalitions of two to three parties must win 7%. If four or more parties were involved, they must attain 10% of the vote. Clearly, if the Hungarian vote was not to be split among four parties and thereby negated entirely, a coalition was necessary, but since it did not seem likely that they would attain 10%, more than three was not sensible. Out of the roughly 350,000 Hungarians who went to the polls, about 290,000 voted for the Coexistence—Hungarian Christian Democratic Movement alliance. The FMK, which ran on the general list of the PAV, received at most 50,000 votes. See Alfred A. Reisch, "Hungarian Ethnic Parties Prepare for Czechoslovak Elections," *RFE/RL Research Report* (May 1, 1992), 12.

39. They also called for the establishment of Hungarian literary, linguistic, ethnographic, and sociological research institutions, and for the reestablishment of institutions that were suppressed by the previous authorities. *Uj Szo* (December 14, 1989) and *Nepszabadsag* (February 8, 1990).

40. The immediate issue of expanding Hungarian-language education, however, is made somewhat moot by the shortage of teachers; yet this simply shifted the point of contention between Hungarians and the Slovak government to the issue of training of Hungarian-language teachers. *Nepszabadsag* (August 14, 1990).

41. Alfred A. Reisch, "The New Hungarian Government's Foreign Policy," *RFE/RL Research Report* (August 26, 1994), 46–47.

42. Both Hungarian organizations in Slovakia and the Hungarian government denied any desire to change their borders, but did note their support for some form of cultural and political autonomy for the Hungarian minority, not something that would gain favor from the Slovak government. *Nap* (March 30, 1990); *Magyar Hirlap* (February 28, 1990); *Nepszabadsag* (September 18, 1990); *SZER/MTI* (September 18, 1990).

43. This was allegedly based on information obtained from southern Slovakia. Meciar himself did little to assuage this friction, since he accused Hungary of trying to take land from Slovakia, and declared that Hungarians in Slovakia were traitors to Slovakia. *Nepszabadsag* (August 15, 1990); *Budapest Domestic Service* (March 27, 1991).

44. *AFP* (October 26, 1990); *Mlada Fronta* (October 30, 1990); *CTK* (October 26, 1990).

45. Havel's warning was supported by a letter from the Christian Democratic Group in the European Parliament disapproving any attempt to make Slovak the only official language. The Slovak National Party responded to all of this by stating that Europe could wait. *DPA* (October 26, 1990); *Prace* (October 10, 1990); *CTK* (October 26, 1990).

46. Jiri Pehe, "Bill of Fundamental Rights and Liberties Adopted," *RFE/RL Report on Eastern Europe* (January 25, 1991), 1–4.

47. Indeed, Slovak nationalists continued to use concerns about Hungary and the Hungarian minority to inflame support, as seen by the warning made, in April 1991, that the crisis in the government was primarily in the *Hungarian* government's interests. Jiri Pehe, "Political Conflict in Slovakia," *RFE/RL Report on Eastern Europe* (May 10, 1991), especially page 4.

48. This was at least partly motivated by the government's desire to raise its popular support, since it had begun to move toward pluralism. Alfred A. Reisch, "Hungarian-Slovak Relations: A Difficult First Year," *RFE/RL Research Report* (December 17, 1993), 16–23.

49. Given Hungary's opposition, the Danube could only be dammed or diverted where both sides of the river were in Slovak territory. On Hungarian doubts about the dam project, see Vera Rich, "Central Europe II: The Battle of the Danube," *The World Today* 48 (December 1992): 216–18.

50. Hungary has argued that the wetlands area of northwestern Hungary is an "inland delta" that would be destroyed if the dam project is completed and water diverted from the riverbed in this area. Rich, "Central Europe II," 217. See also Reisch, "Hungarian-Slovak Relations," 17; Debora MacKenzie, "Slovakia Presses Ahead with Danube Diversion," *New Scientist* 136 (October 31, 1992): 7.

51. Czechoslovakia washed its hands of the project by the fall of 1992, since it was clear that the federal government would dissolve shortly.

52. "Case Concerning Gabcikovo-Nagymaros Project (Hungary/Slovakia): Summary of the Judgement of 25 September 1997," International Court of Justice, Press Communiqué 97/10 bis, September 25, 1997, available from http://www.icj-cij.org/Presscom/ipr97/10bis.html.

53. Alfred A. Reisch, "The Central European Initiative: To Be or Not to Be?" *RFE/RL Research Report* (August 27, 1993), 30–31.

54. Reisch, "Hungarian-Slovak Relations: A Difficult First Year," 18–20; Reisch, "The Central European Initiative: To Be or Not to Be?" 33–34.

55. Hans J. Binnendijk and Jeffrey Simon, "Hungary's 'Near Abroad,' " *Strategic Forum* 93 (November 1996), 2.

56. Indeed, better relations with Slovakia became a priority, in good part because of Hungary's strong interest in improving its image in the West. *RFE/RL Research Report* (August 26, 1994), 50.

57. See, for example, Commission on Security and Cooperation in Europe, *Human Rights and Democratization in Slovakia* (1993), 4.

58. Alfred A. Reisch, "The New Hungarian Government's Foreign Policy," *RFE/RL Research Report* (August 26, 1994), 46–47.

59. Larry L. Watts, "Ethnic Tensions: How the West Can Help," *World Policy Journal* 12 (Spring 1995): 92–93.

60. Only in May 1994 did the Slovak government pass laws that made possible the official use of Hungarian names in Slovakia, and permitting bilingual road signs, which had been removed after Czechoslovakia's split. See Reisch, "The New Hungarian Government's Foreign Policy," 52.

61. Ibid., 52–54.

62. Meciar again relied heavily on nationalist themes in his political campaign. Nonetheless, the strong nationalist sentiment in the state has lessened, as Slovaks have lost interest in politics or become estranged by Meciar's pro-Slovak rhetoric. See Fisher, "Making Slovakia More 'Slovak,' " 14.

63. This remains unresolved, despite Slovak, promises to amend the law. See *The Economist* (September 13, 1997): 56; and Fisher, "Making Slovakia More 'Slovak,' " 14.

64. Watts, "Ethnic Tensions: How the West Can Help," 89.

65. *The Economist* (September 13, 1997): 55–56.

66. On internal problems in Slovakia, see Adrian Evtuhovici, "Slovakia Courts the European Club," *Transitions* 4 (July 1997): 72–74; Simecka, "Slovakia's Lonely Independence," 14–21. See also *The Economist* (16 August 1997): 41–42.

67. Again, this assumes to some degree that attaining some level of affluence can ease tensions. On this point, see Thomas Carothers, "Democracy without Illusions," *Foreign Affiars* 76 (January/February 1997): 85–99.

68. "The Council of Europe in Central and Eastern Europe: The Programmes of Assistance with the Development and Consolidation of Democratic Stability," available from the Council of Europe web site http://www.coe.fr/eng/act-e/dap.htm.

69. Alfred A. Reisch, "Slovakia's Minority Policy under International Scrutiny," *RFE/RL Research Report* (December 10, 1993), 37–39.

70. Reisch, "The Central European Initiative: To Be or Not To Be?" 32–35.

71. Reisch, "Slovakia's Minority Policy under International Scrutiny," 39.

72. *Assistance with the Development and Consolidation of Democratic Security: Cooperation and Assistance with the Countries of Central and East Europe, Programme for 1997* (Strasbourg: Council of Europe, 1997), 93–97.

73. The quote is from the High Commissioner's mandate, cited in Max van der Stoel, "The OSCE High Commissioner on National Minorities," *OSCE ODIHR Bulletin* 3 (1995): 41.

74. "Proposals by the CSCE High Commissioner on National Minorities, Max van der Stoel, upon His Visits to Slovakia and Hungary," *Human Rights Law Journal* 14 (June 30, 1993).

75. Van der Stoel, "High Commissioner on National Minorities, Slovakia," 1–2, available from www.osceprag.cz/inst.

76. "Recommendations by the CSCE High Commissioner on National Minorities, Mr. Max van der Stoel, upon Visits to the Former Republic of Macedonia, Slovakia, and Hungary," *Human Rights Law Journal* 15 (September 26, 1994), 238–42.

77. See Open Media Research Institute (OMRI) *Daily Digest,* Part II (February 14, 17, and 21, 1997).

78. Fisher, "Making Slovakia More 'Slovak,'" 14–17. Meciar was defeated in elections in October 1998, when his party failed to gain enough support to form a new government.

79. *What Is Phare? A European Union Initiative for Economic Integration with Central and Eastern European Countries* (Brussels European Commission, 1996).

80. U.S. Department of State, *Congressional Presentation for Foreign Operations, Fiscal Year 1997* (Washington, D.C.: Congressional Information Service, 1996), 309.

81. Ibid., 146.

82. Many East European states have come to view the PFP program as a means by which to fulfill the conditions necessary to achieve eventual NATO membership. Yet NATO officials also stress that it is a useful partnership with states that do not intend to join NATO, but want to improve coordination with the alliance. For some discussions of PFP and NATO enlargement, see Strobe Talbott, "Why NATO Should Grow," *New York Review of Books* (August 10, 1995); Gebhardt Von Moltke, "Russia and NATO," *RUSI Journal* (February 1995): 8–13. See also U.S. Department of State, *Report to the Congress on the Enlargement of the North Atlantic Treaty Organization: Rationale, Benefits, Costs and Implications* (Washington, D.C.: U.S. Government Printing Office, 1997); Michael E. Brown, "The Flawed Logic of NATO Expansion," *Survival* 37 (Spring 1995): 34–52; Dana H. Allin, "Can Containment Work Again?" *Survival* 37 (Spring 1995): 53–65.

83. The Council of Europe's portion of this expenditure was 50 million French francs; the remaining 20 million is from joint programs with the European Commission, and national voluntary contributions. See "The Council of Europe in Central and Eastern Europe: The Programmes of Assistance with the Development and Consolidation of Democratic Security," 2–3; *Assistance with the Development and Consolidation of Democratic Security: Cooperation and Assistance Programmes with Countries of Central and Eastern Europe,* Annual Report 1996 (Strasbourg: Council of Europe, 1997), 149.

84. *Assistance with the Development and Consolidation of Democratic Security: Cooperation and Assistance Programmes with Countries of Central and Eastern Europe,* Programme for 1997 (Strasbourg: Council of Europe, 1997), 175.

85. Based on discussions with the U.S. Mission to the OSCE, February 28, 1997.

86. Max van der Stoel, "The OSCE High Commissioner on National Minorities," *OSCE ODIRH Bulletin* 3 (1995): 40–41.

87. It is difficult to determine how this budget was allocated without more information from the High Commissioner's office, so this seems the most reasonable assumption to make.

88. This figure includes both multicountry programs and funds spent directly in individual countries. *What Is Phare?* p. 5. The exchange from ECUs to dollars is calculated at a rate of 1 ECU = US$1.158. From the *Financial Times* (February 26, 1997).

89. *Official Journal of the European Communities* 39 (January 29, 1996): 1402.

90. 1995 is the latest year for which actual expenditure figures are available. SEED-funded activities are expected to be completed in FY1997. Of the 1995 expenditure, 2.6 million was earmarked for programs promoting democratic governance; $6 million to Enterprise funds; $5.7 million directly to economic restructuring; and 7.4 million to environmental programs. The remainder went to miscellaneous projects. See *Congressional Presentation for Foreign Operations, Fiscal Year 1997,* 61.

91. Figures on IMET and the PFP program were provided by personal contacts at the U.S. Department of State.

92. Based on private discussions with U.S. Department of the Treasury representatives, February 27, 1997.

93. World Bank, *Slovak Republic: Country Overview*, available from http://www.worldbank.org/html/extdr/offrep/eca/svkcb.htm.

94. UNDPI, *Demographic Yearbook 1994* (New York: United Nations, 1996).

95. Joseph Held, *Dictionary of East European History Since 1945* (Westport, Conn.: Greenwood, 1994).

96. International Institute for Strategic Studies, *The Military Balance 1996–97* (London: Oxford University Press, 1996), 298–99.

97. See chapter 7 by Bradley Thayer in this volume for a detailed evaluation of the costs of the operation.

98. Figures and statistics on UNTAES are from *The Blue Helmets* (UNDPI; New York: United Nations, 1996), 554–55, 760–62. *The Military Balance 1996–97* calculates the costs for 1996 at $292 million (p. 301).

99. See James T. Quinlivan, "Force Requirements in Stability Operations," *Parameters* 25 (Winter 1995–96): 59–69.

100. See chapter 2 by Andrea Talentino on Bosnia and chapter 7 by Bradley Thayer on Macedonia for comparable estimations.

101. See chapter 7 by Bradley Thayer for cost estimates.

102. Indeed, the map of conflict in the former Soviet Union also illustrates the distinction between states that expect to participate in wider economic and political organizations and that have avoided ethnic conflict, such as the Baltic republics, and states with little hope of inclusion in or even attention from external organizations. The latter category includes the states of the Caucasus, Central Asia, and to some degree Russia itself. Russia is particularly interesting in this regard, since its desire to participate in Western institutions is widely believed to have moderated its behavior prior to and after the Chechen conflict.

103. This is particularly true given the renewed debate about necessary "preconditions" for democracy to succeed; while there is no agreement on this, it seems increasingly obvious that democratization efforts in the "third wave" of democratization that began in the 1970s have been more successful in more affluent states—as well as states with links to Western ideas. See Carothers, "Democracy without Illusions," 85–99. On the ongoing debate about modernization and democratization, see Adam Przeworski and Fernando Limongi, "Modernization: Theories and Facts," *World Politics* 49 (January 1997): 155–83.

Chapter 9

1. Michael W. Doyle, *UN Peacekeeping in Cambodia: UNTAC's Civil Mandate* (Boulder: Rienner, 1995), 67.

2. Background information on Cambodia's history comes from David P. Chandler, *The Tragedy of Cambodian History* (New Haven: Yale University Press, 1991); Mats Berdal and Michael Leifer, "Cambodia," in *The New Interventionism 1991–1994: The United Nations Experience in Cambodia, Former Yugoslavia, and Somalia,* ed. James Mayall (Cambridge: Cambridge University Press, 1996); and Steven Ratner, "The United Nations in Cambodia: A Model for Resolution of Internal Conflicts?" in *Enforcing Restraint: Collective Intervention in Internal Conflicts,* ed. Lori Fisler Damrosch (New York: Council on Foreign Relations Press, 1993). Information on Cambodia since peace talks beginning in 1990 is gathered from sources noted below.

3. Chandler, *The Tragedy of Cambodian History,* 140.

4. Ibid., 122.

5. Ibid., 178.

6. Ibid., 203.

7. Ratner, "The United Nations in Cambodia," in *Enforcing Restraint,* ed. Damrosch, 243–44.

8. Chandler, *The Tragedy of Cambodian History,* 229.

9. Berdal and Leifer, "Cambodia," in *The New Interventionism,* ed. Mayall, 30–32.

10. Ibid., 32–33.

11. Ratner, "The United Nations in Cambodia," in *Enforcing Restraint,* ed. Damrosch, 245–50.

12. UNTAC was composed of 12 enlarged battalions with integral first- and second-line support, plus 485 military observers physically verifying adherence to the provisions of the accords. It also had an air-support group composed of 10 fixed-wing aircraft and 26 helicopters, and an engineering unit of 2,000 soldiers responsible for support such as water purification, site preparation, and track and road maintenance. Berdal and Leifer, "Cambodia," in *The New Interventionism,* ed. Mayall, 39.

13. Ibid., 38.

14. Doyle, *UN Peacekeeping in Cambodia,* 35.

15. Berdal and Leifer, "Cambodia," in *The New Interventionism,* ed. Mayall, 42–43.

16. Doyle, *UN Peacekeeping in Cambodia,* 56.

17. Ratner, "The United Nations in Cambodia," in *Enforcing Restraint,* ed. Damrosch, 253.

18. Berdal and Leifer, "Cambodia," in *The New Interventionism,* ed. Mayall, 55: and Human Rights Watch/Asia, *Cambodia at War* (New York: Human Rights Watch, 1995), 14.

19. Human Rights Watch, *Cambodia at War,* 20–27.

20. Doyle, *UN Peacekeeping in Cambodia,* 73.

21. Anthony Spaeth, "Out of the Darkness," *Time* (August 26, 1996).

22. The military component of UNTAC consisted of 15,900 troops, which compromised the force headquarters and sector headquarters staff. This number was divided into 10,200 troops, all ranks and infantry, 485 military observers, 376 naval personnel, and 4,500 troops in logistics and specialized support elements. UNDPI, *The United Nations and Cambodia 1991–1995* (New York: United Nations, 1995), 179.

23. UNDPI, *Yearbook of the United Nations 1993* (New York: United Nations, 1994), 375–78.

24. Trevor Findlay, *Cambodia: The Legacy and Lessons of UNTAC,* Stockholm International Peace Research Institute Research Report No. 9 (New York: Oxford University Press, 1995), 33.

25. Central Intelligence Agency, *World Factbook 1990, 1995* (Washington, D.C.: CIA).

26. United Nations, *World Economic and Social Survey 1996* (New York: United Nations, 1997), 192.

27. Ibid., 193.

28. Ibid., 192, available from www.info.usaid.gov/pubs/cp97/countries/kh/htm.

29. UNDPI, *Yearbook of the United Nations 1993* (New York: United Nations, 1994), 377–78. The four funds were Trust Fund for the Cambodian Peace Process; Trust Fund for a Human Rights Education Programme in Cambodia; Cambodia Trust Fund for Rehabilitation Activities; and Trust Fund for the Demining Programme in Cambodia.

30. Information on NGOs comes from www.interaction.org. For the World Bank's contributions see UNDPI, *The United Nations and Cambodia 1991–1995,* 297–300, and United Nations, *World Economic and Social Survey 1996.* Information on the OECD comes from *Development Co-operation: Efforts and Policies of the Members of the Development Assistance Committee* (Paris: OECD, 1996).

31. Available from www.unicef.org/sowc96pk/hidekill.htm.

32. Berdal and Leifer, "Cambodia," in *The New Interventionism,* ed. Mayall, 48.

33. Human Rights Watch, *Cambodia at War,* 96–105.

34. This information is drawn from UNDPI, *The United Nations and Cambodia 1991–1995,* 262–65, and Human Rights Watch, *Cambodia at War,* 132–35; www.info.usaid.gov/pubs/cp97/countries/kh.htm and www.tradeport.org/cgi-bin/banner.pl/ts/countries/cambodia/index.html.

35. *Japan's Official Development Assistance, ODA Annual Report 1995* (Tokyo: Association for Promotion of International Cooperation), 304. Information on Germany, Italy, France, the Netherlands, Sweden, and Italy also comes from this source, 304–5, and *ODA Annual Report 1994,* 289–91.

36. Malaysia leads all investors with $1 billion; other nations have collectively invested at least $2.2 billion. See Frank Gibney Jr., "The Trials of Living in Peace," *Time* (November 27, 1995); and United Nations, *World Economic and Social Survey 1996,* 192–93.

37. United Nations, *World Economic and Social Survey 1996,* 193.

38. OECD Development Assistance Committee, *Development Cooperation: Efforts and Policies of the Members of the Development Assistance Committee,* (Paris: OECD, 1996), A55–56.

39. United Nations, *World Economic and Social Survey 1996,* 192–94.

40. UNDPI, *Yearbook of the United Nations 1986* (New York: United Nations, 1987), 206.

41. Available from www.tradeport.org/ts/countries/cambodia/bnotes.html.

42. Berdal and Leifer, "Cambodia," in *The New Interventionism,* ed. Mayall, 37.

43. UNDPI, *The Blue Helmets: A Review of United Nations Peace-keeping* (New York: United Nations, 1996), 480–81.

44. United Nations, *Information Notes, United Nations Peace-keeping* (New York: United Nations, 1995), 158.

45. "Unlocking the Secrets of the Last Rebel Stronghold," available from www.pathfinder.com/time/asia/magazine/1998/980427/anlong.html; and "Could the World Have Had Its Trial and Punishment?" available from www.pathfinder.com/time/asia/magazine/1998/980427/Khmer.html.

Chapter 10

1. UNDPI, *The United Nations and El Salvador 1990–1995* (New York: United Nations, 1995), 7.

2. Ibid.

3. Liisa North, *Bitter Grounds: The Roots of Revolt in El Salvador* (Toronto: Between the Lines, 1981), 94.

4. ONUSAL's actual strength never reached the numbers authorized. The maximum deployment included 368 military observers by February 1992 and 315 civilian police by May 1992. The Electoral Division composed the greatest number of personnel and included 900 electoral observers, many of them volunteers, during the elections. UNDPI, *The Blue Helmets: A Review of United Nations Peace-keeping* (New York: United Nations, 1996), 737.

5. Tommie Sue Montgomery, *Revolution in El Salvador: From Civil Strife to Civil Peace* (Boulder: Westview, 1992); North, *Bitter Grounds.*

6. Montgomery, *Revolution in El Salvador,* 25–30.

7. North, *Bitter Grounds,* 19.

8. Ibid.

9. Ibid., 22.

10. Montgomery, *Revolution in El Salvador,* 32; North, *Bitter Grounds,* 22–25.
11. North, *Bitter Grounds,* 29–34.
12. Ibid., 19.
13. Ibid., 48–50.
14. Ibid., 42–54.
15. Cynthia Arnson, *El Salvador, A Revolution Confronts the United States* (Washington, D.C.: Institute for Policy Studies, 1982), 29–31.
16. Ibid., 31.
17. Ibid., 34.
18. Ibid., 38.
19. UNDPI, *The United Nations and El Salvador,* 302.
20. Arnson, *El Salvador,* 60
21. North, *Bitter Grounds,* 87.
22. Montgomery, *Revolution in El Salvador,* 152; Dana Priest, "US Instructed Latins on Executions, Torture," *Washington Post* (September 21, 1996), A1.
23. Montgomery, *Revolution in El Salvador,* 165.
24. Ibid., 171–73.
25. Arnson, *El Salvador,* 45.
26. Montgomery, *Revolution in El Salvador,* 190.
27. Ibid., 219–20.
28. UNDPI, *The United Nations in El Salvador,* 36–37.
29. Ibid.; see www.un.org/Depts/DPKO.
30. UNDPI, *The United Nations in El Salvador,* 31.
31. See the "World" section of the UNHCR web site: www.unhcr.ch.
32. See the "Regions and Countries" section of the USAID web site: gopher.info.usaid.gov.
33. See the web sites of the International Committee of the Red Cross [www.icrc.ch] and the Norwegian Refugee Council [www.nrc.no]. See also UNDPI, *The United Nations in El Salvador,* 437.
34. Central Intelligence Agency, *World Fact Book 1990* (Washington, D.C.: CIA).
35. See the "Countries and Regions" section of the World Bank web site: www.worldbank.org; Eurostat, *Europe in Figures* (Luxembourg: Office for Official Publications of the European Communities, 1995), 414. The EU amount listed here excludes bilateral commitments from member states.
36. See the "Countries and Regions" section of the World Bank web site: www.worldbank.org.
37. UNDPI, *The United Nations in El Salvador,* 488–506; www.usaid.gov70/00/regional_country/lac/elsalvador/speech.249.
38. Available from www.icrc.ch.
39. *Japan's Official Development Assistance, ODA Annual Report 1994* (Tokyo: Association for Promotion of International Cooperation), 425–27; *ODA Annual Report 1995,* 290–91, 449–50.
40. OECD Development Assistance Committee, *Development Co-operation: Efforts and Policies of the Members of the Development Assistance Committee* (Paris: OECD, 1996), A82.

41. Marvin Amador, "A History Is Written with Blood," *Isthmus Comm,* 195 (online magazine). See the 1995 archives under www.sirius.com/~isthmus. This figure is corroborated by Douglas Farah, "Death Squads Flex Muscle," *Washington Post* (October 13, 1996), A42.

42. Central Intelligence Agency, *World Factbook 1990*; Montgomery, *Revolution in El Salvador,* 117.

43. UNDPI, *Yearbook of the United Nations 1984* (New York: United Nations, 1985), 676.

44. United Nations, *Information Notes, United Nations Peace-keeping* (New York: United Nations, 1995), 40–56. Although the strength of the mission was authorized at 1,000, the number of personnel deployed never reached this number. The bulk of personnel were to be employed by the Police Division, which was authorized at 631 members but remained somewhat below this figure.

45. UNDPI, *The United Nations in El Salvador,* 53.

Chapter 11

1. See Alexander L. George and Jane E. Holl, *The Warning-Response Problem and Missed Opportunities in Preventive Diplomacy* (Washington, D.C.: Carnegie Commission on Preventing Deadly Conflict, 1997).

Index

About the Contributors

Mike Blakley is a principal research fellow at the Center for International Relations at the University of California, Los Angeles, and a Ph.D. candidate in the Political Science Department. His dissertation explores the link between political economy and security. Previously he was assistant director and project manager for the Oregon Survey Research Lab at the University of Oregon. Before coming to academia, he was a marketing and sales executive with Telerate Systems, Inc., in New York and Los Angeles.

Michael Brown is associate professor and director of research for the National Security Studies Program at the Edmund A. Walsh School of Foreign Service, Georgetown University. Previously he was adjunct lecturer and associate director of the International Security Program at the John F. Kennedy School of Government, Harvard University. His research focuses on international conflict and security issues. He was the managing editor of the journal *International Security* and has written or edited numerous publications, including *The International Dimensions of Internal Conflict* (Cambridge: MIT Press, 1996) and *Flying Blind: The Politics of the U.S. Strategic Bomber Program* (Ithaca: Cornell University Press, 1992). He is currently at work on a book about the causes of civil wars.

Renée de Nevers is a program officer in arms reduction and security in the Program on Global Security and Sustainability at the John D. and Catherine T. MacArthur Foundation. She has been a fellow at the Belfer Center for Science and International Affairs at Harvard University, Stanford University's Center for International Security and Arms Control and the Hoover Institution, and has worked at the International Institute for Strategic Studies in London. She has published articles and monographs on Russian foreign policy, European security, and Western efforts to assist democratization in former Communist states.

Richard Rosecrance is professor of political science and director of the Center for International Relations at the University of California, Los Angeles. From 1970 to 1988 he was Walter S. Carpenter Jr. professor of international and comparative politics in the Department of Government at Cornell University. He served on the Policy Planning Council of the State Department during the Johnson administration and is the recipient of Guggenheim, Rockefeller, Ford, and Fulbright fellowships. His publications include *International Relations: Peace or War?* (New York: McGraw-Hill, 1973); *America as an Ordinary Country: U.S. Foreign Policy and the Future* (Ithaca: Cornell University Press, 1976); *The Rise of the Trading State: Commerce and Conquest in the Modern World* (New York: Basic Books, 1986); *America's Economic Resurgence: A Bold New Strategy* (New York: Harper & Row, 1990); and *From Territorial to Virtual States: The Eclipse of War in the 21st Century* (forthcoming).

Andrea Kathryn Talentino is a Sawyer Seminar Fellow at the Center of International Studies at Princeton University. She received her Ph.D. from the University of California, Los Angeles. Her research focuses on conflict and security issues and the role of international and regional organizations, as well as the subject of her dissertation, collective security and multilateral intervention into civil conflict.

Bradley Thayer is visiting assistant professor of government at Dartmouth College. He was a fellow at the Belfer Center for Science and International Affairs at Harvard University and a consultant to the RAND Corporation. He was awarded his Ph.D. from the University of Chicago. His dissertation examines great power behavior in the aftermath of great power wars and the feasibility of collective security systems. He has published articles on the causes of nuclear proliferation and the effects of the spread of nuclear weapons on international politics.